Canine
Warrior

Canine Warrior

How a Vietnam Scout Dog
Inspired a National Monument

John C. Burnam, Master Sergeant,
United States Army (RET.)

LOST⁓
COAST
PRESS

Canine Warrior

How a Vietnam Scout Dog Inspired a National Monument

Copyright ©2014 by John C. Burnam

Lost Coast Press
155 Cypress Street
Fort Bragg, CA 95437
(800) 773-7782
www.cypresshouse.com
Cover and Book design: Michael Brechner / Cypress House

PUBLISHER'S CATALOGING-IN-PUBLICATION DATA

Burnam, John C.
  Canine warrior : how a Vietnam scout dog inspired a national monument / John C. Burnam. -- Fort Bragg, CA : Lost Coast Press, c2014.
    p. ; cm.
  ISBN: 978-1-935448-24-2
  "Portions of this book were previously published in 'Dog tags of courage: combat infantrymen and war dog heroes in Vietnam.' 2nd edition."--T.p. verso.

  SUMMARY: During his second tour as a US Army infantryman in the Vietnam War, John Burnam became a scout-dog handler. On combat missions, he learned of the dogs amazing ability to find enemy caches of ammunition and supplies, hidden base camps, and concealed tunnel entrances; saving countless lives by enabling American troops to avoid booby traps and ambushes. After retirement from the military, he became passionate about the idea of a national monument to honor them. Thanks to his efforts, the U.S. Military Working Dog Teams National Monument has been built at Lackland Air Force Base, where all of America's military dog teams are trained.--Publisher.

  1. Dogs--War use--Vietnam. 2. Dogs--War use--United States. 3. U.S. Military Working Dog Teams National Monument. 4. Soldiers' monuments--United States. 5. Burnam, John C. 6. Vietnam War, 1961-1975--Personal narratives, American. 7. United States. Army. Infantry Scout Dog Platoon, 44th--History. I. Title.
    UH100 .B87 2014   2013956681
    355.4/240973--dc23

MIX
Paper from
responsible sources
FSC
www.fsc.org   FSC® C011935

Printed in the USA

9 8 7 6 5 4 3 2 1

Dedication

I DEDICATE MY STORY to the exceptionally brave and loyal combat infantrymen and the war dogs and their handlers of all wars; to all the men and women who lost their lives while serving America during wartime; and to all those who were wounded in action but never gave up, because they found the strength and courage to carry on in life after the war.

Let us never forget our American servicemen missing in action (MIAs) and our prisoners of war (POWs) of all wars.

Finally, for my daughter, Jennifer, and granddaughter, Ariana, I document my military service and volunteer work, which resulted in the establishment of a national monument for America's military working dogs and handlers of all wars since WWII.

Contents

Acknowledgments

I AM HONORED TO HAVE SERVED with Vietnam German shepherd war-dog partners: Hans, sentry dog; Timber, scout dog; and especially my scout dog Clipper. Had it not been for them, I would not have a story to tell, neither would I have ever founded the National Monument for America's Military Working Dogs and Handlers of all wars since WWII.

A very special thanks to U.S. Representative Walter B. Jones, 3rd District of North Carolina, for sponsoring the congressional legislation to establish a national monument for the nation's military working-dog teams, and having enough confidence in me to promote legislation that placed the John Burnam Monument Foundation in charge of building and maintaining the monument.

My deepest respect and gratitude goes to my Vietnam War buddy Kenneth L. Mook, who inspired me to write my stories about the Vietnam War. Many thanks to the Vietnam scout-dog handlers I served with in the 44th Scout Dog Platoon: Ollie Whetstone, Mike "Mac" McClellan, and Dan Barnett. They helped me fill the gaps in my dog stories.

Thanks to my fellow Vietnam veteran infantry Sky Troopers Bob Dunn, Van Wilson, Marlin Dorman, Billy Smith, Donald Clostio, John Engel, and Dennis Blessing of the 2nd Platoon, Company B, 1st Battalion, 7th Cavalry, 1st Cavalry Division. They helped me survive combat in Vietnam and filled in the gaps of my time with them.

Without Natural Balance Pet Foods, Inc., Petco, and Dave and Cheryl Duffield who founded Maddie's Fund, the national monument would not have gotten the significant contributions it needed to complete the

$2,000,000 project. Thanks also to the countless thousands of dog loving people across America and overseas who contributed time, articles, and money to help support education about and construction of the monument. The national monument was officially dedicated on Monday, 28 October 2013 before a large audience and the national media at Lackland Air Force Base, San Antonio, Texas.

A special thanks to the JBMF board of directors, Larry Chilcoat, treasurer; Richard Deggans, Webmaster/secretary; Kristie Dober, secretary; and Jim Frost, promotions. Without their administrative, operational, and fundraising support, the national monument project would not have been managed effectively.

A very special recognition goes to my partner in life, Fern Zappala, for her loving support throughout the years of our life together.

Heroic War Dogs,
Forever Remembered

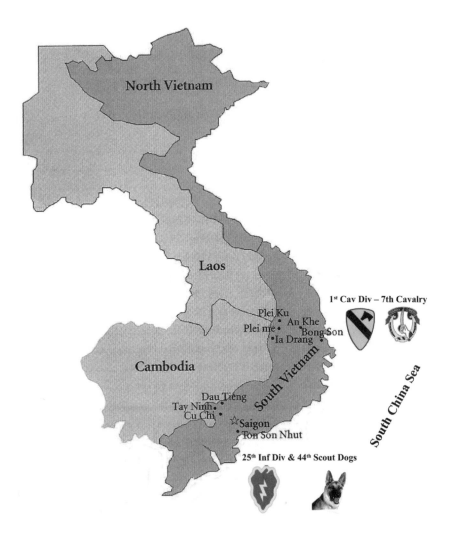

The primary locations, from 1966–1968, where author John
Burnam performed combat missions during the Vietnam War as
an infantryman with the 1st Battalion, 7th Cavalry, 1st Cavalry
Division, and as a German shepherd scout-dog handler with the 44th
Scout Dog Platoon, 25th Infantry Division.

Chapter 1

Camp Alpha

IT WAS MARCH 1966, a few days before my nineteenth birthday. I had five months of U.S. Army service under my bel,; all of it spent training to be an infantryman and paratrooper. I was now aboard a commercial jetliner for the trip from San Francisco to South Vietnam to fight in a war I knew nothing about.

American soldiers took up every seat on the plane. Sleeping was difficult, so I catnapped most of the way. Finally, the pilot announced our arrival at Tan Son Nhut airport near Saigon. It was daylight outside as I strained my neck and eyes to peer through the small porthole for my first glimpse of the foreign land below. I heaved a sigh of relief at the familiar sound of screeching rubber on pavement. The long ride was over.

Armed military policemen (MPs) boarded the plane and ushered us off into awaiting military buses with bars and thick wire mesh replacing glass windows. For the first time, I saw a beautiful German shepherd sentry dog and his handler in combat gear standing a short distance from the aircraft. I thought, *Wow! I didn't know they had dogs over here.* Little did I know that this quick sighting of a war dog was a glimpse into my future.

The driver told us that the wire mesh over the windows was to protect us from grenades that might be hurled at the bus while we traveled through the crowded city of Saigon. I smelled the hot, sticky air with its peculiar odor of stale fish. Raised in the Denver suburb of Littleton, Colorado, I'd never experienced a climate or permeating smell like this. Where I came from the air was dry, fresh, and clear, the land a mile above sea level.

As the bus slowly maneuvered through the crowded streets, I stared at the foreign cars, bicycle riders, and pedestrians. Most of the people wore black or white pajamas, straw hats, and flip-flop sandals. During the ride I didn't hear any shooting, witness any explosions, or see any buildings on fire. In fact, I didn't see anything in Saigon but Vietnamese civilians and soldiers going about their business in peace.

Where is the war? I thought.

The bus finally stopped at the front gate where a sign read CAMP ALPHA. It was a U.S. Army replacement center. Armed MPs quickly herded us into a large wooden building to be in-processed. After handing over our assignment orders, personnel files, finance, and medical records, we were moved into another part of the building. No one talked much. I felt like a robot following orders: "Stop! Wait here! Follow me! That's far enough!"

The camp commander arrived wearing a clean, starched khaki uniform with polished brass and shined shoes, the silver leaves on his collar designating the rank of a lieutenant colonel (LTC). He greeted our group with a smile and gave a "Welcome to Vietnam" orientation. He briefed us on the Vietnamese culture and why we were sent to help stop the spread of communism from North to South Vietnam. Our military presence was stated as no more than a "police action," because the United States had not declared war on North Vietnam.

I whispered to the soldier next to me, "What the hell's the difference between a declared war and a police action if both sides are killing each other?" Getting no response, I shut up and continued to listen. Fresh out of high school, with only a few months' military service and training, I wasn't sure what to expect next.

Camp Alpha consisted of long rows of tin-roofed wooden buildings with screens for windows. It reminded me of the infantry training centers I had stayed in at Fort Leonardwood, Missouri; Fort Ord, California; and Fort Benning, Georgia. I was housed in a numbered wooden building with a concrete-slab floor and several rows of metal bunk beds lining the walls. Each building accommodated about fifty men and had electric lights but no air conditioning. I doubted I would ever adjust to Vietnam's heat, humidity, and persistent smell of stale fish.

John Burnam, Littleton High School graduation photo, Littleton, Colorado, 1965 (author collection).

John Burnam, U.S. Army basic training, Company A, 3rd Battalion, 3rd Brigade, Fort Leonardwood, Missouri, 1965 (author collection).

Like me, most of the replacements were bewildered teenagers, fresh out of training, with a quarter inch of hair on their heads, wearing new fatigue uniforms and army-issue baseball caps. A tall barbed-wire fence surrounded the camp, and armed guards were stationed in towers. I felt like I was living in a small prison.

Camp Alpha had a small store where one could buy soft drinks, candy, cigarettes, toothpaste, and other sundries. A small service club featured live music sung by a Vietnamese rock 'n' roll band. I thought it was hilarious that the musicians couldn't speak English and butchered the words to Rolling Stones and Beatles songs. The club was always crowded, sticky-hot, and filled with cigarette smoke. There was nowhere else to unwind except a small chapel with posted notices for religious services.

Being gregarious by nature, I usually started conversations by asking a soldier where he was from or what his job, or MOS (military occupational specialty), was. I met guys from almost every state in the Union. There were truck drivers, medics, helicopter and vehicle mechanics, personnel and supply clerks, military police, cooks, and construction engineers. Most of them had trained for jobs other than the infantry.

During my stay at Camp Alpha, I met Kenny Mook, a twenty-one-year-old draftee from the farmlands of northern Pennsylvania. I had no idea at the time that we would soon be fighting for our lives in a place called Bong Son, an experience that would bond us for life.

Both Kenny and I were in excellent health and physical condition. Before joining the army, I had played varsity football and baseball at Littleton High School. I had also placed first in several conference and invitational wrestling tournaments in the 122-pound class. Kenny wasn't an athlete, but he was strong from farming in northern Pennsylvania.

We felt a kind of chemistry between us and quickly became friends. And we were both infantrymen, destined to fight in the jungle, defend a base camp, and protect supply roads, airfields, motor pools, and hospitals. Although our mission was a little scary, we liked to talk about how important our jobs were. Kenny was what paratroopers call a leg — a nickname for an infantryman who was not trained as a paratrooper to jump out of airplanes at 1,200 feet. To become a paratrooper, a soldier had to be a volunteer and pass a three-week training course that was physically and mentally taxing and had a high dropout rate.

I said, "I didn't go to three weeks of jump-school hell to be assigned to an infantry leg unit. I'm sure the army will assign me to an elite paratrooper outfit."

Kenny replied, "The only things that fall out of the sky are bird shit and fools. Besides, once you land, you're a leg too."

Throughout our infantry marksmanship training, Kenny and I had both trained on the M14 rifle. We didn't know what standard-issue M16 rifles looked like until we saw camp guards carrying them. I asked one of the sergeants who ran the camp if I would be issued one. He looked at me with a smile on his face and said no. He told me Camp Alpha was well protected, and that I'd get an M16 when I arrived at my combat unit.

As replacements, we were all unarmed and vulnerable if the enemy attacked Camp Alpha. I worried that by the time I was issued a weapon and ammunition during an attack — provided there were enough to go around — I'd be dead. Many frightening thoughts like that ran through my mind while I waited for an assignment to an infantry combat unit.

Less than a week after my arrival, my name was called over the loudspeaker and I was told to report to the personnel office. Kenny's name was also called. By a stroke of good luck, we were both assigned to the 1st Air Cavalry Division, located in the central highlands about 250 miles northwest of Saigon.

Kenny and I were sick of replacement centers, both stateside and in-country, and we were always happy to leave them. We knew their routine all too well: "Hurry up and wait." I'd been waiting six months to get assigned to an active unit that wasn't a training or replacement center. Now, late March 1966, my training was over, the travel had ended, and replacement centers were about to be history. I relished the prospect of fighting in real combat as an elite paratrooper.

There would be some life-and-death experiences before my adventures with German shepherd war dogs, but now, Kenny and I were at last heading for the mountains of South Vietnam. I wondered how it would feel to parachute out of a plane in a war zone for the first time.

Chapter 2

Garry Owen

1st Battalion, 7th Cavalry crest.

IN THE EARLY MORNING light, Kenny and I hauled our duffel bags up the ramp of a C130 military transport plane that quickly filled with troops and supplies. The pilot wasted little time getting airborne. For the first time since arriving in Vietnam, I felt cool air.

Riding in that plane was incredibly noisy; it was nearly impossible to carry on a conversation without yelling. The aircraft flew north of Saigon for several hours before the pilot banked left and began his descent. As I peered through the small window, I saw an airstrip and rows and rows of green military tents and equipment below. Camp Radcliff, home of the 1st Cavalry Division, was directly below us. Kenny pointed out a large yellow-and-black 1st Cavalry Division shoulder patch painted on the mountainside above the camp. I thrilled at the thought that we would soon be wearing that combat patch.

Dense jungle and mountainous terrain surrounded the circular base camp. The small Vietnamese village of An Khe was near the camp's outer perimeter. Trucks, jeeps, and troops moved along the dirt roads that ran through the camp. Helicopters sat idle in neat rows along the airstrip, which was called the Golf Course because it was so enormous. The 1st Cavalry Division, nicknamed the First Team, had more helicopters than any other infantry division in Vietnam.

From the air, the camp appeared well fortified. The vegetation around its outer edges had been bulldozed, leaving a 360-degree dirt buffer that separated the heavily guarded perimeter from the surrounding jungle and made for clear lanes of fire in all directions. Three heavily fortified bunkers were evenly spaced between lookout towers. Strategically positioned artillery pieces and tanks dotted the perimeter.

After the plane landed, we were hustled to the division's personnel and administration building. A clerk collected our individual personnel, finance, and medical records to process us into the division. We had to show our two metal dog tags hanging from chains around our necks. If a soldier was killed, the medic would take one dog tag from the chain and lodge the other between the dead man's teeth. The first tag went to the unit commander for accountability, and the second to the morgue with the body for identification.

The personnel clerk congratulated us as he handed over a set of orders officially promoting us from private to private first class (PFC). The army's policy at the time was to make such a promotion effective upon the soldier's arrival in South Vietnam. That meant a monthly pay increase of at least $50. We also got another $60 per month as combat pay. At the time, I made $300 a month and didn't have to pay taxes. If I were assigned to a paratrooper outfit, I'd get an additional $55 monthly.

An infantry division's organizational structure is layered like a pyramid. At the top is the division commander, a two-star general, who has the ultimate power and authority. The division commander's subordinate commanders, in order of power, are the brigade commander, battalion commander, company commander, and the platoon leader. These are all command positions occupied by commissioned officers.

There may be three brigades in a division, three battalions in a brigade, and four companies in each battalion. In each company, there may be four platoons made up of four squads of enlisted men. There are eleven enlisted men in a squad at full strength. Each squad has two fire teams commanded by a squad leader and two fire-team leaders. A platoon at full strength has a total of forty-four infantrymen.

The enlisted structure is also layered in authority, starting with the division sergeant major, brigade sergeant major, battalion sergeant major, company first sergeant, platoon sergeant, squad leader, fire team leader, and then the riflemen. Kenny and I were riflemen — peons with no authority.

Dennis Blessing (2nd Platoon) in doorway of
Co B 1-7 orderly room, 1966
(photo courtesy of Dennis Blessing).

We were assigned to Company B, 1st Battalion, 7th Cavalry Regiment. General George Armstrong Custer had commanded the 7th Cavalry Regiment in 1876 at Little Big Horn. Whenever we passed an officer outside the cover of a building, the 7th Cavalry tradition was to say, "Garry Owen" as we saluted. Garry Owen was the title of Custer's favorite Irish marching song, which he liked to have the 7th Regiment band play at parades and other festive military functions. I felt a sense of pride that this historical tradition had continued to be observed through the years.

Company B, 7th Cavalry living quarters, 1966
(photo courtesy of James Ertle).

Our new home was a skimpy old green canvas tent held up by two wooden center poles and wooden tie-down stakes. Several empty canvas cots stood on the packed-dirt floor inside. I couldn't believe that this dark and misty tent would be my home for the next twelve months.

Kenny said, "Well, Johnny, we're finally here."

"Yeah, but I wonder where the hell the platoon is? All I saw when we flew in was mountains and very little civilization."

"We're not in Saigon anymore," Kenny said. "We're in a war zone. The platoon is probably out in the jungle hunting for the enemy."

The dining hall, or "mess hall" as we called it, was a large wooden building not far from our tent. Just outside it were large green canvas bags full of drinking water. We ate from metal trays and sat on picnic tables. Breakfast consisted of powdered eggs, powdered milk, fresh-baked bread, and bitter coffee. Lunch and dinner were nothing to write home about either.

After we ate breakfast that morning and were on the way back to our tent, we passed an officer, saluted him, and said, "Garry Owen, sir!"

He returned the salute and replied, "All the way!"

After the officer had passed, Kenny and I looked at each other and chuckled. We thought it was really cool to say, "Garry Owen" instead of "Good morning, sir!"

Kenny and I were introduced to the company supply sergeant, who lived in a tent packed and stacked high with supplies. The sergeant told us that he had everything we'd ever need for fighting a war. He issued each of us a backpack, canteen, ammunition pouches, medical field dressings, a plastic poncho, a nylon poncho liner, a helmet ("steel pot"), a helmet liner, an entrenching tool (field shovel), and a bayonet. He also gave us several division patches like the one we'd seen on the mountainside when we flew in. The insignia on these cloth patches meant that we were no longer trainees in transit — we now belonged to a fighting unit.

The supply sergeant told us we'd get weapons, ammunition, grenades, claymores (mines), trip flares, and other goodies after the platoon returned from its mission in the field. He advised us that our new platoon sergeant would decide when we'd be ready to go on S and Ds.

I asked, "What are S and Ds?"

The sergeant smiled and shook his head and said, "Search and destroy missions. That's what we do for a living around here, young trooper!"

Kenny and I wondered what it would be like to meet the other members of the 2nd Platoon, who were due to arrive aboard helicopters within the hour. I was nervous, yet eager to see real combat infantrymen for the first time. *Will the other soldiers accept us?* I wondered. Kenny appeared calm, but his eyes showed that he too was a bit nervous.

The sound of helicopters filled the air outside the tent. I ran out for a look. Fifteen or twenty ships drifted into view. Fully equipped soldiers clutched their weapons and sat inside the open doors. The door gunners held M60 machine guns mounted on posts.

Dirt kicked up as the first group of ships touched down about one hundred feet away from us. The wind from the helicopters' rotating blades rippled our fatigues and almost whipped the caps off our heads. Dust swirling all around me, I watched, excited, as the men climbed out and slowly walked in my direction. The door gunners stayed aboard as the empty ships lifted off the road and flew away.

I watched, awestruck, while the men walked past me as if I were invisible. Under their steel helmets, I could see the soldiers' tired faces and eyes. Their dirty fatigues and boots looked as if they hadn't been polished since they were issued. The men carried various types of shoulder weapons, some of which I'd never seen before. They wore backpacks filled with items that I couldn't see. As the men walked by, I noticed that they looked and smelled as if they hadn't showered in a month.

Some of the soldiers entered the tent Kenny and I lived in. I was too nervous to follow them inside. Finally, I gathered up enough courage, walked in, and sat on my cot like a little kid, silently watching them unpack their gear. Kenny sat on his cot too, quietly observing everyone. It was easy to see that they were happy to be back in base camp.

A short time later, two men walked into the tent and called our names: "PFC Kenneth L. Mook and PFC John C. Burnam."

Kenny and I jumped to our feet and answered, "Here!"

The men approached us, stopped, and looked us over in silence. We remained standing to show respect as we'd been taught during training. The men looked at one another, smiled, and told us to sit down and relax. They were amused by our innocent behavior. One man introduced himself as Sergeant Savage. He was about five feet seven inches tall, around twenty-three years old, huskily built, and had a hardened, darkly tanned face. Sergeant Savage introduced us to Sergeant Marlin

Sergeant Marlin Dorman,
2nd Platoon squad leader, 1966
(photo courtesy of Billy Smith).

Dorman, our new squad leader, and then excused himself.

Sergeant Dorman smiled and said, "I'm your squad leader. Welcome to the 2nd Platoon and 4th Squad, better known as the weapons squad."

Sergeant Dorman was a thin twenty-two-year-old, five feet eight inches tall, with bright blue eyes, brown hair, and a deep tan. Even though he hadn't cleaned up yet, Sergeant Dorman had the appearance and presence of a leader who spoke with confidence. He reached into his breast pocket and took out a little green notepad. He asked us for our full names, ranks, ages, service numbers, types of training we'd had, hometowns, next of kin, and the dates we'd arrived in Vietnam. He recorded our answers in his notebook.

Sergeant Dorman explained that a weapons squad had two five-man machine-gun teams. Each team had one M60 machine gun, and consisted of one gunner, an assistant gunner, and three riflemen/ammunition bearers.

He said, "That's an ideal fully manned squad. The problem is that I only have two M60 machine gunners and one assistant gunner. My squad is critically undermanned. You men are a sight for sore eyes. Forget whatever you were taught in the States about machine-gun deployment. Even though my squad is undermanned, it's still the primary firepower of the 2nd Platoon. When the shit hits the fan there's nothing better than the M60. Counting you two, I now have three men on the number-two gun and two men on the number-one gun."

As Sergeant Dorman continued, I gathered that the number-one gun provided firepower to the front of the platoon, and the number two gun provided firepower and security at the rear.

We met number-one M60 gunner, Specialist Four John Engel, and his assistant gunner, Private Wildman, and number-two M60 gunner, Specialist Four Bob Dunn. Sergeant Dorman appointed Kenny as Dunn's assistant gunner, and I was assigned as his ammo bearer.

Bob Dunn was five feet seven inches tall, weighed about 170 pounds, had blond hair and blue eyes, and wore a crusty mustache. He was from New York and spoke with a heavy accent. He had arrived in Vietnam in early January 1966.

I asked Bob where the platoon had been. He said they'd searched the jungle for a week but had made no contact with the gooks.

"You mean the enemy?" I asked.

Bob then translated some new terminology for me. He explained that "VC" meant Vietcong, "NVA" was the North Vietnamese Army, and "PAVN" meant the People's Army of Vietnam. Gooks, Cong, dinks, and Charlie were other terms used to describe the enemy. The NVA, he said were the toughest of all to fight.

As we started talking about our duties, Bob explained the importance of keeping the M60 machine gun clean and oiled at all times. Out in the jungle, he said, the gun gets dirty quickly. The rain and humidity quickly cause the metal parts that aren't frequently oiled to rust and possibly malfunction.

Dunn explained the squad's job: "We get an operations order or a mission. We pack up and leave base camp for a week or so. We hunt and kill some gooks. After that, we come home for a few days to shower, rest, and get some hot food. Then it starts all over again. Believe me, you guys will get your share of the action and then some."

When Bob gave me my first M16 rifle, I acted like a little kid with a new Christmas toy. Kenny and I test fired our weapons at a safe location on the camp's perimeter. Bob taught us how to take them apart and reassemble them, and showed us where to put the most oil.

My previous training had taught me how to maintain sight alignment, control my breathing, and squeeze the trigger. I was surprised that the M16 had little or no kick. As with all military rifles and pistols, the M16 was designed for right-handed people. When fired, hot brass casings eject to the right and away from a right-handed shooter. Because I'm left-handed, hot casings eject across my face and body. Not a big problem, but on rare occasions, I'd get a hot casing blown down my collar.

During training in the States, Kenny and I had been awarded Expert Rifle badges for consistently scoring hits in the center of targets at various distances with an M14 rifle. The different qualification levels of marksmanship were, from lowest to highest, Expert, Sharpshooter, and Marksman. The training targets were both pop-up and stationary. Shooting positions — standing, prone, kneeling — also varied based on target distance. Hitting a target dead center was all in the sight alignment, breathing, and trigger squeeze. Kenny had also scored Expert with the M60 machine gun. Most soldiers qualified as sharpshooter or marksman, but you were very well respected when you qualified as an expert with two types of weapons. This was probably why Kenny got to be Bob's assistant machine gunner.

As we trained in base camp, SP4 Dunn gave us some pointers on how to conserve ammunition. He said, "Never switch to full automatic unless there's no other choice. Always carry your own supply of ammunition. The quicker you use it up, the less you'll have when you need it most." The training sessions boosted my self-confidence. As each day passed, Kenny and I felt more like members of the platoon team.

We would need all the confidence we could muster, because we'd soon be meeting Charlie face-to-face on the battlefield for the first time.

Chapter 3

Ia Drang Valley

A FEW DAYS BEFORE my first mission, Sergeant Dorman told Kenny and me a story to fill us in on the history of our new platoon. It was about a mission that took place in the middle of November 1965.

The 1st Battalion, 7th Cavalry had gone looking for a fight near the Cambodian border. The battalion flew into the Ia Drang Valley, a remote area in the northern highlands of South Vietnam, at the base of Chu Pong Mountain. Lieutenant Colonel Harold "Hal" Moore, the battalion commander, had led the battalion into the valley with the 2nd Platoon, making it one of the first on the ground. Immediately, the landing zone, known as LZ XRAY, was saturated with American artillery.

Sergeant Dorman held us spellbound as he recounted the events of that day:

"When our platoon landed, we rushed into the woods, our guns firing. Lieutenant Colonel Moore directed our platoon leader to move the 2nd Platoon about a hundred meters and set up a new position. The platoon fanned out and ran forward toward the base of Chu Pong Mountain. We spotted two or three enemy soldiers moving across our front, and the platoon leader ordered us to chase and capture them. We pursued the enemy for fifty meters and ran into one hundred and fifty NVA soldiers dressed in khaki uniforms and pith helmets, charging down the mountain shooting at us.

"These were hard-core troops from North Vietnam, not your ordinary black-pajama, part-time soldiers/farmers. When they attacked, we took casualties before we could hit the dirt and return their fire. We tried to get behind anything that would provide cover, but we were pinned down by heavy fire and cut off from the rest of the company.

"The platoon spread out. We took cover behind clumps of bushes and trees. Communication was nearly impossible above the noise of blazing machine guns, rifle fire, and grenade explosions. Totally outnumbered, we fought for our lives. We were overwhelmed. Many of our men were already wounded or dead. The gooks screamed at the top of their lungs while they came at us shooting. During one of the enemy's human-wave attacks, our platoon leader, Lieutenant Herrick, was badly wounded and died fighting alongside his men.

"The weapons squad suffered so many casualties that the squad leader took over one of the M60s. He fired it until he was overrun and killed. Then the gooks turned our M60 machine gun on us. We had several more casualties before we took it back. Low on ammunition and grenades, we gathered what we could from our own dead.

"I don't know how we made it after losing the platoon leader, the platoon sergeant, and the squad leaders. Sergeant Savage was the only sergeant left, so he took over the platoon. He got on the radio and found cover behind a log while he called for artillery strikes. We fought on and off, all day and into the night. Sergeant Savage continued to send periodic situation reports over the radio. We received radio reports that the entire battalion was under heavy ground attack by the NVA forces. We were too far out for any immediate rescue attempts. Our orders over the radio were to hold our ground until help arrived the next day.

"It was very dark that first night, but none of us slept. We kept quiet and tried to comfort the wounded as we waited to be attacked again. During that night, I heard a bugle call coming from the mountain, and then all hell broke loose again. We withstood several attacks and survived until Sky Troopers from a sister company rescued us on the afternoon of the second day. The 2nd Platoon became known as the Lost Platoon because we'd been the only platoon outside the battalion lines of defense.

"The battle raged for a third day. B-52 bombers dropped tons of bombs on Chu Pong Mountain and the surrounding area. When the fighting was over, our battalion had taken heavy casualties; our company had forty men left out of a hundred and fifteen. The North Vietnamese Army had lost over a thousand men. At the time, I was a rifleman in the 2nd Squad of the 2nd Platoon. I don't know how I survived. There were bodies all over the place. The dead gooks and Americans were lying next to each other — that was how close the fighting had gotten.

"Our battered troops were relieved by a sister battalion, 2nd Battalion, 7th Cavalry. We were flown out by helicopter for much-needed rest. The 2nd Battalion, 7th Cavalry moved on foot a mile or so away to LZ Albany. They marched in columns, strung out through the woods. We figured the fight and cleanup was over, but the NVA had other plans. They had fresh battalions in reserve — men who were waiting to join the action and kill Americans. The enemy paralleled the American movement until they were in a position to do the most damage. In a matter of several hours, our sister battalion was cut to ribbons and almost wiped out.

"Afterward, I was promoted to sergeant and became the weapons-squad leader. After losing so many men, the replacements we needed in the weapons squad didn't arrive until January. First, SP4 Engel, SP4 Dunn, and PVT Wildman arrived. You and Kenny are the second set of replacements. It's now the first week of April and my weapons squad is still shorthanded.

"I only have to make it a few more months before I go home in August. We haven't been back to Ia Drang since November. I hope I never have to see the place again."

Sergeant Dorman got up, excused himself, and quickly left our company. I was wide-eyed, astounded, and speechless. What could I say to someone like him? I felt honored and humbled to know this brave man with such extraordinary combat experience.

I'd been stateside in Uncle Sam's army for about a month at the time the Ia Drang battle was fought. Now I was assigned to a platoon that was almost wiped out there.

Will I be brave in the face of the enemy, or too scared to fight? Will I be killed instantly, severely wounded, or survive like Sergeant Dorman? I wondered. I found it difficult to sleep that night thinking about the Lost Platoon.

A few days later, Sergeant Dorman came into our tent and said, "Wake up and listen. After you clean up and get some breakfast, meet me here for an operations order."

I got out of my cot, grabbed my shaving gear, and slipped on my "rice-paddy racers" — our nickname for rubber flip-flops. I headed for the showers, which consisted of several green fifty-gallon drums welded together, sitting on top of a wood frame with canvas siding. Flat wooden pallets underneath the showerheads provided a place to stand above the moldy, wet, mosquito-infested ground beneath. A trench was dug around the wooden pallets for water drainage. Towels and clothes hung on nails hammered into the posts that held the shower frame together. A faucet attached to a pipe controlled the flow of cool water; there was no hot. We took quick showers to conserve water for others, and we shaved outside the shower, using our steel helmets as sinks. When the troops were in from the field, water tankers filled the shower-water containers.

After a shower and shave, it was time for breakfast. Kenny and I sat at a picnic table with our new team leader, Bob Dunn. He couldn't tell us anything more about our upcoming mission or operations order. I quickly ate breakfast and returned to my tent. A few minutes later, everyone else in the weapons squad was back from breakfast. Sergeant Dorman arrived and gathered us together. He took out his little green notebook, glanced at his notes, and began to talk in a serious tone.

"We're going back to Ia Drang Valley," he said.

From the story he'd told us only a few days before, Kenny and I knew how Sergeant Dorman must have felt about returning to Ia Drang, but he didn't betray his emotions. Instead, he put his military field map down and pointed to a grid that he knew all too well. The terrain appeared wooded and flat until it reached the base of Chu Pong Mountain. Inside the wooded area, near the base of the mountain, LZ XRAY was clearly marked in grease pencil on the map. The Cambodian border was within marching distance of the LZ. The entire area was completely isolated from any roads and villages.

Sergeant Dorman said, "S2 battalion intelligence reported small concentrations of enemy troops operating in this area. Our mission is to engage the enemy but not pursue them across the Cambodian border. We'll link up with the rest of the company when we get to LZ XRAY, and set up in a company-sized perimeter. Our objective is to check out the area, hike up Chu Pong Mountain, and look for enemy base camps. Then we'll sweep the Ia Drang Valley southeast to LZ Victor, spend the night there, and come back home the next day. We'll be supported by field artillery, gunships, and jet fighters if necessary.

"Pack a basic load and enough food for three days. We'll be re-supplied in the field. Be ready to move out to the road for pickup in an hour. Any questions?"

Sergeant Dorman looked at Kenny and me and said, "You two are about to get your cherries busted." He knew, and now we knew, that we were going to be tested.

Bob Dunn turned to Kenny and said, "Don't forget to pick up the bag of M60 spare parts from my tent."

The spare-parts bag contained one extra machine gun barrel, an asbestos glove used to grab and change the barrel when it got too hot to touch, cleaning rods, metal chamber and bore brushes, small oil cans, and cleaning cloths. The bag had a shoulder strap and weighed about twelve pounds.

I grabbed my pack and filled it with several pairs of socks, underwear, and T-shirts. I checked my shaving kit to make sure I had my toothbrush, shaving cream, soap dish, bottle of after-shave lotion, hand towel, and razor. I decided to pack writing paper and envelopes just in case I had time to write letters home. With my small canvas pack already full, Bob directed me to go with Kenny to the supply tent to pick up a basic load of M16 rifle ammunition (300 rounds), two grenades, two trip flares, one claymore mine, and eight hundred-round belts of machine gun ammunition.

I thought, *Damn! That's a hell of a lot of extra shit to carry.*

When I got back with everything, I had twenty M16 magazines and twenty boxes of bullets. I loaded each magazine clip with eighteen rounds and inserted six clips into a cloth bandoleer with a shoulder strap. I crammed the rest of the magazine clips into my pack. I rolled my poncho as small and tight as I could and strapped it underneath the butt pack.

The M60 machine gun belts held one hundred metal-jacketed rounds. Every fifth round was a red-tipped tracer, which lit up when it left the barrel. Tracers were used to help zero in on a target and for night firing. Each box came with a green cloth bag and a strap so it could be carried slung from the shoulder.

John Burnam, Company B, 2nd Platoon, 1st Battalion, 7th Cavalry, 1966. I was the ammo bearer for Bob Dunn, M60 machine gunner, 1966 (photo courtesy of Bob Dunn).

Kenny put two boxes of M60 machine gun ammunition in the spare-parts bag. He set the other two boxes aside to carry over his shoulder. I brought two hundred-round boxes and Bob attached a hundred-round belt to the feeding mechanism of the M60. My pistol belt held two canteens of water, two ammunition pouches, two grenades, one bayonet, and a field shovel. We attached adjustable shoulder straps to the backpack and pistol belt to help distribute the weight more evenly between the small of the back and the shoulders. Medical field bandages were attached to metal D-rings sewn to the shoulder harness. We placed a plastic bottle of mosquito repellent inside the elastic headband on top of our steel pot.

I lifted the pack onto my back. When I bent over to pick up my M16 and helmet, the weight shifted forward. I nearly fell on my face. Soaking wet, I might have weighed 130 pounds, but the pack added at least fifty more. My feet pressed heavily into the soles of my boots. I didn't know how I was going to carry all that stuff for any great distance, let alone climb Chu Pong Mountain with it.

When I thought I had everything packed, Bob told me to go get a three-day supply of C-Rations. Each soldier was issued a case of C-Rations that contained twelve meals. The case was a little larger than a case of beer and about as heavy. When I got back to the tent, there was little time before I had to be at the road for pickup.

I complained aloud, "How am I going to carry nine meals when my pack is full and I have all this other stuff to carry?"

Bob looked at my gear and asked, "What the hell did you pack?"

"Extra clothes, shaving gear, and ammunition," I replied.

Bob laughed. "Take out the extra clothes and use the room to pack essentials. Put cans of food in your long green socks and tie them to your shoulder harness. By the way, John, I know your pack is heavy. Mine is too. Pack only the bare necessities and as much ammunition as you can carry. Also, take only what you think you'll eat for three days, and leave the rest here."

Although I felt like a complete moron, I did everything Bob said. It was my first mission, so what the hell did I know?

Sergeant Dorman showed up and yelled, "Saddle up!"

I looked awkward, like a fresh-out-of-the-box soldier. When I walked, it sounded like I was carrying pots and pans. Kenny seemed a little uncomfortable too. The other soldiers in the platoon looked at us like the new recruits we were, but didn't say a word. When we reached the road, we joined the other members of the weapons squad. We sat in the hot morning sun and waited for the choppers to arrive.

Sergeant Dorman briefed the squad on the loading plan. We were split into two machine gun teams, one on either side of the road. When the chopper landed, we would board simultaneously from both sides of the ship.

The first group of choppers landed, and SP4 Engel and PFC Wildman climbed aboard with members of another squad. The ships quickly took off and another group of slicks landed. Sergeant Dorman ordered our machine gun team to board the nearest ship. When it touched down, I ran a short distance, climbed aboard, and sat down against the inside wall away from the open door. I felt a little uncomfortable because the doors remained open during flight.

As the ship lifted off, I felt the metal floor vibrate and rattle. I braced myself, thinking I'd slide across the floor and out the open door. My stomach was full of butterflies; it felt like going down the first steep drop of a roller coaster. As the aircraft gained altitude, it joined a column formation of others. I was still a little tense when the helicopter reached cruising altitude. Looking down, I saw the base camp slowly disappear. Several gunships flew escort at a lower altitude — barely above the treetops.

At least thirty ships were in the air. I could see men sitting inside the choppers flying alongside us. Despite my nervousness, riding inside a fully armed formation of flying warships was an awesome feeling and afforded an incredible view of the land below.

The cool air felt good against my face. Looking around, I noticed that no one spoke. Everyone stared out the open doors. The door gunners had their machine guns loaded and tilted down. They wore green flight-crew helmets with intercoms so they could communicate with the two pilots. The formation traveled for about an hour before descending; then the treetops got closer and closer.

Green smoke swirled up from the ground of LZ XRAY in the Ia Drang Valley, indicating that the LZ was cleared for landing. The gunships buzzed around the zone as the choppers approached the landing area. In the near distance, Chu Pong Mountain stuck out like a pyramid covered with tropical vegetation. When our chopper got ready to land, I watched the other soldiers scoot closer to the open doors. As soon as the landing gear touched the earth, everyone quickly jumped out. Kenny and I followed Bob, and we created a small perimeter around the ship until it lifted away.

Sergeant Dorman barked, "Bob, get your gun over to those trees and cover our asses."

Kenny and I followed Bob to a tree line about fifty yards out. My adrenaline spiked. My eyes were wide open, scanning for anything unusual. Bob put the gun down on its bipod and loaded the chamber for firing. He told me to move to my left and link up with the next man in the platoon. I reacted without a word. About twenty yards away, I spotted another member of the platoon. After we made eye contact, I dropped down on one knee and faced outward into the surrounding trees.

Helicopters kept landing with more troops. Bob and Kenny manned the M60 machine gun about forty yards from the landing zone. I was about five yards to the left of the machine gun. Knee-high grass, dried by the hot sun, surrounded the trees. I nervously tapped the bottom of the magazine inserted into my M16 rifle. I loaded a round into the chamber and made sure the selector switch was on "Safe." Everyone lay quietly in a prone position on the hard, dry grass. I scanned my front, trying to see and listen for anything resembling enemy movement. Minutes passed. Nothing happened. Sergeant Dorman was busy going from man to man, checking that each of us was present and in a correct defensive position.

Dorman ordered Bob to follow him to a better position for the gun. Kenny and I briskly followed behind. As I moved, my helmet felt loose on my head and kept moving in front of my eyes. When we finally stopped, Sergeant Dorman positioned the M60 facing Chu Pong Mountain and instructed Bob, "Before you dig in, scout your position thirty yards out." Bob took Kenny with him and I stayed back to cover them. After slowly walking around with the machine gun at the ready, they returned with nothing to report.

There were now over a hundred men on the ground at LZ XRAY. The gunships still buzzed around but weren't firing. Gunships didn't have door gunners because they were heavily armed with machine guns and aerial rocket artillery (ARA) controlled by the pilots.

I felt safe, but still not confident about what I was doing or what to expect. The order was given to dig in. Bob stood guard behind the M60 while Kenny and I dug a three-man foxhole. Sergeant Dorman said he normally didn't put three men in one position, but since we were green, he wanted Bob to teach us how to set up a machine gun position.

After we dug the foxhole, Bob showed Kenny and me how to set up a claymore mine. He said, "The first thing to remember is that the claymore has FRONT printed in large letters on one side. Be sure to point that side in the direction of the enemy. Claymores are real easy to set up, but if you don't do it right, Charlie will turn the mines around and put them closer to your foxhole, and when it's time to squeeze the trigger, you'll blow up your own ass. Remember: surprise is important, so camouflage the mine without disturbing the natural look of the surrounding vegetation. A claymore has a fifty-foot wire. One end is connected to the blasting cap inside the mine. The other end is the trigger mechanism. There's a circuit tester; always use it to make sure the claymore is armed.

"Don't set out trip flares during the day, do it right before dark. Trip flares are a little touchy, but you want them that way. When the enemy trips the wire, the pin should pop out quickly and ignite the flare. To keep Charlie from tampering, attach a second trip wire to the bottom of the claymore. Charlie will be caught by surprise like a deer in headlights. Then we kill him."

Patrols were scheduled for the next morning to search the area and climb Chu Pong Mountain. The sun was setting. I went out with Bob to assemble the claymores and trip flares, while Kenny watched from behind the machine gun. When we got back, I boasted to Kenny with a big smile, saying, "It's a cinch!"

Kenny replied, "Good, then you can do it all the time, Johnny!"

Bob laughed and said, "Kenny, tomorrow it's your turn."

Sergeant Dorman came by to remind us to keep alert and make sure someone manned the M60 machine gun at all times. He also gave us the password for the night. We would use the password, which changed daily, to get back through friendly lines if people got split up during a nighttime firefight.

Bob scheduled two-hour guard shifts. Everyone ate supper before the first watch. I used a tiny can opener called a P38 to open a warm can of beefsteak and potatoes. It tasted terrible, but I ate every bit.

Each box of C-Rations had a dark-brown plastic bag containing a plastic spoon, a tiny roll of toilet paper, a sample-size box of four cigarettes, little packets of sugar, creamer, salt, and pepper packets, one book of matches, and a packet of instant coffee.

To cover our exposed skin, we used mosquito repellent. It was powerful enough to keep the bugs from biting us at night. Each man carried a green plastic poncho to sleep on. I concluded that sleeping in a foxhole was like sleeping in a grave.

✸

Everyone was awake at first light. We used water from canteens to brush our teeth, wash up, and mix powdered coffee. We were required to have clean-shaven faces. When I finished shaving, I slapped on some Mennen Skin Bracer.

To my surprise, Bob blurted, "Who the hell has the after-shave lotion on?"

I confessed, and Bob ripped into me. "You can't go on patrol smelling like a whore. Charlie will smell you a mile away. Charlie has instincts like a fucking animal. He lives out here, for crying out loud. What the hell's wrong with you? You don't need to fucking help him out!"

I was stunned and so embarrassed that I didn't say a word. I also knew the smell would take time to wear off. I quietly dug a hole and buried that bottle of Skin Bracer and wiped my face with dirt, trying to get rid of the scent. When Sergeant Dorman found out what I'd done, he couldn't stop howling. Before long, I was the topic of conversation throughout the platoon. They called me "the Mennen Boy."

What a way to start my first full day in the field with a bunch of combat veterans!

Bob and Kenny went to retrieve the trip flares and claymores. Our orders were to hike to Chu Pong Mountain and scout for enemy base camps. Sergeant Dorman directed the number-two machine gun to bring up the rear of the platoon. The number-one machine gun team moved behind the point man leading the patrol. The platoon spread out and traveled in column formation. Flank guards were placed about twenty-five yards out on each side of the column. With the flat terrain, visibility was good. We walked slowly and cautiously through the trees and knee-high brown grass while avoiding large termite mounds.

I was close to the last man in the formation. As we traveled through a clearing, I stepped over a branch and crushed two huge millipedes crawling near my boot. Red ants (fire ants) were all over the dry vegetation and trees. When they bit, it stung like hell, so I quickly learned to avoid them.

The patrol halted before reaching the base of the mountain. I spotted a helmet on the ground a short distance away. I picked it up. It had a large bullet hole in the front. I examined the inside and saw a piece of dried scalp stuck to the back of the helmet liner. The name on the headband read, "Sgt. Bernard." I put it down and wondered about the man who had worn it, feeling sorry that an American had been killed out here in the middle of nowhere. I looked around and noticed that other soldiers were also finding remnants of a battle that had taken place there.

Shallow foxholes overgrown with grass appeared everywhere. Military web gear from a backpack stuck out from a mound of dirt. Tarnished brass from all types of spent shells littered the area around the foxholes. The positions of everything indicated that the fighting had been fierce — possibly hand-to-hand combat.

Kenny located a splintered human jawbone and a skull with a bullet hole in it. The rains had partly washed away the dirt and exposed what appeared to be human bones. Bob told me, "These aren't American remains, because we don't leave our dead behind."

I wondered how all this had happened. Never in my nineteen young years had I seen anything like it.

The patrol moved out again; eventually, we reached the base of the mountain, which was rugged, dense with vegetation, and dark. The point man used a machete to cut a path. The sunlight barely penetrated to the jungle floor as we started to climb at a snail's pace. My pack snagged on vines every step of the way.

We hadn't traveled far before someone at the head of the platoon spotted a huge enemy base camp built inside a large bamboo thicket. A few soldiers checked for booby traps before we entered the camp, the entire platoon slowly moving inside. Sunlight reflected off the bamboo, creating a yellow glow. We were warned to watch out for snakes, especially bamboo vipers. I shuddered because I hated the sight of snakes.

We set up a defensive position inside the enemy base camp. Half the platoon spread out and searched, but the camp was empty. We did, however, uncover a huge cache of ammunition, mortars, and rockets hidden in camouflaged holes in the ground. We found cooking utensils, a meeting area, and a small hospital with some medical supplies. Bunkers and tiny one-man foxholes dotted the area. Small piles of grenades with wooden handles and strings dangling from them were scattered throughout the camp, which looked as if it could have held several hundred North Vietnamese soldiers.

I thought *This has to be one of the base camps that the enemy used to launch attacks on our company.*

Sergeant Dorman couldn't believe the B-52 bombers had missed this place, though it couldn't be seen from the air. There wasn't a bomb crater anywhere inside the camp. The platoon leader got on the radio to speak with the company commander. They decided to set charges and blow up the enemy munitions.

When we returned to our foxholes that evening, we were dirty and tired. I had to take a crap real bad, so I asked Kenny, "Where do you think I should go?"

"Out in the woods, I guess. I haven't had to go yet."

Overhearing us, Bob said, "We'll cover your ass!"

He and Kenny broke into laughter. It would have been terrible for the enemy to catch me by surprise with my pants down, so I put up with the sarcasm and accepted their protection while I went out to crap.

That night, we set up an ambush at a creek beside the mountain, about 150 yards from my foxhole. Sergeant Dorman teamed me with Ranger Mac, as he was called, a black veteran soldier and a survivor of the battle of Ia Drang. He spoke in a tense voice about not being very happy to be in this place again. After we talked for a few minutes, he set up the trip flares and claymores in front of our foxhole.

While on guard duty in the foxhole, I heard rifle and machine-gun fire coming from the direction of the creek. Ranger Mac woke up and jumped into the foxhole with me. We pointed our weapons into the darkness and listened, waiting to be attacked.

Ranger Mac blurted out, "I hope them gooks trip the flare, so I can blow their asses to hell with the claymore."

He instructed me to put my ammunition in front of me so I could reload as fast as possible. The firing in the distance lasted about half a minute, then total silence. Nothing else happened the rest of the night.

The next morning, Sergeant Dorman told us that the 1st Platoon had killed two enemy soldiers at the creek. He said that the company commander was pissed because someone had sprung the ambush too soon, and the main element had gotten away. The two kills were NVA soldiers who'd been armed with AK-47 rifles.

Later that morning, the entire company swept the valley to LZ Victor, a few miles southeast of LZ XRAY. Our route followed the east side of Chu Pong Mountain, parallel to the Cambodian border. I walked next to Kenny. It seemed to get hotter and hotter as we pushed in the direction of LZ Victor. The water in my canteen was so hot from the sun that drinking it was all but unbearable. I forced it down anyway. The temperature must have been over 115 degrees. My fatigue jacket was soaked with sweat.

Almost out of water, my legs weakening under the heavy load on my back, I kept walking as Kenny pointed out nearby bomb craters. Helicopters flew above to cover our advance through the lightly wooded area. After the platoon stopped for a break, Kenny saw that I was slowing down. Determined not to give in to the heat, I wanted to make it to LZ Victor on my own.

When the platoon stopped again, I drank the last of my water, and found that I was unable to stand. I felt dizzy and went down on one knee, and stayed in that position for a moment. While struggling to rise, I felt a hand on my shoulder and heard a voice ask, "Are you okay, trooper?"

Without looking up, I replied, "I feel a little dizzy and weak."

"How long have you been in-country?"

I finally looked up and recognized Lieutenant Colonel Moore, the battalion commander who had led the ill-fated battle of Ia Drang Valley that Sergeant Dorman had told us about.

I tried to steady my legs, but fell against the tree. LTC Moore grabbed me under the arm and held me up. I thanked him and confessed that this was my first mission.

He gave me some water from his canteen and said, "Where are you from, trooper?"

"Littleton, Colorado, sir."

"It's going to take you a while to get used to this type of heat and humidity, but it's an unusually hot day."

LTC Moore didn't have a pack on, only a pistol belt with a .45-caliber pistol and two canteens of water. He looked fresh, as if he'd just arrived, and he'd hardly broken a sweat. He instructed me to take off the pack.

"Now you'll cool down faster. Grab your rifle and follow me."

LTC Moore picked up my pack and carried it. We walked at a brisk pace, and I finally cooled down. When we got to LZ Victor, I followed LTC Moore to his command post. He gave me my pack and ordered one of his men to fill my canteens and have the medic check me over.

LTC Moore turned and began to walk away, so I said, "Garry Owen, sir!"

He turned and smiled, "All the way, Sky Trooper!"

I made it back to my platoon and didn't see LTC Moore again, but I knew that I'd be forever grateful for that act of kindness from my commander.

Our mission to Ia Drang Valley was over. The helicopters lifted us off LZ Victor and we headed home to An Khe. Even though I never fired a single shot, my first mission had taught me valuable lessons about packing gear, riding in troop-assault helicopters, moving in a tactical formation, and setting up a defensive position. My thoughts of not getting an assignment to an elite paratrooper unit didn't seem to matter anymore. I felt lucky to be with the men of the 2nd Platoon.

Later on, I'd learn the value of relying on a German shepherd scout dog to lead me through more treacherous enemy territory in South Vietnam, but my next mission would teach me the reality of combat, which was something I could never have imagined.

Chapter 4

Operation Davy Crockett

DURING THE FIRST WEEK of May 1966, after several uneventful missions, my company, Company B, 1st Battalion, 7th Cavalry, rested in base camp, cleaning our equipment and oiling our weapons. Sergeant Dorman entered our tent and gathered the squad for a briefing. He told us we were going to Bong Son. On that mission, dubbed "Operation Davy Crockett," our entire 1st battalion was to sweep the Coastal Plains of Bong Son to the South China Sea of the Binh Dinh Province. Our orders were to search, engage, and eradicate a North Vietnamese Army battalion. We would be under the leadership of Colonel Harold G. Moore, commander, 3rd Brigade, 1st Air Cavalry Division.

Sergeant Dorman put his map down on a cot and put his finger on Bong Son. The terrain was composed of vast fields of rice paddies on the coast of the South China Sea. There were numerous streams where a large number of banana and coconut palm trees were under cultivation. The highest peak in the Da Dan Mountains in the west rose to a height of over six hundred meters. National Highway #1 and the railroad ran north and south through about twenty miles of low ground near the coast. An Lao valley, on the west side of the Da Dan range, was a sanctuary and natural corridor for Vietcong (VC) and North Vietnam Army (NVA) movements. Two battalions of NVA were reported operating in the area.

The enemy was using heavily populated villages as safe havens. The entire area was already *hot,* meaning that random firefights between the enemy and our battalion's advance units were underway. A convoy of troop trucks would be used to transport the battalion from our base camp to Bong Son. Upon arrival we would board troop ships and air assault into the valley with gunship escorts to engage and eradicate enemy forces encountered.

Everyone had to pack a three-day supply of food, water, and ammunition. Sergeant Dorman told us that when we reached the beach of the South China Sea, we would be rewarded with a day off to swim in the ocean and eat hot food.

After Dorman left the tent, I turned to Kenny and asked, "Did you hear him say fighting is already going on?"

"Yes, I did."

"Well, I guess this is it, Kenny. We're finally going to see some real action."

For a few seconds, Kenny and I stared at one another, neither of us saying a word.

Then I said, "Kenny, if anything happens to me, please write my family and tell them how it happened. I want them to know from you."

"Johnny," he replied, "if anything happens to me, you write my folks."

At that moment we exchanged addresses and stuffed them into our pockets.

Shortly afterward, I asked Kenny, "Hey, buddy, how do you feel?"

Kenny turned to me with a smile and simply replied, "Fine!"

Having never experienced combat, I hoped that the few missions leading to this one had prepared me to be brave in the face of the enemy.

Billy Smith, M60 machine gunner and rifleman, 2nd Platoon, 1966. Billy was wounded in combat three separate times. (photo courtesy of Billy Smith).

John Engel, M60 Machine-Gunner, 2nd Squad, 1966 (photo courtesy of Billy Smith).

Billy "Smitty" Smith, M60 machine gunner and rifleman, had arrived in the 2nd Platoon in December 1965, a month after the battle of Ia Drang. Smitty had already received three Purple Hearts — all from being wounded by punji stakes (sharpened bamboo spikes). He had lost his best friend, John Paul Travis, in Bong Son on January 26, 1966, so he wasn't too excited about our mission to go back there. I remember walking with Smitty to the battalion aid station to get a bleeding punji wound on his lower right calf re-dressed. He had torn several stitches, and I could hear the blood squishing inside his boot with each step he took. It didn't seem to bother him, and he didn't need to lean on me. Smitty was a tough young soldier from Mississippi who never complained about the pain of those three punji-stake wounds.

While I packed my basic load, Bob Dunn came by and asked me how many more belts of M60 ammunition I could carry. Bob, Kenny, and I had ten belts among us, a total of 1,000 rounds. I told Bob I'd add two more hundred-round belts to my load. I also packed several hand grenades. When I finished packing, my total load weighed at least sixty pounds. I decided not to lighten the load and risk being sorry about the decision later. I was learning to simply deal with the weight and the pain of carrying it.

A few more new men had been assigned to 2nd Platoon since our return from our last mission guarding Route 19. I figured that the new guys probably felt the same way Kenny and I had when we prepared for our first mission, and likely had the same questions and concerns about fitting in. With our platoon pumped up to about twenty men, morale was high. We talked and joked while awaiting orders to move to the pickup point on the road.

In the early morning of May 4, 1966, a loud voice sounded: "Saddle up!" We lifted gear onto our shoulders and headed toward a long column of troop trucks lining the road, bumper to bumper, as far as the eye could see. Each two-and-a-half-ton truck was stripped of its canvas top, except for the cab area. The drivers stood behind the dropped tailgate of their trucks. The smell of diesel fuel hung thick in the air. One by one, soldiers climbed into the beds of the trucks and sat on foldout wooden benches, resting their feet on the solid steel flooring. Each squad leader accounted for his men and then climbed into the cab with the driver.

Company B, 7th Cavalry soldiers riding in a long convoy of
troop trucks to help fight the enemy in Bong Son, May 4, 1966
(photo courtesy of Dennis Blessing).

The trucks rolled slowly down the dirt road. As the convoy moved, more trucks linked up from other roads that led out of An Khe. The distance between the trucks increased as they drove out of the gate.

On the top of each truck's cab was an M60 manned by a gunner. The rest of the troops sat or stood with weapons ready. Overhead, gunships and helicopters flew escort. If Charlie were to attack, the battalion could respond with troops, gunships, artillery, and fighter jets. It was an incredible sight to see so much military firepower assembled for war.

The convoy motored ahead, winding through the mountains and thick vegetation on each side of the road. Several men catnapped; others watched the trees and road for signs of danger. Riding in the back of an open truck made us easy targets. If Charlie wanted to snipe or spring an ambush, he could easily cause a lot of casualties and bring the convoy to a confused halt.

The ride was long. As day turned into night, the drivers turned on tiny nightlights that limited the enemy's ability to see our vehicles at a distance. The lights gave the drivers just enough visibility to see the vehicles in front and behind, as long as they slowed the pace and tightened the distance between trucks.

Kenny kept poking the weary driver of our truck, who would veer left and then right. I wondered if these drivers, unlike us infantrymen, were just not used to working many hours without sleep.

Early the next morning, the vehicles stopped on a huge mountain plateau covered with short vegetation and dense jungle. We dismounted and moved away from the convoy and into a field of wild grass on the mountaintop. My platoon secured an edge of the mountain high above the Bong Son plain.

The sun shone early that morning as we looked into the rice paddies below. The steep cliff, thick with vegetation, made the mountain appear impossible to climb. I could see no path or manmade road leading down into Bong Son. What I saw below my position in the dirt was the water in the paddies reflecting the sunlight like tiny rectangular mirrors. Bong Son looked like a giant mosaic of colorful paddies dotted with palm trees and small straw-hut villages all the way to the South China Sea. It was a beautiful sight from high above the valley.

A steep ravine between the mountains separated us from another company of the 1st Battalion, 7th Cavalry, occupying the ridge on the other side. After we settled in, I accompanied a patrol to check out the ravine. It was another breathtaking view: the ravine was meticulously terraced with rice paddies and dikes all the way down to a rushing river that wound its way into the mouth of the valley. It must have taken hundreds of years to carve this mountainside into giant terraced rice paddies. No Vietnamese farmers were working anywhere in sight. Kenny quipped, "It looks like a picture straight out of *National Geographic*."

Despite all that beauty, a war raged in the valley below. I spotted several navy warships in the waters off the coast of the South China Sea.

From my vantage point, the tiny vessels appeared to be firing their deck guns inland. Puffs of smoke blew from the stationary ships. Seconds later, flashes of light and billowing smoke from the exploding rounds appeared on the faraway ground below. The sound was muffled, like a distant echo.

To the right, air force jets dropped bombs and fired their 20mm cannons, which could only fire on full automatic, expending 2,000 rounds per minute. When the pilot presses the trigger, the air is filled with a burping sound that lasts several seconds. A 20-mm round, from casing to tip, is about five inches long and as thick as a fat cigar. I could only imagine what happened when those huge bullets hit their targets.

Above the valley floor, I could hear helicopter gunships firing M60 machine guns and launching rockets into the trees and rice paddies. On and off during that night, I could see bright flares in the sky above the valley and flashes of fire from explosions. The situation was unlike anything I'd seen in my two months in Vietnam. I commented, "There must be a hell of a lot of enemy troops down there to get the navy, the air force, and the cavalry involved."

Bob replied, "The reason for all the fireworks is to prepare the valley for our air assault tomorrow morning."

Kenny and I didn't get much sleep that night, knowing that in the morning we'd be flying into that valley of death.

✸

In the early morning of May 5, everyone stirred as the sun rose in a sky bright blue and clear of rain clouds. I wiped the morning dew from my weapon, gave it a quick mechanical check, and oiled the exposed metal parts. Breakfast was C-Rations and water. In minutes, everyone in 2nd Platoon was prepared to move at a moment's notice.

Soon, a long stream of choppers flew in and landed a short distance behind our positions. Their rotors turned at idle speed. Each chopper was empty except for two pilots and two door gunners with their doors locked in the open position. The first load of infantrymen from another platoon climbed into the slicks, lifted off, and headed down into the valley.

A familiar voice called, "Saddle up!" The 2nd Platoon scrambled to their feet. A few minutes later, a bunch of choppers roared to a landing. Following Bob and Kenny, I ran to our designated slick. As soon as everyone was aboard, it swiftly lifted off, flying fifteen feet off the ground. When the chopper reached the ravine, the pilot banked sharply to the right and down we went. The ground looked like it was parallel to the side of the chopper, and I thought I was going to fall out through the open door. When the pilot leveled out, he nose-dived into the ravine at breakneck speed. The air escaped from my lungs as I held on for dear life. The chopper swooped so close to the treetops, I could almost reach out and touch the leaves.

We flew into the valley like a swarm of bees. This was the fastest helicopter ride I'd ever had. The chopper suddenly slowed and then landed in a huge, dry rice paddy a mile or so from the mountain we had left behind.

A stream of red smoke, signaling that enemy contact was imminent, marked the landing zone for the pilots. As they prepared to land in the hot LZ, they lifted the noses of their ships slightly and touched down briefly. Lickety-split, everyone was out and rushing for cover. I looked around and saw more and more choppers dropping troops into the dry paddies. Eventually, the entire battalion, several hundred combat infantrymen, would join in the tactical sweep to the South China Sea.

Not far ahead of me, Bob and Kenny lay prone on the ground behind their M60. Suddenly, a voice bellowed, "Move out!"

I rose to my feet and felt the extra-heavy weight of my pack pulling me down and cutting into my shoulders. Rice paddies surrounded us in every direction. Everyone was spread out about fifteen feet apart. As we moved cautiously forward, I kept my eyes on the uneven ground and tried to keep my footing.

American soldiers on the left and right of our platoon slowly faded into the distance. After a while, my platoon was moving as a single unit. Suddenly, a shot rang out, breaking the silence. Everyone hit the ground at once. The shot sounded as though it had come from a wall of trees to our front. We waited a minute, but nothing more happened. The order was given to move out. We carefully advanced toward the tree line from where the shot had come.

7th Cavalry Sky Trooper air assault into Bong Son on May 5, 1966 (photo courtesy Dennis Blessing).

I was positioned close to the rear as our platoon continued its sweep forward. Someone spotted two enemy soldiers in the distance running across our front. The platoon leader ordered us not to shoot or pursue because they were far out of range and because other Americans, whom we couldn't see, were operating in the area. Maybe the lieutenant didn't want a repeat of the situation that had trapped the 2nd Platoon in the Ia Drang Valley where, after chasing a few fleeing enemy soldiers, they ran into a buzz saw of death.

We encountered no resistance as we moved closer to the wall of trees. By late afternoon, we had pushed deep into Bong Son, and halted inside a lightly forested area surrounded by rice paddies. The platoon leader decided to set up a perimeter behind the dike that encompassed the dry rice paddy. Bob found a good spot in the corner of the dike to place his M60.

After the platoon sergeant was satisfied with each platoon's defensive position, he ordered us to dig foxholes for the evening. I had excellent visibility to the front of my position, and clear lanes of fire on flat ground. I could easily see and communicate with adjacent fighting positions.

Before dark, I was about twenty-five yards away from my position, setting up the claymore mines and trip flares, when a loud explosion filled the air no more than a hundred feet behind me. I hit the dirt and saw a small billow of white smoke rising from where the explosion occurred.

Someone yelled, "Incoming!"

Moments later there was a second explosion near the same spot.

I quickly crawled on my belly back to the foxhole. Kenny and Bob were already inside and preparing for the worst. From the direction of the explosions, I heard men repeatedly shouting, "Medic!" In total silence, we waited for the enemy to attack. Several minutes passed; nothing happened — not one shot was fired. It was quiet except for the commotion behind us where someone had been injured.

Bob said that the first explosion was white phosphorus, commonly called Willy Peter. The second was high explosive or "H.E." Bob explained that Charlie didn't use Willy Peter; Americans used it as spotter rounds to mark targets with smoke before unleashing a volley of H.E.

As it turned out, an American mortar squad from another company had launched the mortars accidentally. They had no idea that friendly troops were operating in their test-target area. Our platoon leader, platoon sergeant, a squad leader, and two riflemen had been meeting at the command post (CP) when the two mortar rounds exploded in their midst. They all suffered severe torso and leg wounds, but none had been killed. A medical evacuation chopper landed and lifted them to a field hospital. Though 2nd Platoon was reduced in manpower, Sergeant Dorman reassured us that we could continue the mission. "Stay sharp," he reminded us.

Early the next morning, May 6, 1966, I went out to disarm and retrieve our claymore mines and trip flares. The day was heating up as I packed my gear and buried the trash from the food I had eaten. It was time to saddle up and continue the mission, sweeping on foot to the South China Sea.

As the platoon moved out, the men began to put some distance between one another. I positioned myself with Bob and Kenny's M60 as the rear guard. Being the last man in the platoon formation, my job was to keep an eye on the rear. As we moved across the rice paddies, I spotted the flank guards about fifty yards to the left and right of the column. Searching my surroundings, I saw no other friendly units.

The platoon crossed several large paddies before pausing at a dike. I knelt on one knee and heard aircraft in the distance. Soon the jets were flying about 200 feet directly overhead. Their engines screamed as they flashed by and headed toward the trees in front of us. Bombs released from their wings exploded with tremendous force in the woods. If they'd dropped a hundred yards closer, the bombs would have exploded on top of us. Someone — I didn't know who — had called in the air strike.

Suddenly, gunships appeared and began to fire rocket artillery into the trees. After the air strikes, I scanned for signs of the enemy, but saw nothing. In the distance, other American troops halted and took cover from the air strikes.

Kenny and Bob positioned the M60 on the corner of the dike and aimed it at the trees ahead. I set up a short distance to their right and, without thinking, pointed my M16 toward the inside of the perimeter, my finger on the trigger. Several hundred feet above us, an air force jet screamed in from behind and dropped two bombs simultaneously. They fell into the trees, and an earth-shattering explosion followed. The ground beneath my feet shook violently and, at that instant, I flinched and jerked the trigger of my M16. It was on full automatic and fired a long burst into the center of the perimeter. I watched in fear as bullets kicked up clumps of dirt, and my fellow soldiers scrambled for cover. I realized instantly what I had done; my finger released the trigger, but it was too late — everything had happened in seconds.

Sergeant Dorman rushed over in a crouched position and asked where the shots had come from. Kenny and Bob looked at him and said nothing. I confessed that it was my fault and tried to explain. The sergeant interrupted, screaming, "Are you fucking nuts? Do you have any fucking idea what you just did? You just about fucking killed me and the other squad leaders!"

I froze, rigid with apprehension as I looked into the rage in Sergeant Dorman's eyes.

"Next time you check your fucking weapon and always keep it pointed out and away from anyone. Do I make myself clear?"

"Yes, Sergeant!"

He turned and stomped away, cussing and shaking his head. I had almost killed someone by mistake. I'd never felt so humiliated in all my life. I told Kenny and Bob that I must have left the selector switch on the AUTO setting after oiling my M16 that morning. Kenny saw that I was completely dejected. He put his arm around my shoulder and said, "Shake it off — you didn't kill anyone!"

I recalled the after-shave incident in the Ia Drang Valley and thought *Man, am I prone to making mistakes or what?*

When the bombing stopped, the platoon ended up not going in the direction of the air strikes. Instead, we headed back the way we'd come and circled left toward what appeared to be a village in the distance. We spread out and patrolled very cautiously, looking into the trees and on the ground in front of us. My load kept shifting, which made walking on the uneven terrain difficult.

I kept watching the ground and thinking about what had happened back at the rice paddy. I felt something blunt hit my helmet, and a voice said, "Keep your head and eyes up; Charlie's not in the dirt."

Looking up, I recognized that it was Dennis Blessing, a veteran rifleman. It really was a learning experience to walk on uneven soil with a heavy load, keeping your head up and your eyes constantly scanning for signs of danger. I realized that my months of intensive stateside infantry training had not prepared me for Vietnam. I was learning on the job how to become a reliable combat soldier. My mistakes didn't make it any easier to gain the confidence of the other soldiers in my platoon. I did not want to become undependable.

Our platoon, now somewhere in the middle of Bong Son, was about to enter a Vietnamese village. The platoon stopped and everyone dropped to one knee. A squad of men separated from the platoon and went forward, weapons at the ready. Bob lay behind his M60 machine gun with Kenny at his side. I held my position at the tail end of the platoon and faced the rear.

The rifle squad entered the village and checked out the straw huts as the rest of the platoon waited. From a distance, the village appeared deserted. Not long into the search, however, someone uncovered several Vietnamese hiding inside bunkers and spider holes — these were very narrow and just deep enough to conceal and protect one person. Usually covered with a lid of vegetation, they were difficult to spot. The rest of our platoon quickly moved into the village to support the search and provide security.

Training our weapons on the Vietnamese, we ordered them to move into a group as we rounded up ten elderly unarmed women and some young children. They squatted nervously in a group. It was easy to see the fear in their eyes. An older woman cradled her crying infant. All wore black pajamas and no shoes; the babies didn't have a stitch of clothing on them.

An American soldier spoke in Vietnamese, saying that we wouldn't harm them. He asked where the Vietcong were hiding. An elderly woman kept crying out, "No VC! No VC!" Several men continued the search but uncovered nothing else.

We stayed in the village to eat lunch. The occupants appeared to be simple peasant farmers, and the village was entirely surrounded by rice paddies. I was impressed with how clean the area was and by the beautiful palm trees, coconut trees, and several fruit-bearing banana trees. Wondering where all the men and boys had gone, I speculated that maybe our captives were the families of Vietcong soldiers. Bob surmised that we hadn't found young men, women, and boys because the Vietnamese thought we'd take the young men as prisoners, rape the women, and kill the boys. He went on to say that the men and boys were probably hiding somewhere nearby, and that when we left they would return to their families — a typical reaction when American troops invaded the privacy of a village.

Eventually, the Vietnamese were released to carry on with their daily lives. Several women showed their hospitality by offering us fresh coconuts and bananas. We accepted the gifts with gratitude. I felt safe, and thought Charlie was nowhere near the village as we relaxed in the shade of the trees.

Some of the guys started to horse around, chasing chickens through the village. The Vietnamese children laughed at the crazy Americans. After we ate and rested, it was time to move again. When we departed, an older Vietnamese woman bowed as each soldier passed. I was truly impressed with my fellow soldiers being respectful of the villagers and the hospitality we received in return.

Continuing our tactical sweep to the South China Sea, the platoon headed across another rice paddy. Helicopter gunships overhead fired rockets and machine guns into a forested area just ahead of us. As we neared another village, I heard a machine gun that didn't sound like an M60 or anything else I'd heard before. It had a slower, thudding, firing rhythm. Bob quickly pointed out that this was the sound of an NVA heavy machine gun exchanging fire with our gunships.

Because Bob had been in other firefights with Charlie, I valued his knowledge and combat experience. This was his second mission in Bong Son. The first had been in February 1966, a month before Kenny and I arrived in Vietnam.

My mind filled with crazy thoughts of how I could sneak up with a hand grenade and knock out that enemy machine-gun nest. I wanted to make up for my earlier mistakes and regain the respect of Dorman,

Blessing, and the other members my platoon. My fantasy quickly disappeared when we were ordered to move to the right and away from the enemy machine gun.

Yet another village lay in our path. The platoon entered it much the same way as we had the previous one. The lead squad approached and nothing happened. The rest of the platoon followed in three-man fire teams. One team crouched and rushed forward about fifty feet, then took a knee. The other fire team moved in the same manner. The advance alternated until we were all inside the cover of the village. Specialist Four Engel's machine-gun team positioned itself to provide firepower to support the men searching straw huts for enemy hiding places.

As the platoon poked around outside, they were completely surprised when several Vietnamese men, hands held high over their heads, came running out of an underground hideaway. Some wore black pajamas; others were dressed in khaki shirts and trousers. American weapons quickly trained on the unarmed men. One of the Vietnamese repeated loudly, "*Chieu hoi! Chieu hoi!*" He was referring to the "open arms" program, promising clemency and financial aid to Vietcong and North Vietnamese soldiers who stopped fighting and returned to live under South Vietnamese authority. In essence, "Chieu hoi" meant, "I surrender."

The one man in our platoon who could speak some Vietnamese commanded the prisoners to lie face-down on the ground. They were searched but no weapons or documents were found. Their hands were tied behind their backs and a rope linked them together for security and control. Bob, Kenny, and I were given responsibility for guarding the prisoners. After a short while, the platoon captured several more Vietnamese men who had been hiding in the village. We now had a bunch of Vietnamese prisoners who, after a short interrogation, confessed to being deserters from a battalion of North Vietnamese Army regulars operating in that area.

For the first time, Kenny and I faced the enemy up close. I wasn't afraid to guard them, and they didn't appear to be afraid of me either. They actually stared at me, probably wondering what I was going to do with them. All roped together, the prisoners were positioned near the center of our formation.

I asked, "What if they try to escape?"

Sergeant Dorman replied, "Shoot first and ask questions later."

The platoon headed out of the village to the edge of a clearing to radio for an evacuation of the prisoners. When we spotted a chopper headed our way, Sergeant Dorman popped green smoke in the air to mark a landing site. The chopper, already crammed with gear, took all but two of our prisoners.

I was given sole responsibility for watching over the remaining two. I walked behind them as they followed Kenny and Bob. Not long into the journey, a sniper fired several shots at the platoon from across a clearing. We hit the ground and quickly returned fire. Engel's M60 fired several short bursts. I didn't fire my weapon. Instead, I watched the prisoners to make sure they remained tied up and didn't try to escape. I wasn't going to make another mistake — if they ran, I'd shoot them as ordered, even though I had never shot a man before.

The sniper had shot and wounded our point man. As Doc Bell helped him, the RTO (radio telephone operator) radioed for a medevac (medical evacuation helicopter). With the platoon still in the middle of a rice paddy we formed a hasty perimeter. A few minutes later, the medevac hovered overhead. We popped red smoke and the chopper descended close to the ground. Out of nowhere, an enemy machine gun fired; it hit the chopper, which took off before our wounded soldier could be loaded. As soon as it was airborne, the enemy stopped firing. I thought that the platoon's counter-fire had silenced the enemy machine gun.

It was quiet for a while, and the medevac was radioed to return. As soon as it started to touch down a second time, the enemy opened fire. I couldn't believe what I was witnessing. Here was an unarmed medevac with visible bright-red crosses painted on its nose and doors, and Charlie was determined to knock it out, totally disregarding the rules of the Geneva Convention. The medevac took off, again leaving our wounded comrade behind.

A short time later, two air force jets appeared directly overhead. I checked my M16 to make sure it was on safety and pointed the barrel downrange. One jet dived down to just a few hundred feet above our heads — so close, that I could see the pilot in the cockpit — and released two silver-colored canisters.

Kenny and I watched in amazement as the canisters tumbled over our heads. When they hit the trees, they exploded into a huge wall of orange and red flames. Bob told me that this was napalm, a jelly-like mixture of fatty acids and gasoline that incinerated everything it touched. I could feel the intense heat fifty yards away. A few seconds later, a second jet zoomed over and fired its 20mm cannons, shattering tree limbs and kicking up dirt everywhere. I thought nothing could have survived the barrage. The trees and village were ablaze and smoking.

After the blaze died down, we advanced across the clearing and into the burning hamlet without a shot being fired. Our wounded comrade's arm was in a sling; for maximum protection, he was positioned in the center of the formation, Doc Bell beside him. Smoke billowed everywhere as small fires burned all around us. I kept my weapon trained on the two prisoners, who looked emotionally shaken and remained silent as they moved forward.

As I passed a burning hut, a dark figure stumbled out of a haze of smoke directly in front of me. I froze in my tracks and yelled, "Oh, my God, it's a woman!" Her clothes had been burned off, and her charred body was smoking. Her face was badly burned and bleeding as she raised her hands, cupping them to her mouth as if asking for water or for help. She stood in front of me and spoke softly in Vietnamese. There was nothing I could do; I actually thought of shooting the woman to put her out of her misery. She took a few more steps and fell face-down on the ground. I stared at her motionless body. She was dead.

The incident caused me to lose my concentration, but I soon realized where I was and composed myself. The prisoners hadn't moved and were still secured. I moved them at a quick pace away from the scene and didn't look back.

When I caught up with Kenny and Bob, Kenny asked me if I'd shot the woman. I told him I'd thought about it but hadn't. He asked what had happened to her, and I told him that she'd fallen down and died.

A deep, wide ditch filled with muddy water halted the platoon's advance. The only way across it was a rotting board that connected to the other side. One man at a time, the platoon carefully walked on the board and crossed to the other bank. The weight of our bodies and our loaded packs bowed the plank to its limits.

When Rodrigues stepped onto the plank and got about halfway across, his 200-pound body and heavy pack cracked the rotted wood. He plunged straight down into the muddy water five feet below and sank up to his chest, holding his rifle above his head. He couldn't move anything but his arms and head, and cursed up a storm as the rest of us laughed hysterically. We were able to pull Rod out of the ditch.

Once everyone had crossed, the platoon spread out into a tactical sweeping formation heading into another village smoking from the napalm drop. The air was filled with the smell of fuel and burning debris. My throat and lungs burned from inhaling smoke, so I drank some water and washed my eyes.

Suddenly, the front of the platoon came under attack by automatic weapons. We hit the dirt and returned fire. Being close to the rear with the prisoners, I wasn't in a position to fire my weapon. Bob and Kenny covered the rear of the platoon with the M60. Enemy bullets whizzed over our heads. After a brief exchange we maneuvered away from the attack.

Several VC tried to flank us on the left as we moved right. We had little protection, and it was a miracle none of us was shot. A small clearing on the right led to a group of trees and a straw hut on the other side. We ran in that direction but stopped short of entering the clearing.

Charlie kept up the pressure on our left flank. As the first squad entered and secured the other side of the clearing, the rest of us quickly moved across in groups of four or five. Bullets zipped through the air close to me. I figured that Charlie had spotted the prisoners. Kenny pointed out a water buffalo frantically exiting a dried-up waterhole near where Rod stood. Its horns appeared to scrape against Rod as he desperately tried to get out of its path. The huge beast ran through the middle of the platoon and into the clearing behind us.

When I reached the trees, I passed a fellow soldier lying on his back in the open, his helmet off. His face was covered in dirt and sweat, and blood spurted from his throat in a continuous stream that ran down the side of his mouth. His eyes bulged as he bled and gasped for air. I stopped and knelt beside him to see what I could do, but Sergeant Dorman screamed, "Get your ass and those prisoners under cover before you get shot."

Doc Bell came out of nowhere and began to assist the wounded man. Holding the rope that tied the prisoners, I pulled them along behind me as I rushed into the trees and jumped into the same dry hole the buffalo had left moments before. This pit, chest deep, lay at the edge of a row of banana and palm trees. About ten feet to my right, Kenny and Bob lay behind a banana tree, savagely firing the M60.

From a hastily formed defensive perimeter around a small clump of trees with a straw hut in its center, the platoon made a stand to fight. The heaviest action was on my left flank. From that side, Engel yelled to me, "There they are! There they are!" as he fired his M60. VC clad in khaki uniforms fired back, darting from place to place across our front. Some enemy soldiers fell dead from our hail of bullets and grenades.

For the first time since arriving in Vietnam, I aimed my M16 at enemy soldiers and fired. The VC bobbed up and down and fired back from behind a dike about fifty yards away. I carefully aimed and fired several magazines of rounds just above the dike, trying to hit the VC as they popped up to fire back. I thought I'd silenced some of them, but others held their positions and fought back hard.

Specialist Four Bob Dunn, Weapons Squad, 2nd Platoon, Company B, manning his M60 machine gun, 1966. I became Bob's assistant gunner after Kenny Mook was wounded (photo courtesy of Bob Dunn).

On my right, Kenny loaded another hundred-round belt of ammunition into the M60 while Bob maintained his aim behind the gun. Their machine gun kicked up dirt and debris all over the area, and the lifeless bodies of several VC littered the ground in front of us.

American voices called for a medic; the platoon had taken some casualties. Deadly enemy machine-gun fire had raked our small perimeter. Everyone kept reloading and firing back. I noticed that less shooting and fewer explosions came from the right side of the perimeter.

Someone screamed, "There they are on the left! The left!" This was the direction of the village we had vacated minutes earlier.

Gunships swarmed overhead, firing rockets that exploded almost on top of our platoon. I flinched as shrapnel whizzed through the air, splintering trees and kicking up dirt around me. The noise was intense. Charlie fought from well-fortified defensive positions in the rice paddy dikes, shooting back fast and furiously after each rocket exploded. I fired back in reactive mode, not thinking about what could happen to me.

The extra ammunition I had decided to carry now came in handy, as I had expended about 150 rounds firing on semiautomatic.

Kenny's machine gun jammed with a bullet still in its chamber. If it cooked off, it would explode inside the chamber and damage the firing mechanism, making the weapon useless. Kenny quickly reached back to pull his bayonet out of his pistol belt to pry the jammed cartridge out of the chamber. Suddenly, his arm smacked him in the chest; he fell onto his side and curled up in pain beside the machine gun. Kenny's helmet rolled away from his head.

"I'm hit!"

Bob yelled for a medic and then called, "Johnny, Kenny's hit!"

I looked in Bob's direction and saw Kenny lying still in a curled-up position. Afraid that he was dead, I quickly crawled over to him, leaving my prisoners unattended.

Kenny's first words were, "You're white as a ghost!"

I was speechless seeing my best friend lying there moaning in severe pain. He had open wounds and was bleeding badly. All I could think was *Please don't die.* The medic arrived and we dragged Kenny a few yards into the dry waterhole. He was breathing and alive, but in severe pain.

Kenny had been hit by a VC .30-caliber machine-gun blast. He complained of sharp stomach pains. With one sleeve of his blood-soaked fatigue shirt ripped completely off, I could see that a large part of his forearm muscle was missing and bloody white bone was exposed. There were several bullet holes in his stomach, but no exit wounds in his back.

I carefully removed his shoulder harness and backpack to make him more comfortable. After I got his gear off, he doubled up in pain. Doc Bell placed Kenny's good arm under his armpit to try to slow the bleeding. He then dressed the wounds and gave Kenny a shot of morphine. The two prisoners in the hole with us looked scared but remained tied together, lying where I'd left them.

Doc Bell grabbed my shirt and pulled me down into the hole. He told me that if I didn't keep my head down, I'd be killed. As he dressed Kenny's wounds, I rejoined the fighting. Bob Dunn had changed the barrel and continued firing short bursts at enemy targets. I tossed him a fresh hundred-round belt of ammunition from Kenny's pack.

Above all the shooting and explosions, Sergeant Dorman yelled, "Grab the wounded and dead and get ready to move out!"

The enemy had surrounded our platoon on three sides and was closing in fast. We were about to be overrun and captured or killed. As fast as I could, I untied Kenny's poncho from his pack, rolled it out, and put it under him. Charlie continued pouring it on with AK-47 rifles, machine-gun fire, and grenades. The grenades all fell short and exploded outside our perimeter.

Sergeant Dorman yelled, "Hurry up! We got to go!"

I couldn't lift and carry Kenny by myself. Bob was loaded down with equipment, the M60 machine gun, and ammunition. We each grabbed a corner of the poncho, lifted Kenny a few inches off the ground, and rushed in a crouched position to the far right of the perimeter — away from the enemy. Our platoon carried out all of our wounded and dead. No one was left behind.

Sergeant Dorman said, "The rest of our company is waiting for us in the graveyard on the other side of this rice paddy. They'll provide covering fire as we move to join them. It's about one hundred yards across, so stay low and close to the dike for cover."

From the time the sergeant gave the order, it took us only minutes to grab up the wounded and dead and move into position to cross the rice paddy. The next thing I heard was, "Let's go!"

Almost at once, we started running in a crouched position as fast as our legs could go. Firing continued in front of and behind us. I don't remember anyone stopping for even a short breather. As our ragged platoon came closer to the other side of the paddy, soldiers from our parent company waved us on while covering our advance with a base of fire. When we finally reached the American lines, we were exhausted and breathing heavily. A couple of American soldiers hurried the two prisoners away at gunpoint.

Other soldiers helped us move 2nd Platoon's wounded and dead comrades to a collection point inside the Vietnamese graveyard. The Vietnamese built their graveyards on dry ground above the water levels of the rice paddies. Each grave was a mound of dirt about three feet high. The graves were lined up in rows as in any cemetery back home. The mounded graves provided great defensive positions and security for our wounded and dead.

Medics began to assist the wounded soldiers who lay on ponchos scattered on the ground. Not far off, the lifeless bodies of Specialist Four Robert L. Engberson and Sergeant Earl S. Shelton, two young men from our platoon, were completely covered in green plastic ponchos, only their boots exposed. I stared at them in sadness as they lay motionless, side by side, under the piercing heat of the afternoon sun.

When I saw Kenny again, I looked at him and said, "We made it! How do you feel?" It was difficult for him to speak, but he nodded and said he was fine and that the morphine was relieving much of his pain. Straining to speak, he said, "Thanks for helping me, Johnny. Don't forget to write my folks that I'm okay." I assured him I'd keep my word and tell them what had happened on this day.

The fighting seemed to have stopped. Apparently, Charlie had broken contact or else had been wiped out. Sergeant Dorman, Rod, Dunn, Engel, Blessing, Smitty, and the other survivors of 2nd Platoon came by to pay their respects to the dead and wounded.

I stayed with Kenny until the medics carried him aboard a medevac helicopter. As Kenny and the others lifted off safely into the sky, I watched until the chopper disappeared. After Kenny was gone, I felt alone. *Will I ever see my friend again?* I wondered.

I found Bob sitting behind his M60, staring vigilantly across the rice paddy. I took Kenny's place as Bob's assistant gunner. It was quiet except for the medevac choppers and supply ships flying in and out of the graveyard.

As darkness settled in, we talked about how the events of the day had unfolded. Sergeant Dorman informed us that our sister company had made a sweep of the area we defended and found a lot of dead enemy soldiers. After he left, it began to rain.

I felt empty and alone for the first time since arriving in Vietnam. I felt I had lost my brother. I didn't know whether Kenny was going to live or if he would die before they got him to a hospital. What would I say to Kenny's family? What does anyone say to the families of men who were wounded or killed on the field of battle? I realized how quickly death can come. Tears ran down my face as I sat there in the silence of my thoughts.

Feeling sad and angry only pushed me deeper into depression. I promised myself that I would never forget this day for the rest of my life. Bob and I stayed alert that entire night, waiting for a counterattack that never came. The fighting appeared to have ended — my first combat experience against a determined enemy was finally over.

The next morning I ate my C-Rations, shaved, and prepared to move out. I felt better, but I was ready to get the hell out of that place. The platoon was re-supplied with ammunition, water, and food for the rest of our journey to the South China Sea. Because we had been reduced to about a squad and a half of capable soldiers, we were attached to a sister platoon. No one talked much as we joined the other unit. Sergeant Dorman positioned Bob and me as rear the guard. We moved through a few more burned-out villages that showed no signs of habitation. Everything was quiet on another hot day in Bong Son.

To my amazement, we finally reached the edge of the South China Sea. Some soldiers were already wading in the water without shirts; others relaxed on the sandy beach. The scene lifted my spirits as I stopped and just stood there, staring and listening to the splash of the waves against the shoreline. In the distance, I spotted large, gray ships. I wondered if they were the same ones I had observed from the top of the high Da Dan peak, firing into the valley a few nights before.

After Bob and I settled down on the beach, Sergeant Dorman came by and told us to stand down and enjoy the rest of the day at the beach. As promised, he pointed to some canvas tents where we could get hot food and a cold drink. After nourishing myself, I propped my back against a palm tree on the beach and wrote the letter I had promised Kenny I would send to his parents explaining what had happened to their son.

Bridge over Bong Son, looking toward Shower Point, 1966. Many 7th Cavalry troops were wounded or killed in this place of beckoning beauty (photo courtesy of Dennis Blessing).

Operation Davy Crockett was terminated on May 16, 1966 after all combat infantrymen, support troops, aircraft, and artillery batteries withdrew from the battlefields of Bong Son and headed back home to An Khe. Based on the after-action report, the NVA 9th Battalion had been decimated by the 7th Cavalry Sky Troopers. The number of NVA killed in action was estimated at 250. NVA captured included a medic, ammo bearer, cook, messenger, and supply carrier. The most important captive was apparently a North Vietnamese Army political officer. The 3rd Brigade, 7th Cavalry loses were 27 killed and 155 wounded in action.

The following fourteen heroes were in my unit, Company B, 1st Battalion, 7th Cavalry. Each was awarded the Combat Infantryman Badge and Purple Heart medal for wounds received on the battlefield of Bong Son on May 6, 1966.

Combat Infantryman Badge.

Purple Heart Medal.

Killed in Action

Sergeant Earl S. Shelton, Wayne County, Illinois
Specialist Four Robert L. Engberson, San Leandro, California

Wounded in Action

Second Lieutenant Douglas A. Randles, 2nd Platoon Leader
Sergeant William D. Stephens, 2nd Platoon Sergeant
Specialist Four Salvator Lara, Rifleman
Specialist Four Eddie J. Smith, Rifleman
Private First Class Kenneth L. Mook, Assistant Machine Gunner
Private First Class James R. Belker, Rifleman
Private First Class James Wheeler, Rifleman
Private First Class Gorden E. Yeomans, Rifleman
Private First Class Robert L. Garrett, Rifleman
Private First Class James D. Johnson, Rifleman
Private First Class Terry C. Knudson, Rifleman
Private First Class Leonard E. Payton, Rifleman

My next lesson in Vietnam would involve learning how an ordinary bamboo stick could be turned into a very painful weapon.

Chapter 5

Wounded in Action

I GOT MY FIRST liberty pass to go to "Sin City": An Khe, the dusty little Vietnamese town outside base camp. I went with Sergeant Dorman and Bob Dunn. We had a great time. I bought a small mirror with a frame that was handmade from a beer can. The back of the mirror was part of a cardboard C-ration box. The Vietnamese always seemed to find use for Americans' trash, and sold back to us what we — and they — had originally gotten for free.

Private First Class John Burnam's first liberty pass to An Khe's "Sin City," April 16, 1966 (author collection).

One morning, soon after my trip to Sin City, I grabbed a quick breakfast at the mess hall and returned to the platoon area for an operations order. Sergeant Dorman had directed the platoon to pack a one-day basic load of ammunition and food. He showed us his field map and pointed to several mountains for a combat mission he called hill jumping.

After studying the map, it appeared that several mountaintops had clearings large enough to land a few helicopters. S-2 (Battalion Intelligence) had reported that Charlie had been using the mountaintops to launch mortars and rockets at our airfield, trying to destroy our aircraft on the runways, our ammunition dumps, and our communications towers and bunkers. Retaliatory artillery strikes weren't solving the problem, so our platoon was ordered to search on foot and destroy Charlie's hit-and-run squads.

We were to air assault onto each hilltop and probe the surrounding woods and jungle in an effort to make contact with the enemy and take him out. If the LZ was hot, we were to secure it and radio for gunships and field-artillery support. If we didn't make contact with the enemy, we were to radio for liftoff and air assault into the next LZ marked on the map. The operation was to continue until dark or until all selected targets had been checked out. Each team leader was assigned a radioman.

I was assigned to Van Wilson's M60 as assistant gunner. Van was on Colonel Hal Moore's security team before joining 2nd Platoon. He was from Arkansas and had joined the army in May 1965. After completing infantry training and graduating from paratrooper school, Van arrived in Vietnam in December 1965, four months before I did.

Van told me that the only reason he joined the army was because a North Vietnamese soldier had shot his brother in the ass. Van quipped, "I couldn't let the enemy get away with shooting a Wilson in the ass, so I joined up." Van had a cheerful personality and we got along great.

Specialist Four Van Wilson, M60 machine gunner, 2nd Platoon,
enjoying some leisure time fishing in a Vietnam lake, 1966
(photo courtesy of Van Wilson).

On a hot, quiet day as we sat in defensive posture guarding a road, Van challenged me to a wrestling match. It didn't last long: I took him down to the dirt and pinned him in seconds. He couldn't understand how a little guy like me could have done it so easily.

I joined the service in September 1965, right after graduating from Littleton High School and taking the summer off. I wasn't ready for college, even though I had a potential wrestling scholarship to attend Trinidad Junior College in Colorado. At the time, I was more interested in leaving home and being on my own than in pursuing a college education.

What prompted me was a large poster of a soldier wearing a green beret in the window of the U.S. Army recruiting station. I got excited and decided to inquire about joining the Special Forces. That recruiter told me that the army offered a great way to travel to foreign lands and visit exotic cities and cultures that I'd otherwise have to pay a lot of money to experience on vacation. I was young, trusting, had neither money nor job nor girlfriend, and was eager to make a positive change in my life, so I signed on the dotted line.

The army shipped me by train from Denver to Fort Leonard, Missouri, for basic training, then to Fort Ord, California, for advanced infantry training, and finally to Fort Benning, Georgia, for paratrooper training. After graduating from paratrooper school in February 1966, I was ordered to Vietnam with no specific unit of assignment listed on my paperwork. I was shocked, as I'd had no idea there was a war going on in Vietnam or where on Earth that country was located. I asked lots of questions, but learned little to satisfy my curiosity. I wouldn't have enlisted had I known I'd be sent off to fight in a war, but it was too late — I was now a soldier and I belonged to Uncle Sam.

In preparation for our mission, Van oiled his M60 and packed several hundred-round ammunition belts. I packed 200 rounds of M16 ammunition into magazines and slipped them into the pockets of my shoulder-sling bandoleers. I hung several grenades on the webbing of my shoulder harness. It was the lightest load I had ever packed for a mission.

Three ten-man squads were packed and ready to go. Each consisted of a grenadier with an M79 grenade launcher, a man armed with a twelve-gauge shotgun, four M16 riflemen, a medic, and an M60 machine gunner and assistant gunner. Each squad had enough diversified firepower to handle any small group of VC.

Sergeant Dorman led one of the three squads. We assembled at the pickup point on the road. This would be another mission without Kenny Mook, who'd been like a brother to me. We'd been inseparable from the day we first met at the replacement center in Saigon, and it felt strange not to have him at my side.

The noisy choppers threw dust in our faces as we made our way to their open doors and climbed aboard. I was positioned in the first chopper with Van and several other soldiers. It took only three troopships to lift off our entire squad. As we flew over the perimeter of our base camp, a gunship joined us and flew at low altitude above the trees. I didn't simply fear the possibility of making contact with the VC — I now expected it.

2nd Platoon Sky Troopers air assault into enemy territory, 1966 (author collection).

The morning sun felt good, and so did the fresh air circulating inside the ship. The lush jungle canopy that blanketed the ground below looked peaceful. The choppers climbed toward a small range of hills covered in lush vegetation. We began our descent into a grassy clearing on the first hilltop. As we got closer to touchdown, I scooted to the open door and prepared to jump out. The choppers didn't land in the clearing; instead, they hovered a few feet off the ground just long enough for us to jump.

I dropped to the ground, ran a few feet, and crouched on one knee facing the thick tree line ahead. The drop-off had taken place in less than a minute. After the choppers left it was quiet. The squad leader lifted his arm and pointed in the direction he wanted us to move. I heard birds chirping in the trees as we cautiously advanced in crouched position, weapons at the ready. We were focused on looking for signs of danger.

When we got inside the vegetation beyond the skirt of the small clearing, Sergeant Dorman sent two riflemen to probe deeper into the surrounding jungle. When they returned and reported seeing nothing suspicious, we moved to a different spot and repeated the probing tactic around that entire LZ until we were back to where we had started. We found no indication that Charlie had set up mortars or rocket positions near that hilltop.

Sergeant Dorman got on the radio, reported the situation, and requested lift-off. Minutes later, three choppers landed. The door gunners on each side pointed their M60s at the trees, ready to fire. We quickly boarded and flew off to another hilltop. A gunship escorted our squadron of choppers to the next drop-off point on Sergeant Dorman's map. During the short ride, I scooted on my butt to the open doors to get ready for my second jump. Tall elephant grass covered the entire landing area below. Suddenly, bullets zipped through the air and hit the metal skin of the ship. The door gunner immediately returned fire with his M60. I quickly moved into the open door and looked down at the weaving grass below. I lowered my feet onto the landing skid, my right hand holding onto the side of the ship's doorframe. With its nose up, the ship moved forward slowly but didn't land. I was fully exposed as bullets kept slamming into the chopper's side.

The door gunner tapped my hand and pointed his hand down as my signal to go. I jumped into the elephant grass and hit the ground hard. A sudden sharp pain ripped through my right knee and I fell, twisting onto my belly. I tried to get up, but the pain in my knee drove the idea out of my head. Looking down, I saw a yellow bamboo punji stake sticking right through my knee. It had entered under the kneecap and exited the other side. The rest of the stake splintered below my leg. I tried again to move, but was in severe pain and anchored to the ground.

I knew that the VC carved small bamboo spikes and planted them among the natural vegetation. Worse yet, the VC sometimes dipped the sharp end of the spike into human waste to cause the wounds to become infected. Charlie also placed punji stakes in man-sized holes covered with vegetation and along the sides of well-traveled footpaths. If you took cover by diving off the path and into the brush, punji stakes awaited you. Charlie was a very clever warrior who made good use of his natural surroundings.

I couldn't believe I'd been wounded by one of those primitive, yet debilitating, bamboo spears — I'd always thought I'd be shot. Despite being in pain, I prepared to defend myself. With a round in the chamber of my M16, my finger rested on the trigger, the safety off and the selector switched on AUTO (full automatic).

A lot of shooting and tremendous explosions shook the ground all around me. The tall elephant grass surrounding me blocked my view of anything but the sky above. Over the noise, I heard Van's M60 firing. He was close, but I was unable to move in his direction.

As I tried to prop myself into a better position to shoot, I heard American voices screaming for a medic. Immobile, I lay in agony and tried to remain calm. Soon, I heard movement in the grass nearby. Not knowing the source of the sound, I decided not to take any chances by calling out. I remained silent, my heart pounding a fast and steady rhythm. The noise in the grass moved closer and the adrenaline started to rush through me. I pointed my M16 nervously toward the sound, finger on the trigger. A voice cried out, "Are you okay?" An American helmet broke through the grass near my feet. It was Doc Bell. He crawled to me on his belly as the intensity of the shooting and explosions increased around us. I sighed in relief as I eased my finger off the trigger and lowered the rifle barrel to the ground beside me.

I felt safe with Doc. He encouraged me to lie still as he checked me over and then gave me a shot of painkiller and a drink of water. When Doc Bell moved my knee and snipped away the splintered pieces of bamboo around my wound, I gnashed my teeth and my eyes squirted tears of agony as the blood gushed. With one hand, Doc quickly pulled the large piece of bamboo from under my kneecap. I cried out in excruciating pain. It was hard to lie still while he bandaged the wound. I grew very dizzy, hot, and weak all at once.

Doc Bell talked to me the whole time, telling me that Van had pointed to where I was and that was how he'd located me. He told me to stay calm while he went to help the others. I watched him crawl into the grass and out of sight.

The whole time I lay there, I could hear VC voices through the grass but couldn't see anyone. An hour must have passed, but I didn't fire a single shot. I still couldn't believe I'd been skewered by a damn punji stake. I didn't fear being captured or overrun, but among the many thoughts that passed through my mind, I wondered, *Will I ever be able to use my right leg again?*

Eventually, the firing and explosions trickled to a stop, and a long silence followed. I began to hear other Americans moving through the grass saying, "Watch out for those punji stakes." Then Van Wilson was standing over me, asking if I was okay. Van said he'd seen me go down before he jumped, and that he was lucky not to get stuck too. He said freshly planted punji stakes were all over the place.

Helicopters soon flew overhead like a swarm of bees. The enemy was gone. God only knew how many of them had died during the firefight. Van helped me take off my heavy pack and stand on one foot, but I felt lightheaded. I grabbed Van's shoulder as he pulled me up by my belt. I hobbled on one leg to the waiting helicopter.

*Specialist Four Van Wilson, M60 machine gunner,
2nd Platoon, 1966. I can never thank Van enough for
helping me get on that chopper and safely out of harm's way
(photo courtesy of Van Wilson).*

Van fetched my gear and put it beside me in the chopper, which held two other wounded soldiers. Before long, we were airborne and on our way to a field hospital in Qui Nhom. After being examined there, I was evacuated to a hospital that had better facilities for reconstructive knee surgery.

My recurring concern was *Will I survive this wound and walk normally again?*

Chapter 6

106th General Hospital

I ARRIVED AT THE 106th U.S. Army General Hospital, Ward D in the Kishine Barracks, Yokohama, Japan. The hospital was situated in a former WWII Japanese Army installation. Tall barbed-wire fence surrounded the entire compound. Armed U.S. Army military policemen dressed in heavily starched khaki uniforms and sporting highly polished black boots were stationed at the entrance and exit to the base.

I was assigned to Orthopedic Ward D on the second floor of one of the old buildings. At least thirty other young soldiers occupied hospital beds lined up in rows against the beige walls of a large room. The place was clean and tidy, and the air smelled of medicine. Large fans at each end of the ward circulated the warm late-summer air.

Ward D buzzed with indistinguishable chatter: the voices of bedridden soldiers, and nurses moving about with medicine trays. My bed was near the entrance to the nurses' station. The soldier on my left had to lie on his stomach because of a wound in his back. The man on my right had an L-shaped cast that ran from his neck to his fingers. Other men's arms and legs were covered with bandages.

After I got comfortable, a nurse and a doctor came by to give me a complete examination. They introduced themselves as Dr. George Bogumill and Nurse Nancy Jones. Dr. Bogumill had a gentle disposition and a kind bedside manner. He thought I looked younger than nineteen. He told me that I was too young to be sent to war, and jokingly asked if my mother had signed the enlistment papers that got me into the army.

Nurse Jones, a pretty woman in her mid-twenties, had a comforting smile and a great figure. I liked the idea that she'd been assigned to take care of me. The medical staff asked many questions about when I was injured, how it had happened, and what type of treatment I'd received before arriving. I appreciated their patience and care, especially when they removed the bandages to examine my wound, then cleaned it and re-dressed it from upper thigh to ankle. None of them had a clue about what combat was like or the pain of being wounded in action, but they could no doubt have filled a small library with stories of what they learned at the bedsides of the wounded soldiers they nursed to health over the course of their tours of duty in Japan.

✳

As days turned into weeks, I befriended the guys in the beds around me. We talked about our Vietnam War experiences. Each man told his story of how he'd been wounded. Almost everyone I spoke to came from a different infantry unit.

The man on my right, Robert Lang, had been shot in the arm while on patrol near the Mekong Delta, 250 miles south of where I'd been wounded. Charlie had waited in ambush for Robert's squad as they moved along a trail. Robert happened to be a flank guard. Charlie spotted him first and, Robert said, had been a little faster on the trigger than he was. Several rounds from an AK-47 shattered a bone in Robert's forearm and ripped a hole in his biceps. The impact had spun him completely around and onto the ground. He passed out, having never fired one round. Robert said that he often awoke in the night seeing the face of that VC who shot him.

Robert had been healing in the hospital for several months. The doctor had told him that he'd soon get his cast off and start physical therapy. Robert was one of the few men on the ward able to get out of bed, walk around, and eat in the dining hall.

Gary Morton was the man in the bed on my left. His platoon had been ambushed in the jungle while checking out what appeared to be a deserted VC base camp. As his patrol was leaving, the VC had taken them by surprise. Gary remembered getting down and not being hit by the first volley of small arms fire. He had fired back by emptying an entire twenty-round magazine. While he was changing magazines, an enemy machine gun opened fire in front of him. Something slammed into his upper back and rolled him onto his back. Gary had felt dazed but thought he was okay. When he tried to roll onto his belly, he realized that he had no feeling in his arms. Then he lost consciousness. By the time Gary regained his senses, he was lying on a cot in an army field hospital.

Since Gary's back was in such bad shape, he could lie only on his stomach. A web of silver metal wires was sewn over his open wound, keeping it from tearing open. The bullets had missed his spine, but had torn a very large chunk of skin and muscle from his back and shoulder. The wound was clean, and I could actually see his left shoulder blade surrounded by raw flesh. Every so often, the nurse and doctor would bring small patches of skin they'd cut from Gary's leg, and graft them onto the hole in his back. During my hospital stay, I watched the progress of those skin grafts. They took hold and grew without much infection, and the size of the hole in Gary's shoulder gradually decreased. I wondered if he would ever have full use of his left shoulder or the muscles on the left side of his back.

Even though the men in my ward had suffered wounds as a result of combat in Vietnam, morale was high. Many of the wounded knew that after they recovered they'd be medically discharged from the army and sent home. Like me, most were young and had been in the military less than a year. Now they'd bear scars for the rest of their lives. Everyone was always talking about home, which made a big difference in how they felt about their health and everything else.

Finally, the day came when I was prepped and wheeled away for a surgery that lasted several hours. When I returned to consciousness, I was in my bed again, feeling dry-mouthed and drowsy. I really needed to take a leak but I couldn't move because of the pain, so I called for Nurse Jones to bring me a bedpan. She placed the bedpan under the covers and stood beside me until I used it. Talk about performance anxiety!

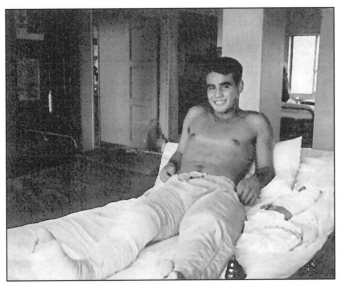

John Burnam recovering from punji-stake wound at the 106 General Hospital, Kishine Barracks, Yokahama, Japan, 1966. After I was wounded, Van Wilson put me on a chopper. I had no photos of my stay in the hospital until I reunited with him in 2003. Van gave me this photo I had sent to him in Vietnam with a note on the back and my signature — thirty-seven years ago.

The operation was successful. Dr. Bogumill said that I'd be able walk normally again, but would have to work hard at physical therapy. A physical therapist came to my bedside a few days later. He encouraged me to start lifting my leg, and helped me do so. The pain was agonizing. The guys in the beds beside me kept joking and calling me a pussy. This was typical verbal harassment — a way for us to help each other to persist in whatever we had to do to heal. Despite the pain, I slowly moved my right knee up and down.

After some success, the therapist draped socks full of sand over my ankles. If I were going to get better, I'd have to ignore the pain and concentrate on strengthening my leg muscles. As the leg strengthened with increased repetitions, the therapist added more weight and encouraged me to keep going. The guys in the beds next to me continued chanting, "More weight! More weight!" Eventually, I could sit on the edge of the bed and bend my leg slightly at the knee.

Oh, man! When the blood rushed down my leg, a whole different level of pain brought tears to my eyes. It was the same old thing each time I tried to sit up and hang my legs over the edge of the bed. Eventually, I learned to expect the pain of therapy.

After a month, I was able to use crutches to move around the ward, eat in the dining hall, and pee standing up. I'd gotten cocky a few times and let go of the crutches. After one step, I'd fallen flat on my face, but that didn't keep me from trying to walk on my own. I wasn't going to be a cripple, and that was that!

My wound seemed to be healing faster than Dr. Bogumill had expected. Maybe it was because I was only nineteen and in great physical shape. The sixty stitches were removed from the sides of my knee, leaving two ugly ten-inch scars. My shaved knee was swollen to twice the size of my left knee and blood oozed from the stitches — not a pretty sight.

By the end of my hospital stay, I was bored. I watched men in the ward get well and go home, and I thought about going home too. I missed riding my motorcycle, going on dates, seeing a scary movie at the drive-in, eating a juicy cheeseburger with crisp French fries, and hanging around with my family and friends. I craved a cold bottle of Coors. Most of the guys I knew had never heard of the Coors beer slogan: "Brewed with pure Rocky Mountain spring water." I hadn't met any other soldiers from Colorado, so no one understood the special things I missed about my home state.

I had a patient take a photo of me while I was propped up on my elbows in bed. I sent that photo to my friend Van Wilson who was still humping the boonies with the 7th Cavalry in Vietnam. He gave it back to me when we reunited in 2003.

As soon as a bed was vacated, it was filled almost immediately with another wounded soldier from Vietnam. The cycle of men entering and leaving Ward D was never-ending. At night, I'd hear the screams of soldiers having nightmares, a constant reminder of the war; I'm sure they heard my nightmares too. No one ever talked much about what went on at night, unless an emergency occurred. Thank God no one died in Ward D while I was there.

Recovered well enough not to need crutches or a cane, I got a liberty pass to Yokohama, the city right outside our military compound. I had to follow the rules and return to the hospital before dark. Civilian clothes weren't authorized for patients, so I was issued a khaki military uniform, a hat, and a pair of shoes. I signed a partial-pay voucher for $50 and suddenly felt rich.

No patient was authorized to go off the base alone. We had to use the buddy system, so I teamed up with another patient; we caught a cab outside the gate, and off we went to visit downtown.

The cab dropped us off on a street near a pier full of boats and ships and a fish market nearby. The streets of Yokohama were crowded with people going about their usual business. The Japanese women wore colorful kimonos; the men were in street clothes and suits. This contrasted with the attire of the Vietnamese, who wore black pajamas and straw hats. We took our time, slowly walking the sidewalks and resting as much as possible. The Japanese acted as though we weren't there. I guess they were used to seeing American servicemen on their streets. I felt quite comfortable even though we couldn't understand a word of Japanese. There was a sense of freedom all around us — something I hadn't experienced in a long time.

We stopped in a bar, ordered a few Japanese beers, but didn't eat anything. Japanese music played on a radio. We sat, talked, and sipped our brews. After a while, we left that bar and roamed the streets and the marketplace. I wasn't much of a fish eater, so I was repulsed by the awful smell of the fish market we passed. Not long after, we flagged a cab and headed back to Kishine Barracks.

The day finally came when Dr. Bogumill and Nurse Jones informed me that my prognosis was good enough for me to be discharged from the hospital. My knee didn't hurt much. The muscles in my right thigh were strong again as a result of physical therapy. I'd also strengthened my upper body by using weights and exercising. I could even jog.

Dr. Bogumill told me that I was healthy enough to return to active duty. This wasn't what I wanted to hear. "How about a one-way trip to Littleton, Colorado, Doc?" I asked, even though my wound wasn't severe enough for a medical discharge.

I sensed from the doctor's manner that he really cared about his patients. He told me to get the hell out of the infantry and find a safer job, and then get out of the army and go to college.

Since I'd joined the army, it seemed that I was always being disappointed. First, I didn't get to go to Special Forces school and was sent to Vietnam instead. When I got there, I nearly killed several of my own squad by accidentally forgetting to secure my rifle's safety. After only two months' service, my best friend, Kenny, had almost been killed. I'd been wounded, and now I couldn't get discharged from Uncle Sam's army because I'd healed too well. I was beginning to think it was my lot in life to be surrounded by tragedy, almost making it to safety, only to get pulled back into chaos again.

While in the hospital, I'd written many letters home mentioning the possibility that I might be discharged. I'd told people to start planning my homecoming party. Now I had to write and tell everyone to put away the party hats. The army was going to keep me on active duty in the Pacific.

Even if I wasn't going home, the news that I'd soon be leaving the hospital made me extremely happy. I'd soon leave Japan for an assignment in Okinawa. Little did I know that my new assignment would change my life in a totally unexpected way.

I'd soon be meeting my first war dog.

Chapter 7

Sentry Dog Platoon

IN JANUARY 1967 the U.S. Army released me from the 106th General Hospital, Kishine Barracks, Yokohama, Japan, and reassigned me to the island of Okinawa to serve out my remaining tour in Southeast Asia.

Okinawa had a huge military supply depot that serviced the war effort in Vietnam. There were no infantry units there, so I was assigned to the 267th Chemical Company because they needed sentry-dog handlers. The personnel clerk must have keyed on the words "infantry" and "sentry" as a close-enough occupational match.

I liked the idea of having a dog of my own, even though it really belonged to Uncle Sam. Training with a sentry dog would prove challenging and exciting. The dogs wouldn't be barking orders at me like the sergeants did. The idea of having a dog to pal around with sounded too good to be true.

When I reported for work at the 267th Company, I met with the 1st Sergeant in his office. I stood at attention in front of his desk. He looked up and saw that I wore a Combat Infantryman Badge. In a soft voice he said, "At ease, soldier." As I relaxed my position, he commented, "A CIB on such a young boy!" I immediately thought, *Here's that "boy" thing again,* but somehow, coming from a salty old veteran, it didn't upset me, so I didn't snap back. He smiled and then offered me a cup of coffee. "Top," as we commonly called the 1st Sergeant, was an infantry veteran who had fought the Nazis in Europe and the North Koreans and Chinese during the Korean War. Okinawa was probably his last assignment before retirement.

After trading a few war stories, Top told me that I was the only Vietnam combat infantry veteran in the outfit wearing a CIB and a Purple Heart, which seemed to make him proud to have me aboard. When he briefed me on the mission of the 267th, Top explained that the unit provided security for and managed the contents of the army's ammunition-storage buildings in a controlled area of the island. The job called for a number of sentry-dog teams — German shepherd and handler — to guard the buildings. He explained the sensitive nature of the mission and how important it was not to discuss the work with anyone outside official channels. That restriction included not taking pictures or writing anything about my work in letters home.

Top advised me to be careful around strangers who offered free drinks in downtown bars. "There are spies out there," he said. "They want classified information about what we do. Don't talk or try to figure them out; they're professionals. Report everything immediately to our security officer. Do you understand, soldier?"

I immediately replied, "Yes, sir!"

He barked back, "And don't call me 'sir' — I work for a living!"

It all sounded mysterious, but what the hell did I know about that type of army business? Top instructed me to read and sign an official military document corroborating that our briefing had taken place. I supposed that if I were suspected of talking with a communist, the army would have been able to use that document against me, lock my young ass up, and lose the key.

I thought, *Hell, man! The army doesn't have to worry about me; I'm a true red-white-and-blue American who'd never sell out my country to some commie bastard.*

Top got up from behind the desk, shook my hand, and told the clerk sitting outside his office to add my name to the roster of sentry-dog handlers. Sitting beside the company clerk's desk, I filled out a long personal-history form so I could get a security clearance. My next stop was to meet the men of the sentry-dog platoon.

A dog handler named Fred escorted me to my new living quarters on the third floor above the company offices. About my size in height and build, Fred had straight black hair, brown eyes, a square jaw, and a neatly trimmed mustache. His uniform was starched stiff and his boots spit-shined. Fred had joined the army two years before I had, and held the enlisted rank of Specialist Four (SP4), one rank above my Private First Class (PFC).

I picked an empty bunk bed and stored my personals. I was issued a set of white sheets, a blanket, a pillow, and a pillowcase. After having slept in about ten different places since leaving my tent in Vietnam, it was a relief to finally have a new home.

I thought about the members of my old combat platoon. *Is Sergeant Dorman still alive? What about my new friend, Van Wilson, who helped carry me out of harm's way? Van had a November 1966 rotation date and must have gone back to Arkansas,* I thought. I closed my eyes and got lost in thoughts of the men I had left in Vietnam. The sound of Sergeant Dorman yelling, "Saddle up!" and the rat-tat-tat of Van's M60 machine gun blasting away on that hilltop remained fresh in my memory.

Fred was anxious for me to meet the rest of the members of the sentry-dog platoon, who were out at the kennel or on guard duty. I asked him about the one-inch-square patch he wore above his nametag. It had the head of a German shepherd sewn in black against a yellow background. Fred told me that all the army sentry-dog handlers wore that patch. I would have to earn my patch through on-the-job dog training. Fred wanted to know what I knew about sentry dogs. I told him that the only sentry dogs I'd encountered guarded junkyards back home.

I was the first Vietnam veteran Fred had met. With excitement in his eyes, he questioned me about my combat experiences. I answered him in very general terms, not yet comfortable enough with Fred or my new surroundings to tell my stories. I felt more comfortable trading stories with the 1st Sergeant: though we were generations apart in age and occupied different stations in life, that CIB seemed to bond us immediately in unspoken respect.

No one I had met since leaving the hospital had served a day in

Vietnam or the infantry. They all had noncombatant jobs in rear-area support, and it wasn't easy to have a one-sided conversation about combat. Most of them told me that they were glad to have been assigned to units not fighting in Vietnam. They were curious and hung on every word I said, treating me like I was something unusual, which made me feel awkward in their company. It felt odd not being around a bunch of grunts carrying weapons. I just wanted to fit in and see those German shepherd sentry dogs everyone was talking about.

Fred informed me that sentry-dog handlers worked night shifts, guarding a highly secured compound. Days off varied, and I would eventually enter the rotation.

One morning I boarded the back of an army troop truck with a bunch of dog handlers. I had no idea what to expect when we arrived at the kennel, greeted by the sounds of a bunch of barking dogs. The dog handlers quickly dismounted the truck and entered the kennels. I lagged behind a little to observe. Inside the kennels, handlers yelled the names of their dogs: Wolf, Mike, Rex, and Lucky.

After the handlers exited the kennel, their dogs attached to neck chains and leather leashes, I slowly entered. The smell of fresh dog shit and urine on the concrete floor permeated the air. The German shepherds were housed behind thick wire fencing. Each dog's name was painted on a piece of plywood attached above his kennel door. A metal choke chain hung on a nail outside each kennel door, along with a leather collar, leash, and muzzle. Metal bowls for water and food sat inside each dog's run.

As I walked by the caged German shepherds, they growled and lunged at me. Had one of those gates accidentally popped open, I'd have been dog meat — literally. It was a horrifying thought. The dogs probably sensed that I was scared shitless. Not one dog allowed me to get close without growling and showing me their big sharp teeth. *Maybe I don't want to be a sentry-dog handler after all,* I thought.

At both ends of the kennel were walls lined with wooden bins; each bore a dog's name. Neatly stored in each bin were a grooming brush, metal comb, and other assorted gear. Large boxes of dog food were stacked high alongside several large metal lockers. Water hoses were connected to pipes at each end of the kennel. Two dog handlers turned the hoses on and washed the waste on the floor through the back of the fenced runs, laughing as they squirted some of the dogs just to piss them off.

Outside, other handlers groomed their dogs on small wooden tables with posts to which the animals were secured. The handlers talked to their dogs while they brushed them, cleaned their teeth, clipped their nails, and checked them for health problems. I watched, impressed, at how muscular and fit the animals appeared, not a bit of fat on any of them. The platoon sergeant approached and instructed me to observe and help around the kennels for the next few days. I became a stable hand, washing the excreta from the concrete runs, cleaning the water buckets, stacking food supplies, and repairing the wooden grooming tables.

The sergeant was responsible for matching dogs to new handlers. Usually, a new guy was assigned the healthiest dog that had spent the most time without a handler. Each dog was already trained in basic obedience, but if a dog didn't work on a regular basis, he became lazy. Keeping the dog through training was an extremely important part of the handler's routine. Sentry dogs were trained for the primary function of guarding and attacking on command. They learn through repetition, and are taught to react to the commands of only one master. I would soon learn an essential rule about working with sentry dogs: don't befriend any animal other than your assigned dog.

Rex held the distinction of being the most ferocious sentry dog. His handler, SP4 Aldridge, was a tall, husky man with scars on his arms where Rex had bitten him several times. He wore his scars like badges of courage.

The platoon sergeant decided to assign me to Hans, the biggest, but not the meanest-looking, German shepherd in the kennel. In fact, none of the dogs was friendly to me; each one charged at me, barking and growling and showing me his teeth as I passed their run. It didn't really matter which dog was assigned to me, because they all wanted to eat me. I think the platoon sergeant figured that if I could handle Hans, I could handle any dog. He was definitely testing my level of fear. The fact was that I feared every one of those dogs, and they sensed it too!

The sergeant said, "Come on, Burnam! Before you know it, you'll have Hans eating out of your hand. The hardest part is overcoming your fear. Besides, this job's a piece of cake compared to what you went through in Vietnam."

I replied, "Yeah, right!"

My first task was to spend quality time with Hans, feeding him, cleaning his cage, and talking to him. During that initial "let's get acquainted" period, I didn't dare go into his run or try to touch Hans through the wire fence. Physical distance was okay with me; I figured I had plenty of time and was in no hurry to put my hands on that big dog. This was so different from what I'd expected. When I arrived in Vietnam, I was eager to fit in and do my job even though I was a "greenhorn" who made some major mistakes at the start, but this dog job was becoming an altogether different kind of challenge.

Someone joked, "Just remember, if Hans bites a chunk out of your ass, you'll be getting a tetanus shot instead of a Purple Heart."

Those who heard the remark burst into laughter. I stood there in silence, realizing that I was going through an acceptance process just as I had in Vietnam.

Every time I visited Hans, he'd growl and try to bite through the wire fence that separated us. The platoon sergeant said Hans's growling was his way of testing my control and my fear. He told me I had to show no fear if I was ever to have a chance at commanding an army sentry dog.

Over time, Hans became accustomed to seeing me and stopped growling. I was getting used to him, too. With each passing day, my fear slowly diminished and the day finally arrived when the platoon sergeant told me to take Hans out of his kennel run.

"Do you think I'm ready, Sarge?"

The sergeant replied, "It's now or never, Burnam! Besides, you survived combat in Vietnam, so handling Hans should be no problem!"

I had to take Hans out of the kennel and deal with him face to face. I kept thinking, *I can't be chicken-shit about it or let that dog control me. I've got to take control of him and just do it!*

I took a deep breath, cleared my mind, grabbed the leather leash, and connected a choke chain to it. All the while, Hans paced back and forth like a hungry lion in a cage. He knew he was getting out. I tried not to think of what could happen after I opened that door.

The platoon sergeant watched me as I kept delaying the inevitable. I spread the choke chain as far as possible, so that the dog's head could pass through easily and quickly. Then I took another long breath and opened the door. Now there was nothing to keep Hans from eating me alive. To my surprise, he quickly put his nose and head through the loop of the choke chain and charged past me through the open door, pulling me behind him toward the exit and the open area behind the kennel.

Running behind us, the platoon sergeant kept yelling, "Yank back on the leash! Command the dog to heel!" I pulled back as hard as I could on the leash and yelled, "Heel! Heel! Heel!" Hans ignored me and pulled even harder. Finally, he just stopped pulling and started walking and sniffing the ground. Then he lifted his leg and took a leak on a fencepost. After he finished, I pulled on the leash and gave the command to heel. To my surprise, Hans moved to my left side and sat.

The platoon sergeant instructed me to praise Hans by saying, "Good dog! Good dog!" Verbal praise was fine; I just hoped the sergeant wouldn't ask me to give Hans a big hug. While we marched around the training yard, Hans stayed at my pace. I had a huge smile on my face, feeling as if I had just won the blue ribbon in a basic obedience contest. My fear had been temporarily replaced with joy.

There was a lot more to learn if I was going to become a respected sentry-dog handler. The platoon sergeant told me I'd have to master the commands for basic obedience and learn to control Hans under all circumstances. Hans already knew what to do but needed a master to make him do it. I had to be consistent in how I handled him. I learned that discipline was extremely important and could be achieved only by practicing with Hans every day. Through effective training, he could become my companion, and maybe we would bond and make a great team.

After several days, Hans and I reached the point at which I could dangle the leash in front of his cage and he would go crazy with excitement. When Hans stood on his hind legs he was taller than I — one of the biggest German shepherds in the platoon. All the sentry dogs were healthy and lean because of their diet and rigorous daily training. There wasn't one fat dog handler either; every man was in excellent health and top physical condition. There were no female dog handlers or trainers in the sentry-dog platoon.

I was issued a military dog-training manual and was expected to learn and practice what it preached. The manual contained illustrations of tools and procedures for grooming, voice commands, hand and arm signals, deployment, and first aid. The other dog handlers were well versed in the commands and advanced dog-training techniques. Most had graduated from a formal twelve-week military dog-training school in the States, so I watched them work their animals. Everything they did appeared simple and smooth between dog and handler, even though each dog was trained to be a lethal weapon.

The platoon sergeant assigned Fred to be my tutor in the finer art of basic obedience training. Fred's happy-go-lucky personality was quickly rubbing off on me. He always talked about the pretty Okinawa barmaids working at Club Lucky, a downtown bar not far from the base, which the dog handlers frequented and considered their special hangout.

Fred taught me that positive reinforcement was critical throughout the training exercises. My first lesson included the voice commands *sit, heel, come, down, stay, no,* and rules on when to praise the dog. Fred taught me how to use voice inflection when calling out commands to Hans. I practiced for hours each day until I could voice the commands with the precision of a drill sergeant.

At first, Hans was slow to commit to action when commanded. When I ordered him to sit, he took his time. When I voiced the command *down,* Hans would get only partway down and then return to a sit. But after several training sessions, he became more responsive, obeying my basic voice commands. The dog that had scared the crap out me before was slowly becoming a partner.

Eventually, I was ready to join the rest of the platoon for regular group training sessions. Uniformity was the key. Each dog handler carried the same equipment attached to specific places on his pistol belt. Each belt held a canteen of water, a six-foot leather leash, a leather collar, a choke chain, a twenty-five-foot nylon leash, a leather muzzle, a first-aid bandage, and a .45-caliber pistol in a black leather holster. Of course our green fatigue uniforms had to be clean and starched; our tarnish-free brass belt buckles gleaming, and our black boots spit-shined.

Outside the kennel, the platoon sergeant, positioned front and center of the platoon, would assemble the twenty dog handlers with their dogs in a formation of four ranks. When he called the platoon to attention, everyone assumed the standing position of attention — feet together, shoulders back, heads high, and eyes straight ahead. The position of attention for the dog was a full and proper sitting position at the handler's left side.

Dogs weren't allowed to slouch or sit leaning on one hind leg. Standing little more than an arm's length from his dog, each handler gripped the choke chain near its end. That way he could easily control the dog if it decided to attack a nearby dog or handler — after all, these dogs were trained to strike and kill.

We practiced many other basic obedience drills: *sit, stay, right face, left face, about face, down, heel, march.* I was not allowed to praise my dog until he successfully completed a movement. When the dogs were warmed up, we performed three or four commands and movements in sequence.

I soon graduated to voice commands with simultaneous hand signals. Hand signals were generally taught with the handler facing the dog at the end of the leash. To get Hans to sit, I'd signal him with my arm and hand and simultaneously voice the command *sit.* We'd practice hand and voice signals for all the movements of advanced basic obedience, including *dead dog, roll over,* and *crawl.*

If there was one command I wore out, it was *No!* But after many weeks of training, Hans would respond with precision when I used hand signals only. It fascinated me that a dog could learn to do so many tricks on command. While training Hans, I often thought that he'd have made a great patrol dog for Vietnam. He was so big that the Vietcong would have run away when they spotted him.

✴

After about a month, I was ready for the next phase of my education: learning how to get Hans to attack and stop on command. This would be the most frightening part of my sentry-dog training. The platoon sergeant marched us into the fenced training yard. He selected one handler and directed him to put on a heavy burlap attack suit. The rest of us buckled the leather collars around our dogs' necks and then removed the choke chains and attached them to our pistol belts. The leather collar was used only when a dog was officially on guard duty.

We formed a single line. The platoon sergeant instructed us to turn around and face away from the platform and the man in the burlap suit. Once the leather collars were buckled on our dogs, they knew what was coming next. The handlers had a difficult time keeping their excited dogs in a sitting position and facing away from the action.

The soldier outfitted in the burlap suit protected his face with a steel mask that looked much like a baseball catcher's mask. Each sentry-dog team would be given the opportunity to perform an attack. There were three commands to the attack phase: *Watch him, Get him,* and *Out.* The command *Get him* meant that the handler released his dog to attack the target.

The platoon sergeant called one of the handlers by name and said, "Attack-dog command!" The man in burlap assumed a crouching position about thirty feet in front of the dog. The handler commanded, "Watch him!" The dog watched the target and moved slowly toward the burlap-suited man, who was raising his arms up and down and growling. When the dog was about twenty feet from the target, the handler commanded, "Get him" and let go of the leash, which remained attached to the dog's leather collar. In a flash the dog charged and lunged at the crouching man's throat and then at his groin.

I had never seen a big dog move so fast. Each time the dog lunged, the force of the hit shoved the man in the burlap suit backward. The dog would bite down on the arm of the suit, back off, and lunge again. At one point, the force of the dog's lunge knocked the man onto his back. The dog would attack a vulnerable area and thrash his head side to side like a shark in a feeding frenzy. The ferocious biting exercises caused the dog's gums to bleed, but they liked it.

The command "Out" meant that the dog should immediately release his bite and back off the target. The handler would then command, "Heel," and the dog would return to his side, at which point the handler praised his dog.

After so many dog attacks the burlap suit was saturated with bloodstains. When it was my turn, I was nervous, unsure how I'd handle Hans throughout the process. The platoon sergeant gave me the signal. The man in burlap began to kick up dirt and wave his arms. From about twenty feet away, I commanded, "Get him." When Hans reached the end of the leash, the force of his charge pulled it right out of my hand. In a flash, Hans was on his target. I ran behind Hans and grabbed the leash while he had the man on the ground, biting, and twisting his entire body in an effort to tear the man's leg off.

The hair on the back of Hans's neck stood straight up and his teeth dug deep into the burlap. The guy in the suit screamed, "Call him off! Call him off!" I frantically yelled, "Out! Out! Out!" Finally, Hans let go. It took every bit of strength I had to keep Hans back and away from the powerless man. I was exhausted, even though the action had lasted less than a minute. The platoon sergeant told me that I'd have to learn to control my dog better during the attack — truly a masterpiece of understatement.

After the attack, Hans's gums were bleeding, and the muscles in his shoulders and legs twitched tensely and were hot to the touch. I praised him as he sat, ears pointed high, eyes locked on the target. It was scary to know that Hans was fully capable of killing a man.

Back in the barracks, several of the dog handlers commented on how well my training was coming along. Fred invited me to go to town for drinks at Club Lucky. I didn't make very much money as a PFC, but being overseas, I didn't have to pay taxes either. A few bucks went a long way at Club Lucky.

Outside the main gate of the base, *skoshi* cabs (small cars) parked alongside the fence. Fred instructed the driver to take us to Club Lucky. The streets were crowded with people walking, riding bicycles, and driving funny-looking little cars. The signs above the bars were in English: Club BC Night, Club California, Club Chicago, Club Texas, and so on. The streets were crowded with American servicemen — sailors, marines, soldiers, and airmen. Japanese hawkers in black slacks and white shirts stood in the doorways of the bars, trying to entice people to step inside.

I was warned not to mess with the hawkers. Although they were little guys, they were also club bouncers, many of them karate and judo experts.

I said to Fred, "You mean these little shits can fight?"

"You bet your ass!" he replied. "I've seen the little fellows take down some big boys." That was enough to convince me. I'd never been one to pick a fight, though I had enjoyed fast one-on-one wrestling competition during high school. It required talent, strength, speed, endurance, training, and a driving desire to win. Since I hadn't heard of any wrestlers from Okinawa, I wondered if I could teach the little bar hawkers a few tricks. *I'd love to take on one of them in a wrestling match,* I thought.

We entered Club Lucky. Behind the bar stood an older Japanese woman who greeted us. Everyone called her "Mama San." Small groups of Asian women dressed in long flowered silk dresses were seated at the bar and a few tables, talking and giggling at one another.

Fred ordered a round of Japanese beers and we moved to an empty table to sit down. The jukebox filled the air with the sound of American rock 'n' roll. One of the barmaids came over and asked for money to put in the jukebox. Someone gave her change and off she went. Soon, several other attractive young barmaids came to our table. I was the only one who didn't know them by name.

When the drinks came, we ordered a round for the girls. I quickly learned that some of the guys considered certain girls their girlfriends, which meant they were off-limits to everyone else. Fred pointed out the women not taken. I wasn't interested in those who were left over, and besides, I was having too much fun watching everyone else.

I quickly learned that if I didn't buy a barmaid a drink, she'd go sit with someone who would. It was their job to rotate to all the customers, which was how they made their tips. The guys all considered the locals poor people who survived on the money we Americans poured into their economy. The bars created big business. Fred told me that none of the women at Club Lucky were prostitutes. I found that hard to believe.

Meeting decent girls as an American serviceman in a foreign country wasn't as easy as back home. Many of the young women on the island were simply looking for a way to get to the United States, and the best method was to marry an American serviceman, which would assure them a home on a military base, money, medical benefits, and a ticket to the States and U.S. citizenship. Many of the high-ranking soldiers paid for their girlfriends' apartments in town so they'd have a place to shack up after duty and on weekends. It was a common practice among those who could afford it. As soon as a soldier got reassigned off the island, another was in line to rent his woman an apartment. None of that was of any interest to me.

Some American servicemen fathered children and then abandoned them when they left the island. It really bothered me to see kids of mixed heritage begging for money on the streets. Most of those kids appeared to be shunned by the people of their own culture.

Midnight was the curfew for all military personnel to be back on base. MPs from all the military services roamed the streets and checked the bars for soldiers who caused problems or violated curfew. The native island police also walked the streets to enforce local law and order. We left the bar, flagged a skoshi, and were back on base before midnight. I wasn't one to get into trouble with MPs or to become involved in a court-martial for drunk-and-disorderly conduct.

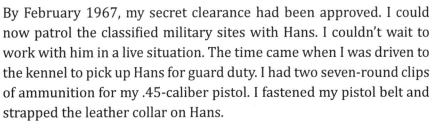

By February 1967, my secret clearance had been approved. I could now patrol the classified military sites with Hans. I couldn't wait to work with him in a live situation. The time came when I was driven to the kennel to pick up Hans for guard duty. I had two seven-round clips of ammunition for my .45-caliber pistol. I fastened my pistol belt and strapped the leather collar on Hans.

There were six sentry-dog teams in back of the troop truck headed for the guard-duty site. Muzzled like the rest of the dogs, Hans sat between my legs for control and protection from fighting with the other animals.

We arrived at the entrance gate of a fully lighted fenced area. The guard checked us over, opened the gate, and waved us into the classified compound. Armed guards patrolled in jeeps between two electric fences that encircled the perimeter. Sentry dogs patrolled the inner fenced perimeter where the munitions buildings were located.

That perimeter contained many munitions bunkers, called igloos because of their rounded mound shape. They were well spaced apart and aligned in rows. Each igloo had huge steel double doors surrounded by windowless concrete walls. The entire structure was buried under dirt on which grass grew. The only exposed areas were the steel doors and the air vents on top. From the sky, the area must have appeared to be a flat grassy field with a grid of roads.

My guard post included five igloos. Fred instructed me to check all the doors to make sure each igloo was secure. When on duty, I was to have my .45 loaded, with a round in the chamber, but holstered until I needed to use it. If a perpetrator entered my guard-post area, my orders were to command the dog to attack, after which I would shoot to kill.

I carried two black rubber gas masks, one for me and one for Hans. I asked Fred what was inside the igloos. He told me that that information was classified. I informed him that I had secret clearance and needed to know just what in hell I was responsible for guarding. Giving in, Fred told me that the military stockpiled chemical warfare weapons inside the igloos. He warned me that I now had a classified secret to protect and that I was not to discuss it with him again.

There were cages near the vents on top of each igloo. I was to check them frequently, and quietly observe the behavior of the rabbits housed inside. I had to do the same with the goats that roamed freely into my guard post from time to time. I thought, *Holy shit!* It didn't take my young-ass brain but one second to figure out why the army put animals in there with us. If any of those chemicals weapons sprung a leak, the rabbits, housed right near the air vents, would be the first to inhale the airborne agent. Hans and the goats had no shoes to protect them from contamination if chemicals seeped through the concrete walls and into the soil they walked on.

If I smelled or tasted anything foul in the air, I was basically fucked. *Whoa!* I remembered several tear-gas drills during my infantry training at Fort Leonardwood, Missouri, and Fort Ord, California. We were escorted into an empty wooden building out in the woods. They closed the doors and forced us to breathe tear gas. I remember coming out of that damn building with my eyes and throat on fire; but it wasn't tear gas stored in those igloos on Okinawa. These were the real killers that no training could ever possibly prepare you for: the horrific effects of nerve gas, choking agents, and blood agents — the type of shit that instantly upset your stomach, burned your eyes out, made you vomit, and caused convulsions, followed by an agonizing death in the fetal position. Even if I were quick enough to get my rubber protective mask on in seconds, I'd still die. What about Hans? He had absolutely no idea that he was a guinea pig too.

I must have practiced putting on my gas mask ten times that night. Hans was getting annoyed with the exercise, so I stopped when he started growling at me. *Hans, if you only knew!* I thought. *If you only knew!*

By the time my first shift ended, I was thankful that all the rabbits and goats were still alive and not doing the shimmy-shake. As I sat in the back of that troop truck heading back to the kennels, I contemplated how long I'd last doing that job with Hans. I thought I'd rather take my chances fighting the North Vietnamese Army in Vietnam than guard a village of igloos full of rabbits, goats, and killer chemicals.

✳

Hans and I had gotten along fine thus far and I'd come to really love him. For many nights over the course of a month, we guarded those igloos with never an incident to report. Even though my fear never subsided, I was growing bored with the whole routine. During those long night hours on guard, I had plenty of time to think of home in Colorado. My house was about forty-five minutes from the tranquility of the Rocky Mountain wilderness. I would reflect on the special places in the mountains, sitting on the bank of a fast-flowing stream, listening to the whispering aspen trees and the water rushing over the boulders. It was peaceful and the air was fresh and cool.

✳

I had met a local barmaid, Kiko, who worked at Club Texas. Kiko was the most beautiful Japanese girl I had ever seen — she looked like a calendar model. It seemed like every time I entered the club, soldiers surrounded Kiko and sat at her table. During my nights off, I'd be at the club, vying for time to sit with her. And I rarely had to buy her drinks to keep her at my table. It wasn't long before I was taking Kiko to the local Japanese theater and dining at her favorite Japanese restaurants off the main bar strip. We enjoyed each other's company, but I wasn't too keen on the taste of Japanese food.

Kiko had never been off the island of Okinawa, but had learned to speak and write English from all the American servicemen she had met working in bars. She was eighteen years old and wanted to have children and make a home with me in the United States. I thought about it many times and even checked into the military administrative procedures. There was a lot of legal paperwork involved, but deep down I knew I wasn't ready for marriage. The only girl I had ever had a crush on before was Tena, who had attended Littleton High School with me. She was *beautiful.* From the letters I had received, Tena was finishing her freshman year at the University of Colorado. I wondered if she'd found a steady boyfriend in college or would ever date me again when I got home.

The more I thought about marrying a shy, petite Japanese girl, the clearer it became that I didn't want to take home a girl from a totally different culture and have to face a huge cultural transition. Like most guys my age, I was lonely for female companionship, but had concluded that marriage would be too big a step for me at nineteen. That relationship had become way too much for me to deal with, and my need to break it off gave me another reason for trying to leave Okinawa.

The army wasn't going to let me off the island for another year, so I pondered volunteering to go back to Vietnam. After Vietnam, I could return home to Littleton and attend a state college. That, I thought, was the perfect remedy for my depressing predicament.

I had assumed that being an infantryman was all I was capable of at the time, and convinced myself that fighting in Vietnam wasn't such a bad job after all. The idea of leaving Hans troubled me, but I felt that requesting reassignment to Vietnam was my only way out. I thought I might even get to select an assignment with an elite paratrooper outfit. With all that stirring in my mind, I made an appointment with the personnel office to volunteer for a return trip to Vietnam.

My friends thought I was out of my mind. Returning to Vietnam as an infantryman was the worst thing any of them could possibly imagine — especially as a way to get off Okinawa. I was told time and again, "You'll be killed if you go back there."

I tried to defend my reasons, but couldn't convince my friends that I wasn't insane. Their words — *dead, killed, blown away, dying, pine box, body bag, POW*—failed to trigger any belief that tragedy could befall me. I had confidence in my decisions and in myself, and I didn't fear the dangers they had predicted for me.

I thought about what I needed to buy in Okinawa to add to my standard-issue combat infantry gear in South Vietnam. Something I regretted about my first tour of duty, with the 1st Air Cavalry Division, was that I had not one photo to document my experience. Now I had a chance to go back and record what I'd want to remember. I bought my first camera, a Canon 35-millimeter half frame that was small enough to carry in an ammo pouch. Then I bought a shiny pair of handmade black patent-leather paratrooper boots. I'd wear them in base camp when I wasn't wearing my army-issue green canvas jungle boots. The last item I bought was a bone-handled hunting knife with a six-inch blade. With those items, I started preparing for my planned return to Vietnam.

When I went to see the personnel clerk, he told me that I had two options. The first was to fill out a request for transfer to duty in Vietnam. That would get me to Vietnam, and the army would assign me according to its needs after I got there. The paperwork, however, could take several months, which didn't appeal to me in the least. I wanted control over where I was going in Vietnam, and I wanted to get there fast, especially if I was to volunteer.

The second option was to reenlist in the army for an additional year and get assigned to the outfit of my choice. The paperwork would only take a week or so, and I could be on my way within a month. I didn't think twice about giving the army another year of my life if it could work that fast for me.

So, I reenlisted to join the 173rd Airborne Brigade, an elite paratrooper outfit operating in the southern jungles of South Vietnam. A week later, my unit of choice was granted and I received official orders to report to the Republic of South Vietnam in March 1967. My paratrooper jump-school training was about to pay off.

Don Vestal was a good friend at the time and was a former infantryman. He had a job operating a forklift at the warehouse loading docks in Okinawa. We met while shopping at the Post Exchange (PX). When I saw he was wearing a CIB, I introduced myself. We became friends and started hanging out together after work. Don told me that I had the balls of a real American fighting soldier. He said, "To go back to that hellhole after being wounded is a choice only you can understand. No matter what happens to you in life, John, I will always respect your decision."

Don had been wounded in Vietnam and had received the Army Commendation Medal for valor in combat. He was counting the days until he went home to Texas. I spent my last days in Okinawa hanging around with Don until I boarded a C-130 cargo plane at Kadena Air Base and took off for Vietnam.

I couldn't have foreseen that my sentry-dog training would be a huge factor in why I survived my second combat tour.

Chapter 8

Return to Vietnam

I ARRIVED BACK IN VIETNAM in March 1967, a few days after turning twenty years of age. The C-130 I rode in was loaded with new recruits getting their first glimpse of Saigon and Ton Son Nhut Air Force Base. Their innocence and fear of the unknown contrasted with my eagerness to get in-processed and on my way to the elite 173rd Airborne.

The airfield was busy with the sounds of equipment moving about and the deafening roar of fighter jets speeding down runways. On the ground, I rode in an olive drab bus with steel mesh over the windows — just like the bus I'd ridden my first time around, a year ago to the month. The climate was the same: hot and humid, and that familiar smell of stale fish permeated the air.

The officers had been separated from the enlisted troops and rode in a separate bus. The vehicles cruised through the airfield, passing armed guards and manned fortified bunkers.

Saigon was still an extremely crowded city, with people, bicycles, rickshaws, strange-looking foreign buses, and tiny cars everywhere. There was no sign of war activity, but I knew it was a different story outside the city limits and deep in the remote jungles.

I soon passed through the gates of Camp Alpha. Stepping off the bus, I surveyed my surroundings and saw that the camp had changed little. In a familiar drill we were quickly shuffled into a large reception building. Personnel clerks greeted us: "Give me a copy of your orders. Wait right here and don't move. We'll get you processed as soon as possible." I was accustomed to this hurry-up-and-wait routine. Whatever those personnel folks did was never fast enough for me. My main objective was to get to the 173rd Airborne, and I didn't like the idea of hanging around a deadbeat replacement camp with a bunch of bewildered FNGs (fucking new guys) fresh from the States, sporting bald heads, new fatigues, and farmer tans.

I heard my name called over a loudspeaker, so I reported to a wooden building where a sergeant sat behind a gray metal desk covered with stacks of brown file folders. He asked me to sit while he prepared my assignment. When he finished, he told me I was going to be assigned to the 3rd Brigade, 25th Infantry Division in Dau Tieng.

I couldn't believe what I was hearing. "What do you mean?" I asked. "Didn't you read my orders? There has to be some kind of mistake here, Sarge. Are you sure you have the right guy? I've got orders guaranteeing my assignment to the 173rd Airborne Brigade."

The sergeant looked at me with a complete lack of interest and sternly stated, "Look, soldier, I process hundreds of men through here each day. You're not so special because you were here before or because you have orders to the 173rd. Remember, the rules are different in a combat zone, and Uncle Sam reserves the right to change your orders anytime it fits an immediate mission requirement. Got it?"

I replied in anger, "Well, I'm not going to accept this. I was guaranteed an assignment to the 173rd Airborne. That's the only reason I came back to Vietnam."

The sergeant didn't respond. He just sat there with his head down and stuffed my papers back into my brown folder.

I shouted, "Are you listening to me? Look, Sarge, I want to talk to the officer in charge here!"

The sergeant pointed to an officer seated behind a desk and reading documents. I marched over to him with the sergeant right behind me, carrying my personnel file folder.

The major looked up from his desk and asked, "Can I help you, soldier?"

I blurted out, "Sir, I have a guaranteed assignment to the 173rd Airborne Brigade. This sergeant just changed my orders and I want to know why, sir!"

The sergeant handed him my file. The major dismissed the sergeant and asked me to sit down. After reading through my file, he explained that under normal circumstances it would have been no problem to process me for assignment to the 173rd; however, the camp commander had directed that the 3rd Brigade, 25th Infantry Division was to be given the highest priority for infantry replacements. He indicated that I had just happened to arrive while that order was still in full effect. The 3rd Brigade, 25th Infantry had recently suffered numerous casualties, and the major was under orders to process all incoming infantrymen into that unit.

Again, I couldn't believe what I was hearing. I said, "This is my second tour. I should be given priority since I reenlisted to come back to Vietnam as an infantryman."

The major listened patiently, but kept telling me that there was nothing he could do to help. Starting to comprehend that I was being screwed out of a promised assignment, I got enraged. I told the major that if I'd known such a thing could happen, I would never have volunteered to come back to Vietnam. He sympathized with me and told me that I was a brave man for going back into the infantry after having been wounded in action, but there was absolutely no way he could change my assignment. He pointed out that he'd processed only a few soldiers who had returned as infantrymen.

"Sir, is there anyone else I can talk to?"

"No! And seeking counsel with the base camp commander is also out of the question," he barked.

The major assured me that he'd give my new assignment top priority for out-processing. I picked up my orders from his desk and stomped out of the building. There was nowhere I could go and no one else I could talk to. The army had me in a straitjacket and had completely neutralized my entire plan. I paced around the camp like a wounded tiger, getting more furious by the minute.

After passing the camp chapel for a third time, I decided to step inside. It was quiet and dimly lit by candles. I sat at the end of a pew and stared at the wooden cross above the altar. Another soldier sat nearby. He turned and smiled at me. I immediately recognized that he was an officer wearing the rank of captain, and I saw the small cross sewn to his collar, signifying that he was a chaplain.

Seeing that I was shaken up, the chaplain came over, shook my hand, and welcomed me to the place of the Lord. I explained my situation and how unfair I thought it was for the army to treat me that way. The chaplain listened without interruption. Then he told me that he'd talk to the personnel officer and see what he could do.

I waited in the chapel and said a few prayers. When the chaplain returned, he told me that he was sorry, but there was nothing he could do to remedy my situation. Distraught, I thanked him and walked out.

After breakfast the next morning, I heard my name called over the camp loudspeaker. I quickly reported to the personnel office where the major told me that my out-processing was complete and a jeep had been dispatched to transport me to the airfield. We shook hands, exchanged salutes, and the major wished me luck. I grabbed my gear and climbed into the jeep for the short ride to the airfield. I still couldn't quite believe I was going to the 3rd Brigade, 25th Infantry Division. My new assignment was in a small U.S. Army base camp of Dau Tieng, sixty miles west of Saigon, not far from the Cambodian border.

At the airfield, I didn't have to wait long before boarding a Chinook re-supply helicopter. Flying over the rice paddies, villages, and jungle terrain felt like old times. Not knowing any of the other soldiers riding with me, I sat quietly, my mind drifting back in time. I thought of Kenny Mook and our first chopper ride with the 7th Cavalry. It had been almost a year to the day since Kenny and I were brand-spanking-new guys from the States. A few months later, we were in deep shit in Bong Son. Now Kenny was home in Pennsylvania, recovering from his wounds, and I was back in Vietnam as an infantryman.

I had a lot of concerns and questions on my mind: *What kind of hell did the 3rd Brigade experience that caused the loss of so many infantrymen?*

What will my fellow veteran infantrymen think of my volunteering to return? What platoon and squad will I end up joining? What am I getting myself into this time?

The second I'd set foot back on Vietnamese soil, my entire plan had taken a detour. Based on what I'd learned and what the army told me, I had begun to question my ability to make sound decisions, and now I was on my way to a remote outpost west of Saigon and close to Cambodia.

I had no idea that this odd twist of fate meant that my involvement with military working dogs wasn't over.

Chapter 9

Dau Tieng Base Camp

THE CHINOOK HELICOPTER BEGAN its descent into a small base camp located in the middle of a huge rubber tree plantation. Raised in the inner city and suburbs of Denver, I had never seen rubber trees. From the air, the camp appeared small, remote, dusty, and temporary. The two huge rotary blades of the Chinook kicked up dust as it landed and then lowered its cargo ramp.

A buck sergeant (three stripes) in dusty jungle fatigues waved us over to him as we stepped off the ramp with our gear. We handed him copies of our assignment orders and climbed into the back of a small utility truck headed to the replacement facility. Traveling along the camp's main dirt road, we passed by a small field hospital, an armored squadron of tanks, a squadron of armored personnel carriers, a few infantry encampments, and a small motor pool of jeeps and trucks. The truck finally squealed to a stop at the entrance of the replacement center. Barbed-wire fencing enclosed its perimeter.

I asked, "Are they trying to keep the replacements from running away, or what?"

No one answered.

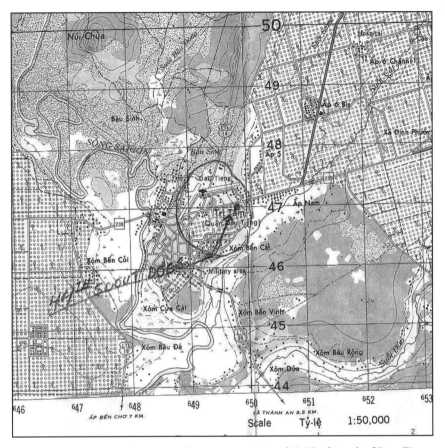

Map section of U.S. Military Land Navigation Map (1965 edition) of Dau Tieng and its surrounding area of jungle, rivers, and the Michelin and Ben Cui Rubber Plantations, South Vietnam (author collection).

After we jumped out of the truck and grabbed our gear, we moved inside the main wooden building, which was surrounded by sandbags piled waist high. As we sat in a small classroom, the noncommissioned officer in charge, a master sergeant (six stripes), stood before us. He was a husky, towering figure with the presence of a seasoned drill sergeant.

In a deep, penetrating voice, he welcomed us and emphasized the importance of the 3rd Brigade, 25th Infantry Division's mission. He explained that the base camp was strategically located as a buffer between Cambodia and Saigon. He called the area "III Corps" and "War

Zone C" and the "Iron Triangle." "Pick any name you like," he said. "It's all dictated by high-level commanders who decide how this area we operate in will be strategically divided for military operations."

The master sergeant explained that the entire area surrounding Dau Tieng had a high concentration of enemy troops who regularly launched mortar attacks at the airstrip from the small hilltops not far from camp. He said that if the VC tried to overrun our camp, we'd be issued the weapons and ammunition stored in bunkers inside the compound. He also explained that on March 21, the 3rd Brigade's 2nd Battalion, 12th Infantry had fought a victorious battle with the North Vietnamese Army in a place called LZ Gold, not far from Dau Tieng. The battle was initiated by the NVA in reaction to a "mad minute."

A mad minute was an operation designed to discard a unit's old and possibly faulty ammunition by firing it at a predetermined time. At LZ Gold, several hidden enemy regiments were preparing to attack the unsuspecting battalion. When the American infantrymen initiated the mad minute, the enemy assumed that the Americans were engaging them and decided to launch their attack, which was a complete surprise to the Americans. In the end, the NVA lost the battle. Bulldozers had to be airlifted into the battle zone to dig mass graves for the hundreds of enemy dead. Although the number of American casualties was low by comparison, the 2nd Battalion, 12th Infantry (Lancers) and the 2nd Battalion, 22nd Infantry (Triple Deuce) were in desperate need of replacements. *Now I know the details of why my assignment to the 173rd was nixed,* I thought.

The village of Dau Tieng was classified as hostile and off-limits to American soldiers. We were required to carry our weapons at all times when leaving the confines of the base camp and entering any of the surrounding villages within the rubber plantation. At night, MPs patrolled Dau Tieng because of its close proximity to the perimeter of the base camp. Inside the village, soldiers of the Army of the Republic of Vietnam (ARVN), our allies, occupied a command post.

Before my release from the replacement center and my duty assignment to an infantry combat unit, I had to put up with some training.

This consisted of orientations, the use and maintenance of the M16 rifle, hearing the history of the 3rd Brigade, memorizing various simple Vietnamese phrases, and recognizing the different enemy uniforms and equipment and weaponry they used to maim and kill Americans. It was similar to the indoctrination I got when I joined the 1st Air Cavalry Division in the central highlands.

The master sergeant used a pointer and a large military map, thumbtacked to the wall, to provide a geographical overview of the areas surrounding Dau Tieng. The 3rd Brigade's encampment split the district village of Dau Tieng into two parts. A dirt road running straight through the base camp connected the east and west ends of the village.

The base camp was large enough to contain three battalions of infantry and an assortment of support and supply units. Each battalion was strategically placed around the perimeter. Less than a mile west of the perimeter, the Song Saigon River snaked its way north and south. The Ben Cui rubber plantation was situated west and south of the river.

Tay Ninh, the next largest populated province, was several miles northwest of Dau Tieng. Southwest lay Cu Chi, home of the U.S. Army's 25th Infantry Division, nicknamed Tropical Lightning, with its American home base on the Hawaiian island of Oahu. The three base camps, Dau Tieng, Tay Ninh, and Cu Chi, formed a large triangle on the map — the Iron Triangle.

After the briefing, I walked up to the master sergeant and boldly stated, "I've been through all this shit before, so why can't I just skip this bullshit and join an infantry unit right away?"

The sergeant replied, "You will be treated like everyone else, with no exceptions for past experience. Besides, you can be of value to me by helping the others learn from your combat experience up north."

I impatiently replied, "I didn't come back to train a bunch of stinking FNGs!"

That really pissed him off. He leaned into my face and shouted, "You, soldier, have a bad attitude. If you don't back the fuck off, I'll put your ass in a sling!"

I got the message and quickly retreated. My only ambition was to get to my unit. Besides, I didn't want any problems or get on his shit list. The master sergeant looked as if he could kick my ass into next week. In those days, it wasn't uncommon for a sergeant like him to take a young trooper like me to the woodshed for a physical eye opener.

The next day, everyone formed up for training outside our hooch (wooden hut). The training area had mock booby traps, mines, and punji pits. There was also a huge ball of dried mud with bamboo spikes sticking out all over it hung from a tree by a vine. Such a ball, rigged by a trip wire or vine, was often camouflaged and suspended above a jungle trail. When tripped by a passing soldier, it would swing down with all its momentum and hit the man about chest high. There was little chance of surviving several bamboo spears piercing the torso.

The enemy was very clever at creating all kinds of nasty booby traps. I already knew what it felt like to be wounded by a punji stake. Dying was something I didn't think about with a fresh twelve-month tour of duty before going home.

To my surprise, as part of our training, two scout-dog handlers with leashed German shepherds showed up to give us a presentation on their mission in Vietnam. They were members of the 44th Infantry Platoon Scout Dogs (IPSD), and their presentation was directed at trying to recruit new dog handlers. I was excited to hear what they had to say. Oliver Whetstone, a handler whom everyone called Ollie, was from Kenosha, Wisconsin. Ollie was a tall, skinny, blond-headed, blue-eyed, friendly guy with a Midwestern accent. He explained the mission of a scout-dog team and how the dog provided an early silent warning while on patrol in enemy territory.

A scout dog used natural instincts and training to alert its handler of a smell, sight, or sound by its body language. It was up to the handler to interpret the dog's alert and pass it along to the patrol leader. Ollie explained that the dogs alerted on things like booby traps, enemy foxholes, ambushes, and even other animals. I was completely fascinated by his talk about what scout-dog teams could achieve in a combat zone. I immediately started comparing the duty of a scout dog with my experience with sentry dogs.

The handlers provided a short demonstration of basic obedience. The discipline between the scout-dog handlers and their dogs thoroughly impressed me and reminded me of my time with Hans. At the end of the demonstration, we were asked if any of us was interested in joining the 44th Scout Dogs. We were assured that we'd be trained before we had to go out on combat missions. The only requirement was to show a genuine interest in working with dogs. Ollie said, "If you don't love animals enough to work with them every day then don't volunteer."

As the handlers talked with the group of replacements, I was interested in learning more. Someone in the crowd asked, "Where is the scout-dog team positioned in a tactical formation?"

Ollie replied, "Good question."

He explained that the dog and handler always walked point, meaning they led the way. Handlers and scout dogs were first in a combat formation, first in the jungle, first across clearings, first down roads and trails, and, it was hoped, first to find the enemy before the enemy found them. He went on to explain that, after the dog had alerted and contact with the enemy had been made, the dog and handler pulled back inside the safety net of the perimeter.

Ollie said, "Our job is done after we make contact. Remember, we're just the early warning system, but we're still infantry and we fight the enemy when we have to."

Ollie concluded that walking point was the most effective way of deploying a scout-dog team, and that they saved lives.

Another replacement asked, "How many dogs and handlers have you guys lost?"

"A few have been wounded," Ollie replied, "but no one has been killed."

Every new replacement in that small training area was quiet. Ollie broke the silence by asking if any of us had experience working with dogs. I stood up and said that I'd had some sentry-dog training in Okinawa. Each handler asked me several questions. Apparently, I answered to their satisfaction. Finally, they asked if I wanted to join the 44th.

"Yes!" I said without hesitation.

I was the only one who volunteered to join the K-9 platoon. The others thought I was crazy for coming back to Vietnam, and doubly crazy for volunteering to be a point man. Maybe I was a little different in the head, but I wasn't crazy. I figured I'd take my chances with a well-trained dog leading the way and maybe have a better shot at surviving the war in one piece.

Chapter 10

44th Scout Dog Platoon

I LEARNED THAT THE 44th Scout Dog Platoon was the last war-dog platoon to be activated and sent overseas during WWII. They had served with the 811th Military Police Company on the island of Saipan. Japanese soldiers had hidden in the vast number of caves and bunkers throughout the island. The German shepherd scout dogs helped locate and capture them. The 44th had remained on Saipan until the end of the war. When the dog unit and its flag returned to the United States on January 6, 1946, it was deactivated.

In 1966, the 44th Scout Dog Platoon was reactivated at Fort Benning, Georgia. The unit was reorganized with a new generation of young soldiers and German shepherds. They underwent extensive training at Fort Benning for deployment to Vietnam.

After training school, the fresh graduates with their frisky young dogs arrived in Vietnam in early January 1967. The army engineers had built their kennel inside the Michelin rubber plantation near the perimeter of the Dau Tieng base camp.

I walked to the K-9 compound from the replacement center in the company of Ollie Whetstone and his scout dog, Erik. As we neared the entrance I could hear the dogs barking in the kennel. Their smell filled the air, reminding me of the sentry-dog kennel on Okinawa.

After stowing my gear in my quarters, I was introduced to the platoon leader, Lieutenant Robert Fenner, a thin man, about five feet seven inches tall, with short blond hair. We shook hands and he began to tell me about the dog platoon. I learned that the entire platoon had graduated together from a twelve-week scout-dog training course at Fort Benning. They arrived in Vietnam in January 1967, three months before I did. There were fifteen scout-dog handlers and twice that many dogs. They were shorthanded for the mounting number of missions they had to support.

Dirt-road entrance under the sign 44TH SCOUT DOGS
with kennel in background, 1967 (author collection).

Lieutenant Fenner didn't ask why I had returned to Vietnam. His demeanor was friendly, and my first response was respect for his rank and position. Besides, he was my new boss. I had no problem following his orders — I knew I had to pay attention and learn all I could.

Lieutenant Robert Fenner, 44th Scout Dogs platoon leader, Sergeant Walter Shelton, and Sergeant John Burnam in front of sleeping quarters, 1967 (author collection).

I had learned that most of the handlers had attended some college, and some were even college graduates. The majority had failed to finish the U.S. Army Officer Candidate School (OCS) at Fort Benning and subsequently reassigned to the 44th Scout Dog Platoon to train for deployment to Vietnam.

Lt. Fenner briefed me on the dog platoon's tactical mission and deployment. He stated that their primary mission was to use the dog teams to save American lives. The teams were used extensively on combat patrols and sweeping the village outside the camp perimeter.

Casualties had been light for both dogs and handlers. A few dog teams had even participated in the major battle at LZ Gold.

The mission assignment policy was simple: one scout-dog team per tactical unit. Lt. Fenner maintained a schedule to ensure equitable rotations so that no dog team would perform more missions than any other.

The German shepherd was the only breed of dog assigned to the 44th. The only other breed the military deployed was the Labrador retriever; they had worked exclusively as tracker dogs in CTTs (combat tracker teams). Dau Tieng had no CTTs assigned to support the 3rd Brigade's combat missions.

All the military services — army, air force, navy, and marines — collectively used military working dogs in South Vietnam. They performed a variety of jobs: scout, sentry, mine and booby-trap detection, patrol, and tracking. The primary breed was the German shepherd, with a very small number of Labrador retrievers used exclusively for tracking.

Lt. Fenner explained that, over time, an infantryman could acclimate to his surroundings and develop animal-like instincts, but he could never match the natural instincts of a dog. He stated that I would learn that a scout dog working in the jungle, open terrain, woods, and dry and wet weather has natural senses that are incredibly keen and far superior to any human's.

The German shepherd breed was known for its adaptability to almost any climate and environmental condition. Their black-and-brown coats blended well with the terrain and vegetation. Their intimidating size allowed them to take a man down quite easily, and they could be trained to be aggressive for sentry duty or to be passive for scouting. Also, they could quickly adapt to changing from one handler to another. The army had decided wisely that the German shepherd was the best breed for use in Vietnam.

A single mission for a scout-dog team could last from one day to a week or more. The K-9 platoon had compiled a record of highly successful combat missions without loss of life. They had earned the respect of the infantry patrols they supported by proving they could save lives.

The platoon had its own veterinarian technician, Specialist Five Robert Glydon, who lived in a hooch by himself. It was fully equipped with medical supplies and a small operating table. Doc was qualified to perform minor surgery on the animals. For major health problems, he would call on a veterinarian.

Specialist Four Wade Evans and Robert Glydon, veterinary technician, giving scout dog Buckshot a shot. Buckshot was killed in action after Wade returned home to the States, 1967 (author collection).

The Army Corps of Engineers had built the dog kennels between rows of rubber trees. The floor was a long slab of concrete, with wood and metal fence sidings and a tin roof. The kennel was wired for electricity and overhead lights. It had the capacity to house forty dogs. Several empty runs were used for food, supplies, dog crates, and other equipment. Metal chain-link fencing separated each dog's run. To protect the dogs from deadly shrapnel and small-arms fire, sandbags were stacked waist high around one side of the kennel. There was nothing to protect the dogs from an aerial attack of mortars and rockets.

Shortly before my arrival, the platoon had employed local Vietnamese laborers to fill and stack the sandbags around the kennel. One day, several hours after the Vietnamese departed the area, one of the sandbags exploded. No one was hurt, but after that incident, Lieutenant Fenner never allowed Vietnamese laborers inside the K-9 compound. Filling and repairing sandbags was strictly the job of the dog handlers.

After dark, the dogs were kept inside the kennel, and the handlers slept in their own quarters close by. During the day, each dog was taken out of his run and leashed to his own rubber tree, his water bucket nearby. The dogs were fed, groomed, and exercised in the morning and afternoon.

The handlers had brought a tiny mixed-breed dog from the States to serve as their pet and mascot. Her name was "44." Her shorthair coat was a shiny black, and she had a long snout, floppy ears, and a long skinny tail. Forty-four was a friendly dog and ran all over the compound.

John Burnam posing with "44." She was the unit mascot and came over with the original dog platoon from Fort Benning, Georgia, in January 1967. Later that same year, she died in Vietnam (author collection).

As I listened to Lieutenant Fenner describe the work and the organization, I knew that my new assignment, relying on a dog to save lives in combat, was far beyond what I'd imagined I'd be doing during my second tour in Vietnam. I realized that my sentry-dog training would prove very useful in preparing me for my first experience handling a scout dog.

Chapter 11

Meet Timber

MY FIRST GERMAN SHEPHERD scout dog was named Timber. He was two years old and had a beautiful tan-and-black mane and perfectly shaped ears that stood at attention. Timber was a little on the thin side and shorter in height than some of the other dogs. He had a high-spirited and aggressive temperament, and he didn't like to be disciplined. Ollie told me that Timber would settle down after he got used to being handled by me. It seemed that Timber was kin to my old friend Hans. *Why do I always get the mean ones?* I wondered.

Base-camp training was essential in my preparation to lead combat infantry patrols with a dog. The handlers of the 44th had built an infantry-blue obstacle course behind the kennel to train and exercise the dogs. Among the obstacles were a five-foot wall with a window opening big enough for a dog to jump through and a seesaw of the type you might see in a playground. The dogs learned to walk up one side, balance the board in the center, and then walk down the other side as the board hit the ground. Hurdles had been built to teach the dogs to jump on command. Several fifty-gallon drums were welded together to teach them to crawl through tunnels.

A twelve-foot section of wire-mesh fence, staked about two feet above the ground, was used to teach the dogs to crawl through tight spaces. For balance training, there was a long log — trimmed of branches and bark — to walk across, and a narrow wooden plank for the dogs to climb up to a horizontal ladder about five feet above the ground. Since dogs aren't as sure-footed as cats on this type of obstacle, it was amusing to watch them walk across so carefully.

Basic obedience was the root of all training. Timber was reluctant to obey me at first, but we practiced every day until he started to respond to my voice commands and hand signals. It was all about repetition, discipline, and concentrated focus on the dog. Since I hadn't attended the formal twelve-week training course at Fort Benning, I tried hard to make up for it with on-the-job training with a seasoned dog handler.

As Timber and I worked through the obstacle course day after day, his confidence, balance, strength, muscle tone, and obedience grew to precision. Scout dogs had to learn to maneuver on command — to go over, around, under, and through whatever terrain, vegetation, or water hazard they might encounter during a combat mission. Timber was soon performing admirably, and our bond was developing.

Timber's only reward for his performance was my verbal and physical affection. I was told not to give my dog treats because the dogs were kept on a basic diet of water and canned and packaged food issued, approved, and monitored by Doc Glydon. In combat situations, it was easy to imagine running out of treats and being in deep shit with a disobedient dog and Charlie lurking in the jungle shadows.

During my training, I learned that you get out of a dog what you put in. Dogs adapt to the personality and behavior of their handler. If the handler is lazy, his dog will act accordingly; if the handler is an energetic go-getter, he'll have an A-1 canine partner.

The scout dog has to learn his master's scent, the pitch of his voice, what type of physical gestures he uses, the pace at which he walks, his general disposition, and which commands are the most important ones he gives. The more the handler and his dog work together, the more responsive they'll be to one another. Consistent training develops understanding, teamwork, and unconditional loyalty.

One of the harder parts of being a handler was interpreting what a dog already knew. I learned more about scouting from my fellow handlers, Ollie and Mike "Mac" McClellan, than from anyone else. The key, they taught me, was to keep my eyes on the dog at all times. A dog's natural instincts and body language will tell you what he smells, sees, and hears, and when danger is near.

Timber would be the real point man, with me walking behind holding the leash. It would be my job to translate Timber's body language into English, so I could convey to everyone else what I thought he was telling me. When Timber and I worked together, he was the one in charge; I was his interpreter and pack mule. That was a funny revelation for me, because, before joining the dogs, I thought I'd be in charge. Boy, was I wrong.

Ollie and his dog, Erik, worked with precision as a team. They were something special to watch. Ollie used silent arm and hand signals to control Erik at distances well beyond the length of the standard-issue leash. Ollie worked Erik off leash while in base camp and on combat missions. Erik responded quickly to each of his commands. Their movements struck me as an art form. I hoped I could teach Timber to be as disciplined and well trained as Erik.

Mac McClellan was considered the platoon's top off-leash handler. Watching Mac and his dog, Achates, work was an excellent learning experience as well as great entertainment. To see the communication and movements between handler and dog was like watching dance partners who'd been together for a long time. Like the other handlers, Mac and Ollie were formally schooled in handling military working dogs and had mastered scouting techniques.

Training was my key to successful preparation for combat missions. The more I trained with Timber, the more I learned about what he could see, hear, and sense. Between missions, I was told, training was expected and at my discretion. The only hard-and-fast rule was that I had better be prepared to go on a mission when scheduled.

I felt less prepared than my fellow scout-dog handlers because of a lack of time and experience with a dog. Sentry-dog training had given me basic knowledge, but it hadn't prepared me for anything like working with a scout dog. The functional use of sentry dogs was vastly different from that of scout dogs.

A sentry dog's deployment was straightforward — guard and attack. Scout-dog training and deployment was more diversified and complex. To be effective, it required much more knowledge, concentrated skill, and training. I was eager to learn as much as possible because I knew that Timber and I would soon be going on our first scouting mission.

Chapter 12

Ambush

I STRAPPED ON TIMBER'S body harness and connected the leash. With a fully loaded pack strapped on my back with my CAR-15 rifle, and my helmet on my head, I left the K-9 compound and walked a short distance to join the infantrymen I was assigned to support. I reported to the commanding officer of Company B, 2nd Battalion, 22nd Mechanized Infantry. The unit dated back to 1866. Their motto was "Deeds Not Words," and they were commonly referred to as the Triple Deuce.

I was the only dog handler assigned to their mission. It was my job to brief the company commander (CO) and platoon leader on the capabilities and limitations of the scout-dog team and where to best deploy Timber in a tactical formation. When I arrived, the CO directed me to brief the platoon leader and platoon sergeant I was ultimately assigned to support.

The platoon leader told me that the brigade's long-range reconnaissance patrol (LRRP) had recently located a large concentration of VC operating several miles west of Dau Tieng. Using his map he pointed out the area where the platoon would dismount and patrol on foot to search for and engage the enemy. The platoon leader had never worked with a scout-dog team before, so I briefed him on what we could do.

A long column of APCs (armored personnel carriers) had assembled on the main road leading out of Dau Tieng. The first leg of the mission was to travel on dirt roads until we reached a point near the target area. I knew that riding inside or sitting on top of an APC would neutralize Timber's effectiveness, at least until we were able to dismount and work on the ground.

Upon reaching the target area, we were to get off the road and break trail through the jungle for about half a mile until we reached a large clearing where the APCs would form a defensive perimeter. When that was set up, Timber and I would join foot patrols in search of the bad guys. The area on the map was remote and without visible manmade structures, roads, or landmarks.

I explained to the platoon leader that negotiating my way with Timber through dense jungle rather than open areas would be more difficult. One problem was that it shortened the distance of Timber's alerts on potential enemy targets and allowed for little reaction time if the enemy engaged us at close range. One of the objectives would be to locate and check out the narrow trails that zigzagged through the terrain. These were dangerous, but I knew that we had a better chance of getting an alert from Timber than from sending a soldier to check them. At least that tactic had worked during my training in base camp.

The APCs were lined up on the road, one behind the other, engines running and ramps up. They were all ready to move out through the main gate. On top of each APC sat several armed grunts wearing helmets and flak vests. Fifty-caliber machine guns were manned in their turrets, and radios squawked as we prepared to roll out.

The platoon leader stopped close to the front of the column, turned, looked at me, and pointed to an APC. Its ramp was already down, so Timber and I climbed aboard. The driver yanked a hand lever, and a greasy cable slowly pulled the heavy metal ramp door up until it locked in a closed position, eliminating the light from outside. Inside the cabin we had to shout to be heard above the engine noise.

I wasn't fond of APCs because I felt vulnerable to VC rocket-propelled grenade (RPG) attacks. RPGs could destroy helicopters, bunkers, buildings, ammunition dumps, and whatever else they hit. Nonetheless, I had no choice about the assignment — it was my first scouting mission with a mechanized infantry unit and I would have to make the best of it.

The elusive VC didn't make as easy targets as we Americans did; they didn't ride around in jeeps, trucks, tanks, or helicopters. Their strengths were knowledge of their home terrain and the ability to strike without warning, and make a quick escape.

M-113 U.S Army Military Personnel Carrier. Pictured are Erik (Ollie Whetstone's dog), 44th Scout Dog Platoon, and members of 2nd Battalion, 22nd Infantry (Mechanized), better known as Triple Deuce. This was the type of vehicle Timber and I were riding in during the ambush, 1967 (photo courtesy of Ollie Whetstone).

Inside the APC troop compartment, two other infantrymen accompanied Timber and me. The manually operated hatch overhead was locked open. If you didn't mind standing, you could look out over the top of the vehicle as it motored down the road. Sometimes the riflemen would sit on top of the APC to enjoy cooler air and view the countryside. If the enemy attacked, the men on top could quickly pile inside and return fire from a standing position. I sat quietly inside on a metal bench, with my back against the metal wall. Timber was lying down on the cool metal floor and touching my boots.

Timber would growl and bare his teeth each time one of the crew tried to touch him. They'd quickly back off as I shouted, "No, Timber! No!" I assured them that Timber would get used to them over time. That was a white lie! Timber was an aggressive dog, period. He had even bitten me a few times during our getting-acquainted phase. I don't think Timber liked his job or Vietnam. He had the temperament of a grumpy draftee whose attitude was *"Let's get this crap over with!"*

One of the grunts commented, "I have a dog at home. He's a Lab. No way would I send his ass over here to fight this fucking war."

Another said, "Fuck that! I don't know shit about what you and your dog are supposed to do for me. All I know is that the dog wants to bite my ass."

This crew had never worked with a scout-dog team before. I did my best to explain how scout-dog teams worked in the field. The looks on their faces indicated they were not convinced.

While the long, noisy column of APCs clattered down the road, I couldn't hear any combat activity. When we came to a stop, the radio started to squawk with chatter; from what I could hear, we were to break up the convoy, get off the road, and head into the jungle. I stood up through the open hatch to take a peek. I saw nothing unusual, and the road dust irritated my eyes, so I sat down inside.

The APCs moved off the road and into the jungle, heading for a clearing. I had no field map, so I had no way of knowing exactly where we were or how far we had traveled. The tracks under the APC slowly cranked and ground their way through thick brush. Leaves and small branches, along with bugs and fire ants fell, through the open hatch; one of the grunts got up and buttoned it down. I quickly brushed off Timber and smashed the stinging fire ants with my hand and boots.

The APC moved forward, bulldozing everything in its way and leaving a wide path of mashed brush and a newly created trail in its wake. The engine roared and the exhaust pipe spewed plumes of black smoke. It was slow and bumpy as the tracks struggled to get over rocks, stumps, stubborn trees, and bushes.

There was no doubt in my mind that if Charlie was in the area he was tracking us. After about half an hour of trailblazing, the APCs entered a huge clearing. Looking out at the surrounding area, I saw that the APCs were assembling into a giant defensive perimeter. It reminded me of a wagon train circling the wagons in that Old West TV show *Rawhide.*

With all its radio antennas sticking out, the commander's APC was easy to spot. I watched it set up near a clump of trees toward the center of the perimeter. We had reached our first objective. Timber and I would finally get our chance to show what we could do.

When my APC stopped and the driver lowered the ramp, I took Timber outside. I saw APCs strategically spaced on either side of ours. The gunners on top of the APCs pointed their guns to the front. I introduced myself to the track commander, a sergeant, and asked him about the next phase. He said we'd set up camp for the night, send out some outposts, and deploy foot patrols in the morning. I told him I was ready to take the lead when the patrol assembled and the sergeant nodded his approval.

It was late afternoon and hot as hell sitting in the open. Crews milled around, talking, assembling their gear, checking their weapons and ammunition, and setting up defensive positions. I tied Timber to the track and poured him some drinking water into my steel pot. I had carried four canteens of water — three for Timber and one for myself.

My CAR 15 was a modified model of the M16. It had a retractable metal stock. When extended, the weapon served as a rifle. It fired the same 5.56-caliber steel-jacketed bullets as the M16. Internally, it had the same mechanism as the M16, but the CAR-15 was much shorter, lighter, and easier to carry. It was the perfect weapon to allow me to simultaneously manage Timber on the leash and shoot from a shoulder sling.

Most of the grunts carried the standard M16. Some carried M79 grenade launchers, M60 machine guns, or 12-gauge shotguns. I was the only one sporting the new CAR-15. I felt like hot shit because my weapon got second looks from the grunts hanging around the track.

I had backpacked twenty clips of ammunition, which amounted to 200 rounds; two grenades, a hunting knife, food, water, a poncho, and a poncho liner to wrap up in at night. My backpack held enough food for three days. The grunts stored all their food and water and extra gear inside the APCs. *Leave it to grunts,* I thought. *If there were any way not to have to carry their shit, they would capitalize on it.*

I was getting hungry but decided to feed Timber first. I checked his food package for bugs before giving it to him. Bugs were everywhere in Vietnam, and they'd get into anything except metal cans of C-Rations. Timber ate the semi-moist packaged chunks of meat as fast as I put them down, and he slurped the water I poured into my steel pot.

I took a can of beefsteak and potatoes from my stash and soon realized that I hadn't packed a can opener. Most of the time, I had a P38 attached to the dog tags chained around my neck. Now the damn thing was missing. I felt embarrassed to ask a grunt for one, especially since I'd just met them. To have no P38 might make them think I was a greenhorn. They didn't know that I was a veteran or know anything about my first tour as an infantryman.

I thought, *Aw, what the hell, I gotta eat.* So I asked the guy from New York if I could borrow his P38. He was about five feet seven, weighed a husky 175 pounds, and had jet-black hair and a crusty black mustache. He spoke in a heavy New York tough-guy accent.

He replied loudly, "My P38? Sure, you can borrow it, but I'll have to kill you if you don't give it back." He immediately burst into laughter and told me to keep it as a souvenir of the 2nd Squad. Then he asked me to join him for chow. As we ate our C-Rations, we talked about home and girls. Timber lay quietly on the ground beside the APC, sheltered from the hot late-afternoon sun.

Suddenly, activity on the radio picked up. Troops quickly moved around the two tracks on either side of me. My track commander yelled, "Saddle up! Hurry! Let's go! Come on! Go! Go! Go!"

I hustled to gather Timber and my gear, leaving my half-eaten can of C-Rations on the ground. Clutching my backpack in one hand and Timber's leash in the other, I scrambled up the ramp into the track. I put Timber between my legs on the bench seat near the hinged ramp. The other guys quickly loaded their gear and sat facing us.

Within seconds the driver had started the engine, raised the ramp, and moved forward. The sergeant was on the radio. I leaned over to ask him what was going on. He told me that a bunch of NVA troops had been spotted from the air, heading away from our location. His squad was the closest to them, so he'd been ordered to close in and engage. The sergeant laid his compass on the map and pointed to a strategic area not far from where the enemy appeared to be heading.

During the pursuit, Timber and I were in the lead APC, which was moving as fast as it could go. We bounced around and hung on. The APC crashed into the brush. Small trees and bushes splintered as we plowed over them. When the terrain became rougher, the APC slowed down, mashing whatever was in its way. Suddenly, the front end of the APC dipped down with a jolt when the treads hit something solid. It felt as if we were stuck in a ditch. The treads kept grinding underneath us. The driver tried to climb up and over the obstacle. A thick pall of diesel fumes and smoke filled the air as the engine revved and the metal treads spun in place. The driver backed up and then slammed forward repeatedly, trying to break free. Inside, we rocked back and forth. Finally, the APC climbed free and into more jungle growth.

The machine gunner on top ducked under tree limbs. Looking up, I could see only a green canopy of jungle growth as splinters of vegetation fell in on us. Then there was a deafening BANG! The APC stopped dead in its tracks. My ears were ringing. The explosion's force ripped through the thin panel covering the engine. Black smoke streamed from the driver's compartment, filling the inside of the cabin. I noticed that the driver was wounded in the right leg as he quickly scrambled up through his escape hatch and out of the APC. Simultaneously, the .50-caliber machine gun on top began firing. I looked at the two soldiers across from me. They looked startled and said nothing. All this took place in a matter of seconds.

There was no way to reach the handle to lower the ramp because it was in the driver's compartment. Survival instinct took over and I grabbed the small emergency door handle and yanked it open. With my boot, I pushed the heavy metal door as hard as I could. It swung out on its hinges and latched itself open.

With Timber's leash in one hand, I grabbed my CAR-15 and a

bandoleer of magazines. I dove through the open door and lay flat on my belly in the dirt behind the smoking track. I realized I was in the middle of a narrow dirt road. I pulled on Timber's leash as I tried to crawl away, but the end of the leash was trapped between the ramp and the door — it must have gotten caught when the ramp door closed as we rushed inside.

The other two grunts had already dived through the opening and were crawling away into the jungle. I frantically pulled and yanked to free the leash, but it wouldn't budge, so I cut it with the hunting knife I'd bought in Okinawa. Only about ten inches of leash remained to connect me with Timber. Timber was panicking; he jumped up and down trying to free himself from my grip. The shooting and explosions increased to my front and on the left.

I crouched on my knees, leaned against the back of the APC, and tried hard to control Timber. The APC sat perpendicular on the dirt road; its front end was on fire and receiving incoming small-arms fire. I didn't detect any shots coming from the left or right of the road.

Another stationary APC stood directly behind me in the path we'd made in the jungle. The rest of the column was stopped behind it.

The enemy started firing on the APC column from the front and left side. I saw my track commander lying on top of the burning APC, firing the .50-caliber machine gun directly to his front. The vegetation on both sides of the dirt road was thick and dark. I couldn't see the enemy through it, but could feel his bullets hammering the APC close to my position.

I aimed and fired into the thick jungle to the front. Charlie returned fire immediately, but I couldn't see the enemy troops. I realized I was exposed kneeling behind the burning APC, so I decided to seek better cover. I got on my stomach and quickly crawled toward the jungle, dragging Timber away from the flaming track. We reached the cover of the jungle about fifty feet behind the APC without being hit. Timber continued to growl and jerk away from my grasp. I was determined not to let him run off and get killed. *We're in this together and we'll stay together,* I thought.

I scanned the jungle for signs of enemy movement. Charlie was still firing at us from invisible positions. The column of APCs was to my left. I could hear American weapons firing, and the turret-mounted heavy machine guns kept blasting away. Small-arms fire from Americans and VC filled the air with constant cracking noises and shredded the vegetation. There was another loud explosion nearby followed by black smoke and red flames coming from a second APC. The enemy had knocked out two of the four APCs during the first few minutes of the attack.

No enemy fire was coming from my right side, which led me to believe that we were in an L-shaped ambush. The short leg of the L was the front of my APC; the long leg was the left side of the column of our four APCs, which were now to my front. The VC we had chased had clearly maneuvered us into the kill zone of their trap.

Timber was going crazy. Crawling around to find a better fighting position, I discovered a wounded American soldier. Timber growled at him, but I kept my dog at bay. Timber was scared, and he didn't want to be in that situation any more than any of us did. In shock, the wounded soldier sat on his knees, eyes glazed over, staring blindly into nothingness. He had no weapon and no helmet on his head. I recognized him as one of the crew who'd been in my APC. A chunk of shrapnel stuck out from his forehead. I pulled the wounded man to the ground and tried to comfort him. I had no first-aid bandages — only my CAR-15, a bandoleer of ammo, and Timber. With my free hand, I tore a strip of cloth from my fatigue jacket and used it to soak up the blood dripping down the soldier's face, then helped him to crawl to a nearby tree.

Still struggling desperately to get away, Timber kept nipping at me. I was getting pissed off, so I quickly reacted and slapped him hard across the snout with my free hand. That only upset him more. I realized that I had lost my composure. I shouldn't have struck my dog. There was too much confusion in the heat of that moment, and too many things to concentrate on at once. The situation seemed out of control, and for the first time since I had been in Vietnam, I began to wonder if I would get out alive.

The constant rifle fire, exploding grenades, and chatter of machine guns were deafening. I fired into the jungle in front of the track that was still blazing in the road. Although the shooting was to my left, I didn't want to shoot over the heads of the Americans positioned around the APCs. I was fortunate to have a good firing position from behind the thick base of a tropical tree whose large roots grew a few feet above the ground and connected to its base. For protection, I wedged between the tree roots with Timber and the wounded soldier. Even if the wounded soldier had had his weapon, he was incapable of defending himself.

There was another APC on fire to my left behind the one I'd vacated. It bothered me not to have both hands free, but I kept returning single-shots into the thick jungle to my front, aware that I needed to conserve what little ammunition I had left.

I figured Charlie would eventually surround and trap us all. I had no idea how large a force we were up against. The nonstop firing was brutal. I thought there must be more than a platoon of VC for them to be putting out so much firepower. Maybe there were fifty enemy soldiers attacking us — I couldn't be certain.

We had started out with four APCs. Now I could hear only two of them firing their machine guns. Charlie used interlocking fire to maximize his effect on us, and it was working. My mind was running wild with crazy thoughts. *Charlie's going to come around on my side any time now. I'm not prepared to hold off an all-out assault. He's definitely got the advantage and will overrun us and kill me and Timber.*

On the right side of the burning APC, I was receiving intense fire from across the road to my front. I could tell from where the bullets were landing that Charlie knew my exact location. I couldn't see him through the jungle but he was there. I had no idea whether I was hitting any of them when I returned fire. Charlie appeared to have been dug in, and seemed to know where all the Americans were positioned. I kept reloading and firing on semiautomatic.

Trying to maintain my confidence, I thought that Charlie probably suspected that American reinforcements would be here soon. On the downside, I kept thinking that reinforcements wouldn't get here in time if Charlie decided to launch an all-out assault.

The attack wasn't typical of how Charlie operated. Usually, he'd hit fast and run like hell before we could regroup and reinforce. This time, Charlie wasn't running. I figured he was preparing to move in for the kill.

Timber kept on fighting to get free. I refused to let him go and tried talking softly, hoping he'd calm down. The wounded soldier was still alive, lying quietly on the ground between the tree roots. If Charlie charged across the road, I decided I'd switch to full automatic and take out as many of them as I could before they wasted me.

I didn't see any other Americans nearby, so I assumed that I was the only one defending our right flank. My mind raced: *If Charlie realizes I'm the only man defending this side, he'll overrun my position. Why hasn't he attacked already? Maybe he's getting ready to. Maybe he knows I'm low on ammo. I'll make every shot count! Reinforcements have to get here soon. I can't hold out much longer. My grenades are in the burning APC — going to get them would be suicide. Timber's gone mad.*

All these thoughts were driving *me* mad. For the first time while serving in Vietnam, I felt completely isolated and vulnerable.

BOOM! A tremendous explosion filled the air. The ground shook. The APC I'd escaped from had just blown sky-high. Timber let out a pained cry and went down on his side. At the same instant, I felt the heat of stinging shrapnel burning my face and left hand. I could feel small cuts on my face. Blood trickled down my cheeks. My hands and arms had tiny cuts too. My muscles were tense. Timber was bleeding badly from his right rear flank. I had no bandages, so there wasn't much I could do to cover his wound. Timber lay on his side in pain and panted quietly. I'd been lucky once more; I was still alive. The tree had taken the brunt of the shrapnel. I looked to my left-front where the explosion had occurred. The APC had been reduced to a smoking slab of metal resting on its tracks in the middle of the dirt road.

Then it became strangely quiet for a few moments. My eyes anxiously darted around looking for any kind of movement. I saw nothing, but I heard groans nearby. The shooting started again on the left side of the column of APCs. The soldier firing his .50-caliber machine gun on top of the burning APC had disappeared with the explosion. I knew there was no way he could have survived. Several .50-caliber brass casings, hot to the touch and split wide open from the exploding powder, were scattered near my feet, the black metal links still connecting them.

The other APCs on my left were too close for comfort. One was still smoking, and I figured it was only a matter of time before it blew up. Soldiers moved around on the ground, using the protection of the APCs to defend themselves. I decided to help another wounded soldier nearby, so I left Timber and crawled over to him. Timber, too hurt to move, didn't follow me. I recognized the soldier as the fellow from New York who'd given me his P38 to open my C-Rations. He was the most mind-boggling sight I'd ever witnessed in combat: that poor soldier, suffering from severe wounds, slowly crawled aimlessly on his hands and knees. The sleeves of his shirt were torn away, exposing nothing but the remains of his arms — white bones and joints, most of the flesh gone. Chunks of flesh had ripped away from his thighs and back. I couldn't understand how that man could still be alive and crawling around in such a state.

The wounded soldier grabbed me by the shoulder and stopped crawling. He looked as if he recognized me. Then, slowly, he rolled over on his back, his eyes staring up at me. He moved his mouth, trying to talk, but I couldn't understand a word he said. I couldn't stop staring at him either.

Then something happened that I'll never forget for as long as I live. As the wounded soldier stared at me, his body began to glow a soft white, as if a light fog were slowly covering him. That lasted only a few seconds. When it disappeared, the soldier wasn't breathing anymore. I knew he was dead. I closed his eyes and slowly moved away. I'd seen my share of men die in Vietnam, but I'd never seen anything like that before. Had I watched that man's spirit leave his body?

Then I thought about the tragedy of the situation. A man I'd barely known was now dead, his face forever burned into my memory. I knew I'd never recall this experience without feeling the profound sadness and senselessness of that moment. I felt helpless and hopeless. The shooting seemed to never stop. I returned to the tree to check on Timber and the other wounded man. Timber wasn't moving anymore, but he still breathed. I told him he was going to be okay, and assured him that I'd get him out of there. I don't know whether Timber understood a word I said, but he didn't move.

The other soldier was alive and in shock. Small-arms fire poured in on us. Spotting movement in the jungle across the road, I fired on semi-automatic. The movement stopped. I might have silenced one VC, but I surely wasn't going out to confirm the kill. I kept firing single shots at invisible enemies wherever I heard something. I looked around and spotted more wounded Americans huddled in the vegetation behind nearby trees. Some were curled up on the ground, crying in pain and unable to continue fighting.

I left the safety of my position again to try to help. I found the platoon leader I'd met at the start of the mission. Badly burned, he sat with his back propped against a tree. His smoking fatigue jacket had welded to his flesh. His right arm was mangled. With the numbness of a man in shock, the lieutenant asked, "Do I look okay?"

"You look fine, sir. Everything's going to be all right," I said, trying to give him a shred of hope to hang on to.

The lieutenant said, "Before we abandoned the burning APC, I radioed for air strikes on our position."

There was nothing I could do for the lieutenant, so I returned to the tree to check on my dog and the other wounded man.

American artillery and air strikes zeroed in on our position and dropped their loads. Nothing is more frightening than the incredible thunder of exploding artillery shells and bombs within a stone's throw of a soldier's position. Those jets couldn't possibly see where we were under the jungle canopy. I hugged the earth near a tree, kept my head down, and held Timber to the ground. Even though Timber had lost some blood, he came to life when the artillery and bombs exploded, but he quickly wore himself out struggling to get away from me again, and finally gave up and lay still.

The fighting seemed to last forever, and I was in a state of sensory overload trying to absorb all that was happening and stay alert. It was hard to believe that anyone would make it out of there alive. I knew it was only a matter of time before I'd be shot. I tried to keep my wits about me and stay focused on the enemy who were still out there.

Body numbness began to overcome me. I'd never experienced such a feeling. For some reason I now felt mentally and physically strange. I was exhausted and thirsty, and the numbness spread quickly through my entire body. Something weird was happening to me and I couldn't shake it off.

Suddenly, I heard a commotion in the brush to my right. It was the first time there had been noise on that side of the jungle. The numbness intensified. *This is it!* I thought. *The gooks are coming for me now. It's all over! Charlie's at my doorstep, and he won't be taking prisoners. I'll fucking kill myself before I let those fuckers get me.*

The noise grew closer. My adrenaline spiked. Nervously, I aimed my CAR-15. My body shook uncontrollably as I listened, waiting, eyes wide open, for something to happen. Then I heard voices call out from the brush: "Don't shoot! We're Americans!" I lowered my weapon and sat there shaking and staring aimlessly. American soldiers poured into the area; they were going to prevent us all from being wiped out — I had been saved!

I was still in a daze when one of the soldiers came over. He stooped and brushed the ants and dirt from my naked arms and offered me water from his canteen. I couldn't speak or stand, still unable to shake that strange numbness. The soldier told me to stay where I was and that he'd be back. Another soldier tended to the wounded man lying next to me. Fresh troops moved all around the area.

I could hear the leaders shouting, "Let's get these wounded men some help over here! Check out those APCs for survivors! Help that man over there! Set up a firing position! Oh, my God, we have some dead Americans here! Cover them with ponchos!"

The shooting and explosions had stopped. The only sound was the American voices. Silently clutching the short leash still attached to Timber, I sat and watched helplessly as American troops helped the wounded and covered our dead. It was a complete mess.

Why is this happening to me? Why can't I get up?

A huge armored wrecker drove past the tree where I sat. Right in front of me, without warning, it ran over a land mine, which exploded. Everyone hit the ground in an instant. I didn't even flinch. Dirt and debris flew everywhere. I just sat there and watched, not responding or talking, as if I were locked deep inside myself, looking out.

Our rescuers loaded the dead and wounded into APCs idling on the road. Two soldiers approached me. I recognized Mac McClellan, my fellow dog handler from the 44th Scout Dog Platoon. Mac said, "John, I'm going to take care of Timber. You need to let these guys get you into the APC and to a hospital."

I shook my head and yelled, "No! No! No! I can take care of him!"

Mac pried my hand open and took hold of Timber's leash. He picked up my wounded dog and carried him away. Two soldiers helped me to my feet and into an APC. As we rode off, I sat quietly, not moving a muscle, feeling totally useless.

When the APC stopped, the soldiers helped me get up and put me down on a stretcher. I lay very still, staring up at the darkening sky. A face appeared and looked down at me, eyes fixed on mine. I glanced at his collar and noticed the white cross. My eyes welled with tears that blurred my vision. The chaplain hugged and blessed me. He told me that the Lord was with me now, that I was safe and needn't worry. The chaplain walked beside the stretcher as two soldiers carried me to the waiting medical evacuation chopper. The medevac lifted off to a field hospital. My body felt paralyzed, but my mind was now clear and active.

When the chopper landed, I was carried into a tent that smelled like medicine. Looking up at the bright lights overhead, I realized I was in a field hospital. Wounded men on stretchers and tables were all over the place. A nurse with a mask over her mouth asked me where I hurt. I couldn't speak; I lay there on my back and stared at her. The nurse shined a bright light into my eyes. I didn't even blink. She cut away my fatigue jacket and trousers and checked my entire body, cleaned the cuts on my face and arms, and then stuck me with a needle. I passed out.

I awoke the next morning on a cot in a recovery tent. Feeling a little sore, but otherwise fine, I sat up and looked around the room. I no longer felt the strange numbness. *What the hell happened to me out there?*

The room was filled with soldiers all bandaged up and lying on cots. A doctor came over and told me to lie down. I explained that I felt fine and wanted to check on Timber. The doctor said they had no patient by that name, and that I had no serious wounds. He said that I had suffered a bout of traumatic combat shock and battle fatigue and would soon be released. I told him that I'd been on many missions and seen plenty of combat, but no such thing had ever happened to me before. "Why this time?" I asked.

The doctor believed that this type of medical condition occurred when a soldier's resistance to combat has worn down and his system has had enough. He explained that the consequences of combat could linger for a while, but that I would soon recover. Cautioning me to take it easy for a few weeks before heading out on another mission, the doctor said he'd release me from medical care the next day.

When I arrived back at the 44th, Mac welcomed me and said that Doc Glydon had patched up Timber. Most of my gear had burned up in the APC, but Mac had put my weapon on my cot. I went to my hooch to rest. It was hard to believe that I'd been gone only a few days.

I pondered the events that had led to the ambush and all those casualties. I thought about Timber and how difficult he'd been to control. I was still pissed off that he'd tried to run away, but I felt even more upset at having struck him. I didn't want to ride in another APC for as long as I lived.

I looked at the P38 attached to my dog tags and instantly flashed back to that poor soul from New York who'd given it to me. That soldier had died in the middle of nowhere, and there'd been nothing I could do but watch. I replayed that battle over and over in my mind. The faces of all the nameless men I had fought beside flashed through my head. *God rest their souls,* I prayed.

I briefed the K-9 platoon leader, Lieutenant Fenner, on the mission. After listening intently, he said he was happy that I was okay. That was about it. The lieutenant wasn't one to dwell on the details; as a leader, he wanted me to recover and try to forget.

Doc Glydon told me that Timber had been a frightened animal when he was brought to him. Shrapnel had badly chewed up Timber's right rear flank. Doc said that the dog had lost some blood but would recover.

I went to the kennel and found Timber lying on his concrete run. He didn't respond much when I called his name, so I went inside and sat beside him, talking to him and stroking his soft, furry body. I apologized to Timber for striking him and asked his forgiveness.

Timber showed no liveliness the whole time I was there. It was too early to expect much. Timber was obviously having a hard time dealing with all that had happened to him. Hell, I knew how he felt! I wondered if either of us would ever get over what we'd been through in that jungle. Would Timber ever be the same dog as before? I knew I'd go on other missions, but would I be okay? Only time would tell.

A week passed. I continued to feed and care for Timber, and his wounds appeared to be healing. I took him out of his run several times and tried some basic obedience exercises, but he didn't respond to commands as before. He had no snap and lacked his usual aggressiveness. My instincts told me that Timber wouldn't be ready for any missions in the near future. I wasn't sure what I wanted to do.

As much as I loved Timber, and felt sorry for him, I decided that the best thing for both of us was for me to ask Lieutenant Fenner for a different scout dog. The lieutenant agreed: if I didn't feel comfortable handling Timber anymore, I could replace him with any other available dog.

I thought about that APC mission many times during the days I spent recovering in base camp. I never had the chance to work Timber the way we'd trained to operate. Regardless of my title as a scout-dog handler, I was, in reality, an infantryman.

Mac McClellan, the 44th's poet, expressed so well what it had been like to ride in an APC and become an easy target.

Kaiser Coffin

Aluminum-hulled hearse, carrier of cattle.
Made by Detroit to take men to battle.
Gas tank high on the left-hand side.
Charlie found out, and a lot of men died.
Gasoline tanks in the floor and wall,
One rocket hit, and you're in a fiery ball.
Beer-can aluminum, two inches thick,
A browning fifty will go through slick.
Can it stop anything except a trifle?
You're safe as can be from a Daisy air rifle.

— Michael "Mac" McClellan, 44th Scout Dogs, 1967

Chapter 13

Meet Clipper

John Burnam and his partner, scout dog Clipper.

IT TOOK ME SEVERAL days to decide which of the available dogs I wanted as my next partner. I selected a fine-looking dog whose name was Clipper. I was excited from the first time I saw that dog, and he took to me as if we'd worked together before.

We both had to wear dog tags — mine were metal and hung from a chain around my neck. The military had permanently marked Clipper as its own by tattooing the serial number 12X3 inside his left ear.

Clipper had an official military medical record, as did each dog in the 44th Scout Dog Platoon. It contained information such as who had donated or sold him to the military, the date and place of his entry into military service, age, weight, height, training record, and a photo of him in profile. Doc Glydon maintained a record of all the medical treatment provided to each dog.

Clipper was docile and very smart. A handsome dog of about eighty pounds of toned muscle, he had a healthy black-and-brown coat, big brown eyes, and great-looking ears. Clipper walked with a sense of pride, intelligence, confidence, and control. In my opinion, he was a perfect specimen of a German shepherd, even though he wasn't a pure-bred animal by show-dog standards. He'd let any American soldier pet him, no matter where we were.

Whenever Clipper was around the local Vietnamese people, friendly or otherwise, he became agitated and aggressive. One reason was that the Vietnamese looked, talked, smelled, walked, and ate differently from Americans. Secondly, all the scout dogs were trained to hunt those characteristics, and were rewarded with love and affection when they alerted on them. Besides, to keep the dogs from getting used to them, the Vietnamese were not allowed to enter the K-9 compound.

Between missions, Ollie and I decided to do some dog training together. We found a perfect place inside the base camp's outer defensive perimeter, within the rows and rows of tall rubber trees behind the kennel area. The trees offered the added advantage of shade from the hot and humid climate.

I wanted to teach Clipper how to recognize trip wires and alert me to their presence. Also, I needed to learn how to clearly recognize when and how Clipper's body language alerted to specific targets, so I could quickly relay that information to the other soldiers on the mission. I had to learn what Clipper would do when he sensed different kinds of danger. How would he alert when he suspected that there were enemies hiding in foxholes, behind or up in trees, or standing in full view? At what distance from the stimulus would Clipper alert when he detected human or metallic movement, noise, or smell? Did he alert the same way on a man as he would on an animal or a booby trap? To learn the answers, I had to work with Clipper on each training situation, and keep a sharp eye on what I thought his body language was telling me.

During our training sessions, we set up a different mock situation each time. Often, we'd use captured enemy clothing, equipment, and weapons to prepare our dogs to alert us on specific sounds and scents. In one scenario, we'd send a fellow dog handler far enough into the woods so that I wouldn't know exactly where he was. While our decoy hid behind a tree or some other form of cover, I'd keep Clipper distracted by walking and playing with him in another area, allowing several minutes to pass before we'd begin the hunt. Then I'd command Clipper by slapping my hand against the side of my left leg — the signal to heel and sit.

When it was time to go, I'd work Clipper on a six-foot leather leash. I'd tug the leash, signaling him to move to the end of it, and then give the command "Search!" Keeping the pace slow, as if we were walking point on a live patrol, I'd walk behind Clipper, my eyes on the back of his head and ears at all times, monitoring any physical reactions outside his ordinary behavior.

As we headed toward the hidden target, I observed Clipper's neck and head rising sharply and his ears popping straight up and forward. Clipper stopped, stood erect with his mouth closed, and stared straight ahead for just a tiny instant. Then the alert was relaxed. If I hadn't had my eyes on him at that instant, I would have missed that first quick signal, giving me a distance to a target.

When Clipper turned and gave me a quick glance, I interpreted his reaction as a strong alert. I quickly got to one knee, as I was taught, and looked in the direction Clipper's head had pointed. He would sit quietly and await his next command. I put my weapon on the ready and scanned our front. I saw and heard nothing. We moved another twenty or thirty yards toward where I had expected the target decoy to be hiding.

We continued to move forward, and Clipper gave the same strong alert again. I knew he'd spotted something to the front, but I could tell only the target's direction, not how far away it was.

There were hundreds of trees all around. The question was always which tree hid the decoy? I decided to keep moving forward. Clipper continued in the same direction; finally he stopped and stood erect, ears up, and refused to go any farther. Then the decoy came out from behind the tree. I grabbed Clipper around the neck and hugged and praised him for doing such a great job. As it turned out, Clipper's first alert had been about a hundred yards from the decoy.

Using these training techniques helped me learn how Clipper alerted on a human hiding behind a tree. I repeated the exercise over and over, even in the rain. I learned that wind, heat, humidity, density of vegetation and terrain, surrounding noises, and the movement of others influenced how strongly and how far from a target a scout dog could alert.

During our training sessions, Ollie was a terrific tutor, always patient and understanding, as he thoroughly explained and demonstrated the techniques.

Sometimes, we'd dig foxholes and have men hide in them, or we'd hide military equipment in the woods and in foxholes to see how the dog would alert on a scent carried through the air or wind, or heavy rain. Over time, I learned to read Clipper's reactions by concentrating on the movements of his body, head, and ears. I was gaining confidence in what Clipper could do and was always amazed at his consistent accuracy.

We couldn't conduct training missions outside the Dau Tieng base camp because everything beyond the barbed wire was considered hostile. To really learn whether Clipper's alerts would be the same in the various terrain conditions outside camp, we had to go on a real mission. I wondered how Clipper would work when fatigued by the heat, and how he'd handle marching long distances through the jungle or moving across a lot of open terrain. After all, Clipper wasn't a machine; he was a dog, and before his induction into the army he'd been a family pet.

Walking point was one of the most dangerous jobs in Vietnam. Since that's what dog handlers did, we had to stay focused constantly. The enemy usually had the advantage of spotting the American point man first. With a scout-dog team, though, the tables were turned and we gained the advantage, because a dog's instincts, vision, and senses of smell and hearing were hundreds of times more acute than any human's on the battlefield. Clipper was like a walking radar beam.

Even though I expected to go on many missions with Clipper, always knowing that we would be leading a combat patrol, I was still a little apprehensive about the job. Clipper relied on me to recognize when he was thirsty, hungry, tired, hurt, or sick. We bonded as a team because we always took care of one another. Over time our bond would only grow stronger.

When Clipper alerted, my job was to drop immediately to one knee, determine what his alert meant, and, as quickly and quietly as possible, relay the information to the men behind me. The platoon leader would then assess the situation and determine whether the patrol should act on the alert and check it out, ignore it, or proceed with caution. Even though I would brief the platoon leader ahead of time, if he had never worked with a scout-dog team, it was difficult to predict how he'd react when Clipper alerted.

Most patrol leaders trusted the dogs' instincts and my assessment of the situation; some, however, didn't like the idea of a scout-dog team making such judgments, and would often ignore the team's warning. Sometimes they'd get away with it; other times they paid a price in casualties. When I worked Clipper on point, I insisted that every strong alert he gave be checked out. I didn't like the crapshoot of ignoring his signals.

If soldiers checked out Clipper's alert and didn't make enemy contact, Clipper and I would resume the lead and continue pushing in the mission's direction. If the alert resulted in enemy contact, and if the situation allowed, we'd quickly move back inside the patrol's main body, our job considered complete once the enemy was engaged.

Standard operating procedure for every mission was that when the fighting was over, and if casualties were light, the scout-dog team would resume the job of point man and continue the mission. If casualties were heavy, a fresh unit usually replaced the entire platoon. Things didn't always go as planned. Sometimes, the handler and his dog were so far out in front of the patrol that they got trapped between the enemy and American lines when all hell broke loose.

Since I'd been in combat before, I took my base-camp training with Clipper seriously. I knew I'd have to rely on him and he on me. I'd had experience with jungle conditions, open terrain, rivers, creeks, villages, hills, valleys, rice paddies, nighttime operations, and various kinds of weather. Now I had to adjust to working with a different dog in diverse combat situations.

My goal was to come home alive, and I hoped Clipper would save some lives in the process of leading us.

Chapter 14

Tinzer's Alert

FELLOW SCOUT-DOG HANDLER Fred DeBarros and his dog, Tinzer, were original members of the 44th Scout Dog Platoon that had trained at Fort Benning and arrived in Vietnam in January 1967. They were next on the rotation schedule to scout for an infantry unit on a search-and-destroy mission in the jungles surrounding Dau Tieng. After a few days in the bush with no enemy contact, Fred was ordered to join a small detachment of the platoon on a night-ambush operation that would set up alongside a narrow dirt road the Vietcong had been using.

It was dusk when Fred's detachment of ten infantrymen reached a suitable ambush site inside some thick vegetation a few yards off the dirt road. Complete silence was the norm; everyone quietly settled into hidden positions for what Fred thought would be a long, boring night, like most ambushes he'd supported.

When it was totally dark, the surrounding jungle came alive with its characteristic nocturnal noises. That was when Tinzer started fidgeting; he kept turning to face the rear of the ambush rather than in the direction of the road like everyone else. Fred thought it was probably just an animal moving through the darkness behind them, which was a common alert, so he ignored Tinzer's movements and kept pulling him around to observe the road. This went on for a while before Fred realized that Tinzer was really trying to tell him that something other than an animal might be moving behind them.

As a precaution, Fred quietly passed the word down the line to advise the detachment leader that Tinzer was alerting to the rear and that it could be human scent and movement. The leader was quick to react, passing the word back along the line to quietly change positions and train their weapons rearward.

Shortly after they were all in position to defend the rear, a small force of Vietcong attacked with small-arms fire at close range. The firing was intense from both sides as muzzle flashes and tracer bullets lit up the night. As Fred kept shooting through the darkness in the direction of the muzzle flashes, Tinzer lay by his side without moving or barking.

After a long exchange of concentrated fire from both sides, the enemy broke contact. Everyone stayed vigilant the rest of the night, nervously waiting for the Cong to launch a counterattack, but it never happened. At dawn the weary detachment found three dead enemy soldiers nearby and some blood trails leading off into the jungle. The Americans were extremely lucky to have suffered no casualties.

Fred thought that Charlie must have spotted the detachment—including the dog and him—setting up the ambush, and decided to wait nearby in the bush until the Americans got settled before sneaking up behind them. It was apparent that the enemy could easily have surprised them and possibly wiped them out had it not been for Tinzer's unwavering attention to the rear, even though Fred's reaction was a bit delayed. Tinzer got lots of hugs and praise from Fred for saving lives. Fred learned to pay closer attention to his dog's alerts!

Chapter 15

Death in the Kennel

MISSION AFTER MISSION, German shepherd scout dogs alerted American patrols of ambushes, snipers, and booby traps. Their courage and hard work under the adverse conditions of treacherous jungle terrain, tropical heat, and monsoon rains was often met with hostile enemy contact and the deafening impacts of American firepower. Throughout their difficult and dangerous life in the field, the dogs grew toughened and saved a lot of American lives. The enemy tried to counteract the dog teams' success by offering rewards to any soldier who killed a scout dog and his handler.

On November 9, 1967, several scout-dog teams from the 44th Scout Dog Platoon in Dau Tieng were out on combat missions in support of local infantry units. It was a typical quiet evening in base camp, with all the dogs sheltered in the kennel for the night. As it got dark, I walked to the kennel to say goodnight to Clipper. Then, after hanging out in the K-9 Klub until after ten o'clock, I hit the sack. Most of the other dog handlers had already turned in.

After midnight, I awoke to the deafening sound of a nearby explosion. I could hear and feel the shrapnel splintering the walls of my hooch. I jumped up, grabbed my CAR-15, slipped my bare feet into jungle boots, and as I dashed through the screen door, tripped and fell to the ground outside. It was pitch-black except for the blinding flashes of light coming from a barrage of exploding missiles. Clad only in underwear and unlaced boots, I dashed for the shelter of one of the two bunkers outside our quarters.

The bunkers were huge rectangular steel boxes partially buried in the ground and protected by sandbags. Portholes had been cut through the steel walls on all four sides to provide ventilation and create a 360-degree field of fire. After entering the doorway, my hands and body shook uncontrollably; it was terrifying to be abruptly awakened in the middle of the night to find my life in immediate danger and our kennel area being bombarded with mortars and rockets.

I heard at least ten explosions as the rest of the dog handlers crammed inside the shelters and huddled tightly in the limited floor space. Looking around, I realized I wasn't the only one in underwear and unlaced boots — hell, some guys were barefoot! We were all wide-eyed with shock: this was the first time our K-9 compound had come under surprise attack and taken direct hits from enemy fire. Another volley of mortar shells whistled down, exploding in the trees and on the ground. I shuddered with fear at the metallic sounds of shrapnel striking objects all around us.

On the K-9 compound, which was several hundred yards inside the primary defensive perimeter of Dau Tieng, the bunkers provided the only safe area to fight from. The enemy was somewhere inside the nearby rubber trees and not far from the base-camp perimeter. There was no easy way to account for all the dog handlers since we didn't have radio communication between the bunkers; however, everyone inside my bunker appeared to be okay.

Each bunker was fully stocked with weapons, grenades, and plenty of ammunition. Between barrages of mortar fire, the dog handlers nervously waited to see the silhouettes of enemy soldiers assaulting the compound. If we spotted the VC, it would mean that they'd breached the perimeter defenses.

With loaded weapons pointed out through the portholes, we waited for targets to appear. During the relentless VC barrage, one round exploded on the top of the bunker I was in, and we all flinched simultaneously. The bunkers had never been tested like that, but ours held up, making us feel more secure.

The kennel was across an open area from the bunkers; we couldn't see it very well through the shadows of the rubber trees that surrounded the compound. Months before the attack, we had filled and stacked sandbags waist-high on the side of the kennel facing the bunkers. On the night of the attack, the back of the kennel was still unprotected: no sandbags shielded the dogs from shrapnel or bullets on that side.

During the bombardment, the dogs barked in panic. They were used to their handlers being with them during dangerous situations. I knew Clipper felt confused, wondering where I was and when I'd come and take him out of harm's way. Because of the frequent explosions inside the compound, it was too dangerous for us to leave the bunkers. As long as the dogs kept barking, we assumed they were okay, though several of the handlers wanted to get their dogs and bring them inside the bunkers. Lieutenant Fenner ordered us to quiet down and stay where we were.

We could hear small arms and machine guns firing in the near distance. We assumed that Charlie had decided to assault our camp's perimeter of defense, which was well fortified and manned twenty-four/seven/365. If Charlie somehow got through the perimeter, the K-9 compound was the second line of defense. I wondered how long we'd be able to hold off an assault.

The scout dogs were the only ones unprotected from a ground attack. Caged inside their runs, they couldn't get out. If Charlie got to the dogs, he could kill every one easily without their having a chance to fight back. Every dog handler's worst fear became reality when several 82mm mortar rounds hit the tin roof over the kennel and exploded, sending deadly shrapnel in every direction.

"They hit the kennel! They hit the kennel!" one handler screamed.

"Oh, my God!" another yelled.

The scene inside the bunkers was chaotic. We strained to see through the portholes. The roof of the kennel had been visibly damaged. We knew that one or more of our dogs had been wounded or killed. The question was: which dogs? Several of us started to leave. Lieutenant Fenner screamed, "Everyone stay in the bunkers! That's an order!" It would have been suicide to go outside at that time.

Indescribable dismay filled the eyes of my fellow dog handlers. We couldn't do anything but wait as more volleys of missiles exploded outside. I worried that Clipper had been wounded or, worse yet, killed. Several more explosions damaged trees near the entrance to our small compound. I figured there was a VC spotter hiding nearby, zeroing in on the compound and directing the attack with deadly accuracy.

To our surprise, a jeep, its lights on and with no doors or canvas top, suddenly roared through the compound entrance. Someone shouted, "That's our jeep! Who the hell is it?"

A man jumped out of the vehicle and ran toward the bunkers. Sergeant Barnett was halfway out of his bunker, motioning the man to hurry, when a mortar shell landed and exploded near them. We watched in horror as the impact blew the driver to the ground face-down. A large piece of flying shrapnel shattered Sergeant Barnett's elbow. The jeep lurched forward from the blast, its engine dying when it was a few yards from the bunkers.

Sergeant Barnett and another man dragged the driver inside the bunker. Someone turned on a flashlight to identify him. It was "Kentucky," one of the new men in the platoon. The front of his body and his hands were unscathed, but his backside, from head to buttocks, was bleeding and peppered with gray-and-silver shrapnel slivers. He looked more frightened than racked with pain. A closer look at his wounds indicated that Kentucky wasn't in life-threatening condition, but he definitely needed medical attention. A dog handler got some field dressings from the first-aid kit and wrapped up Kentucky's larger wounds and Sergeant Barnett's injured elbow.

Had he sat down or lain on his back, Kentucky's pain would have been unbearable. Two dog handlers helped him to stand, as that position would be less painful. Kentucky didn't complain — he tried to tough it out. Most of the handlers had experienced the brutality of combat, so it was easy for us to imagine how bad Kentucky must have felt. We knew that when the blood from all those splinter wounds dried, Kentucky had better not try to move or he'd suffer pure agony.

Lieutenant Fenner asked Kentucky why he'd driven a jeep into the middle of a mortar attack. Kentucky explained that he'd been visiting a friend across the compound when he saw the flashes of light and heard the explosions. The area Kentucky had been in wasn't under attack; wanting to help us, he'd driven the jeep as fast as he could. "Hey," he said, "I almost made it before that mortar hit me from behind."

A voice in the bunker blurted, "Kentucky, you're fucking nuts! You should have stayed put!"

Shortly after we brought Kentucky into the bunker, the shelling stopped. The only noises we could still hear were the pitiful sounds of our scout dogs crying out in the kennel. In underwear and boots, carrying our weapons at the ready, we darted one by one from the bunkers. We moved quickly over shards of glass from the jeep's blown-out windshield and debris from the trees and kennel.

After a shelling like that, there was always the danger that one of us might step on an unexploded mortar round lying on the ground. We also knew that the VC might have breached the perimeter and could be waiting behind the rubber trees or lying in the weeds seeking targets. Even so, we braved the unknown to reach our dogs. The closer we got to the kennels, the louder the dogs howled. They knew we were coming and were frantic to get out of their runs. I couldn't imagine how they must have felt, trapped and helpless while awaiting rescue.

A few of us stepped inside the open entrances at either end of the kennel while others checked the surrounding area for signs of the enemy. We could hear dogs groaning in pain.

A voice cried out in the darkness, "My dog's hit!"

Just a few feet inside the kennel, I stopped in my tracks, afraid of what I might see. Clipper's run was close to the middle of the kennel. I took a deep breath and hoped I'd find him alive and unhurt. I moved closer to his run. Someone flipped on the overhead lights, revealing a sickening sight: large pools of blood marked the entrances of several dog runs. Splinters of wood and structural debris littered the concrete floor, and the tin roof had gaping holes.

The repaired roof of the 44th Scout Dog kennel after a deadly enemy mortar attack on the night of November 9, 1967 (author collection).

By now, most of the dog handlers had made it inside the kennel. Several sobbed as they held their wounded and bleeding companions. Some of the dogs lay in pools of blood inside their runs. Others limped with wounds.

I hurried to Clipper's run. He was pawing at the door and trying to get out. I opened the door and went inside. Clipper jumped all over me. I touched and examined every inch of his body. Although Clipper's paws were bloody from clawing at the door, he had no wounds at all. He was so excited to see me that he couldn't keep still. I sat on the floor, hugged him tightly, and cried like a child. Feeling partly responsible for his having been helplessly caged during the attack, I told him how sorry I was that I hadn't been able to protect him.

The sight of the other dogs' suffering devastated me. The smell of their blood saturated the air. Doc Glydon was away on R&R (rest and relaxation), so he wasn't available to tend the wounded and dying.

On that awful night, Ollie, who was scheduled to rotate back to the States in just a few months, found his dog, Erik, bleeding to death in his kennel run. Erik had severe shrapnel wounds, and both his lungs were punctured. Ollie held his limp friend in his arms and cried, crushed to know that his best friend was slowly dying in agony. No one could have saved Erik's life at that point.

Mac came over to Ollie, who sadly offered him his weapon and told Mac that he couldn't bring himself to use it, even to relieve Erik's suffering. He asked Mac if he'd take care of the awful task. Visibly shaking, tears streaming down his face, Ollie stood on unsteady legs. Without looking back, he walked away from Erik and Mac. After Ollie left the kennel, a single shot rang out.

Ollie had made the hardest decision of his life in releasing Erik to heaven. The thought of losing his best friend must have been unbearable. Ollie had trained with Erik back in the States and had worked with him on countless missions in Vietnam. We considered Ollie and Erik one of the best-trained scout-dog teams in the platoon.

*Specialist Four Ollie Whetstone and his beloved scout dog, Erik, 1967
(photo courtesy of Ollie Whetstone).*

I'd learned a great deal about scout dogs from Ollie, and I held him and Erik in the highest regard as soldiers and as friends. They'd been through lots of scrapes with the enemy over the past ten months, and there was no telling how many lives Erik had saved with his alerts and courage under fire.

Dan Scott's dog, Shadow, was in the run next to Clipper's. Barely breathing, Shadow lay in a pool of blood. Dan had been on the other side of the base camp during the mortar attack and couldn't get back to the K-9 compound in time to do anything for his dog; Sergeant Dan Barnett tended to Shadow after making sure his own dog, Sergeant, was okay.

Shadow and Clipper, 44th Scout Dogs, were friends and lived next door to one another in the kennel, 1967. Shadow's handler, Dan Scott, was devastated because he was not there during the enemy mortar attack that took the life of his beloved dog (author collection).

Doc Glydon's absence was deeply felt that awful night. Doc was used to making medical decisions about the dogs; now it became our duty to make tough choices about the injured and dying. Sergeant Barnett stood over Shadow, struggling over whether to put him out of his misery or allow the dog to suffer in hopes that he'd somehow recover. Barnett assessed Shadow's wounds and decided that he was too badly hurt to be saved. Shadow was slowly dying from massive blood loss. In the absence of Dan Scott and the veterinarian, Barnett decided Shadow's fate. He fired a single bullet into the dog's head. Barnett was clearly shaken — this was one of the hardest calls any dog handler ever had to make.

When Dan Scott returned later that night to find Shadow dead from a gunshot to the head and covered in a poncho in his run, he went berserk. Several dog handlers had to restrain him from physically attacking Sergeant Barnett. Scott believed that Shadow hadn't been mortally wounded and hadn't needed to be killed, that with proper medical attention and a blood transfusion he'd have still been alive. He pointed out that Ringo had been saved despite having suffered severe face and jaw wounds.

Sergeant Barnett felt that he had done what he thought was best for the dog. He stood his ground and defended his decision. Nevertheless, Dan called Barnett "the Dog Killer." Having worked together for eight months, Dan and Shadow had become inseparable. I wondered if Dan would ever recover from Shadow's untimely death.

A medical vehicle took Kentucky and Sergeant Barnett to the Dau Tieng field hospital. We all pitched in to help clean wounds and patch up the surviving dogs. I helped wash the kennel's bloodstained concrete floor; other handlers picked up debris and hunted for unexploded mortar rounds.

Before long, the morning sun was shining. Even with all we'd gone through, none of us looked tired, probably because we'd been so keyed up all night. We paid our respects by giving Erik and Shadow proper burials. While someone led us in prayer, Dan and Ollie interred their lost friends. We marked their graves in the scout-dog cemetery, which was in a quiet spot under the shade of rubber trees, away from the kennel and sleeping quarters.

Staff Sergeant Dan Barnett, squad leader, 44th Scout Dogs,
having coffee and a cigarette early in the morning,
somewhere in the bush, 1967 (author collection).

Later that morning, someone yelled, "Formation!" and we assembled in front of the orderly room next to the K-9 Klub. Lieutenant Fenner announced that Major General F. K. Mearns, commander of the 25th Infantry Division, was flying in from his headquarters in Cu Chi. MG Mearns had planned to visit the 44th and evaluate the damage to our K-9 compound. Lieutenant Fenner ordered us to clean up, shave, and get into clean and proper uniforms.

Later that day, someone spotted a jeep heading to the compound. Alerted, we gathered in the parking area in front of the K-9 Klub. Several jeeps drove under the 44th Scout Dog sign that marked the entrance of our compound. When the vehicles stopped, Lieutenant Fenner walked to the lead jeep, which had two white stars on small red flags attached to the front bumper. Major General Mearns returned his salute, stepped out of the vehicle, and shook the lieutenant's hand. It was the first time a distinguished military officer had visited the K-9 compound since its construction eleven months earlier.

Fifteen dog handlers gathered to greet the general; we hung out in a very loose group that anyone would have hesitated to call a military formation. We weren't showing disrespect, but we weren't used to showing snappy protocol either. At least we were all properly dressed and we all had our baseball caps on.

Major General Mearns addressed us, expressing his sorrow about the scout dogs who'd been lost and the handlers and dogs who'd been wounded. He explained how important scout dogs were to the infantry's mission in Vietnam. He praised the successful contribution of the 44th to the mission of the 3rd Brigade, 25th Infantry Division. It was obvious that the CG was well informed about several recent K-9 missions that had saved American lives. His brief speech over, the look in his eyes was sincere as he shook hands with every dog handler.

The general took Ollie Whetstone and Dan Scott aside. Speaking to them privately, he asked Ollie how long he had before he rotated back to the States. Ollie told him his rotation date was in January, just two months away. Major General Mearns promised Ollie that he'd be home for Christmas. Then he asked Dan the same question. Dan replied that he was scheduled to rotate in four months. The general told Dan that, regrettably, he had too much time left to justify ordering an earlier rotation date. After talking to Ollie and Dan, the general toured the damaged kennels and the rest of our compound. He ordered his attending staff officers to make sure that repairing the kennel was given top priority for the engineers.

Having quickly grasped the advantage the dogs gave us, the VC were now doing all they could to eliminate them. I was very grateful that Clipper had lived so that he could help me and others make it through the battles yet to come. Deeply saddened over our losses, I prepared for my next mission — to hunt down the enemy with extreme prejudice.

Chapter 16

Trapped

A FEW WEEKS AFTER the demoralizing attack on the compound, the camp engineers had repaired the kennel. We were back in the business of supporting the infantry's requests for scout-dog teams.

On Sunday, November 25, 1967, Dan Scott, Mike Eply, Ed Hughes, Ollie Whetstone, Mac McClellan, Dan Barnett, and a few other dog handlers were socializing in the K-9 Klub when a fight suddenly erupted between Eply and Hughes. Eply went flying through the screen door and hit the ground outside. Hughes ran out to punch him again. Lieutenant Fenner came out of nowhere and stepped between them to end the scuffle.

Eply complained to the lieutenant that his ankle hurt so badly he couldn't go on his assigned mission in the morning. Lieutenant Fenner, clearly angry, ordered Ed to take Mike's place.

Ed turned to Mike, hostility in his voice, and said, "Eply, if I get killed out there tomorrow, I'm gonna come back here and kick your fuckin' ass."

Mike said nothing as he limped away.

Despite their brawl, Ed and Mike were both good men. We nicknamed Ed the "California Boy." He and I were good friends. Before joining the canines, Ed explained that he'd been assigned to the Old Guard to provide security for the Tomb of the Unknown Soldier at Arlington National Cemetery in Virginia. He boasted that, for a soldier to be an honor guard, he had to project the image of a Hollywood model with exactly the right height and weight and physique. Short, stumpy guys weren't considered for that assignment, he said. The public visited the tomb every day, he said, and the guards had to stand tall and always look clean-cut. There were no excuses for failing to strike the right pose.

Ed was tall and had the ideal physique for that job; I could picture him in a perfectly tailored army dress-blue uniform, his shoes and boots spit-shined every day. Most of us dog handlers had never even seen dress blues.

Ed demonstrated how to march properly with stiff, sharp, snappy movements as he paraded around like a toy soldier. He'd learned a marching rhythm that the rest of us had never seen before, and we got a kick out of watching him demonstrate Old Guard rifle drills with his M16. Yup, among the scraggly scout-dog handlers of our platoon, we had ourselves a true blond-haired, blue-eyed California boy.

I got up early the next morning and greeted Ed in the kennel while he was with his dog Sergeant. I let Clipper out of his run. As usual, Clipper raced past me and headed to his tree, where he'd sit until I arrived to hook him to the twenty-foot leash and fetch him a fresh bucket of water.

Each dog had a tree with his name on it. I nailed a small piece of wood from an ammunition box to Clipper's tree and painted CLIPPER on it in large black letters. Below his name I wrote in small letters, WAR IS GOOD BUSINESS – INVEST YOUR DOG. At the time, I thought that was a pretty clever slogan.

While cleaning Clipper's run, I couldn't help noticing the faded blood-stains in Shadow's and Erik's empty runs — a constant reminder of what had happened to them. I wondered if they'd be replaced. We hadn't had any new dogs in the eleven months the platoon had been in Vietnam.

When I returned to Clipper's tree with my field gear, he became excited, wagging his tail and pacing back and forth. It always amazed me how a dog knew when it was time for a mission.

I met Ed near the compound entrance where he and Sergeant were ready to leave. As the sun rose over the trees, we walked onto the main dirt road leading to our respective units of assignment. Along the way, we talked, agreeing to get together and exchange stories after the mission. I didn't ask Ed about the fight with Mike because it didn't seem appropriate to raise the issue at the time.

Ed and I split up when we reached the infantry battalion area so I could search for the "Company A" unit sign while Ed looked for his outfit. They weren't hard to find. Because unit pride was such an important part of army life, every unit marked its territory with its name, unit crest, patch, and logo. We knew we'd found our mission assignments when we saw soldiers milling around and preparing their field gear.

When I arrived at Headquarters, Company A, I recognized the company commander by the two black bars attached to the front of his helmet. He finished his conversation with several lieutenants, acknowledged my presence, and introduced me to the platoon leader Clipper and I would be assigned to support. After the lieutenant and I shook hands, he knelt to pet Clipper. He seemed pleased to have a scout-dog team with his unit, and Clipper loved the attention.

The platoon leader briefed me on the mission. Choppers would fly the platoon into a landing zone close to the Cambodian border and west of Dau Tieng. My platoon was to hit the ground first and serve as the company's point platoon, the scout-dog team in the lead.

Other platoons were to follow after the first platoon had secured the LZ. Then each platoon would split up and traverse the area in sweeping tactical formations. Our orders were to sweep the South Vietnam side of the Cambodian border for several miles. Battalion reconnaissance teams had reported large numbers of North Vietnam Army regulars and Vietcong throughout the area. No other American units were operating in that remote area, which was considered a primary NVA infiltration route from Cambodia into South Vietnam. The infamous Ho Chi Minh Trail was just inside Cambodia and extended all the way to North Vietnam.

On the field map, the terrain appeared to be fairly flat with thick vegetation and jungle. A few large natural clearings ran alongside the border. American troops were never to cross into Cambodia to search for or pursue the enemy. I told the lieutenant that someone needed to direct my forward movement while I was working the point position, to make sure I didn't venture into Cambodia. He smiled and assured me that I'd stay advised as long as I didn't get too far ahead of the platoon.

The border between South Vietnam and Cambodia may have been clearly designated on the map, but it wasn't marked on the ground. Where we were going, there would be no villages, signs, fences, walls, outposts, or roads to identify the boundary separating the two countries. On the ground, Vietnam and Cambodia looked the same. Looking at the map, I knew it would be easy to cross into Cambodia accidentally. Besides, who'd have reported us if we accidentally crossed the border?

The area of operation (AO) we were going into was designated as a hostile free-fire zone, which meant that I could lock and load, fire first, and ask questions later. I preferred that scenario to the limited-fire zones where I could only lock and load after the enemy had fired at me first. Operating in no-fire zones, usually in densely populated areas, just plain sucked; it was like walking around with a target on my chest. I doubted whether the people who made up these rules had ever served as infantrymen. The enemy had the upper hand to begin with because he blended right in with the population. Sometimes it felt like we were fighting ghost soldiers.

American and Vietnamese government leaders made and controlled the rules of war. Vietnam was classified as a *conflict,* not a war, but soldiers were killing each other just the same. The ground rules for fighting the "Vietnam Conflict" should have been left up to the men who were fighting it. If Charlie didn't abide by any rules of war — and he surely didn't — why handicap us Americans with all these restrictions? Vietnam was no gentleman's war. Soldiers on both sides were serious and used every trick possible to hunt and kill each other. I believed that American soldiers put themselves at a disadvantage by fighting within the confines of those multiple fire-zone rules.

I told the lieutenant, "Get real! It's a bunch of bullshit that we can't pursue Charlie into Cambodia. Those fire-zone restrictions are a crazy idea!"

He replied, "Just do your job, soldier!"

I learned that the company was at full strength, with four platoons of about 150 fighters. My platoon would be breaking trail when we reached the landing objective; the other three would follow not far behind.

Ed Hughes and his dog, Sergeant, had been assigned to the same mission, but to a different platoon. I had no idea where they would be deployed relative to where I'd be operating.

My platoon split up into chopper-sized groups for transport. The morning sun was heating the air; I knew it was going to be a hot one humping around. My backpack was crammed full of the usual stuff. I had at least a hundred rounds of ammunition for my CAR-15, but I'd forgotten to pack any grenades.

We moved out to the Dau Tieng airstrip with my chopper group and the rest of the platoon. The choppers were warmed up and ready to fly; their door gunners' M60s freshly oiled and loaded. I climbed aboard with several infantrymen I didn't know.

When we were airborne, Clipper stood up and leaned forward, sticking his head out the open door, his usual tactic when riding in a chopper. His eyes squinted, his mouth hung wide-open, and his tongue dangled to one side. This was his favorite position, and who could blame him? He was a dog, and dogs liked that natural air conditioning as much as the troops did. Clipper knew I had a solid grip on his leash as he leaned out the open door, stretching the leash taut. We'd done this before, and he felt confident that I wouldn't let go of him.

On these helicopter rides, the weight of Clipper leaning out for the entire ride really tired my arm. After a while, I'd yank on his leash to pull him back inside. When I did, Clipper would back off and lie down beside me for about a minute. Because he enjoyed the view, and the cool air felt so good, he would then get back up and again assume the leaning-out-the-door position. Again, I would yank him inside, a back-and-forth routine that went on during every ride. What was a dog handler to do?

On this mission, I thought of a possible solution: I decided to take up a little slack in Clipper's leash and clutch it tightly in my fist. I figured that when Clipper got up and assumed the leaning-out-the-door position, I'd just let the slack go. Well, I did, and Clipper freaked out. He fell forward enough to think he was falling out of the chopper. His ears and the hair on the back of his neck stood straight up like the quills on a porcupine. When he turned to me, his eyes were as big as golf balls. Clipper dropped to all fours so fast that he scared himself. On his belly, he hugged the metal floor of the chopper, and scooted backwards to get next to me. He gave me that doggy dirty look, which I interpreted as "Hey, John, have you lost your freakin' mind? You just about got me killed!"

I just hugged Clipper and said, "Hey buddy, are you okay? I just saved you from falling out of the chopper. You must have slipped on something. Let me check your paws."

Clipper was really too frightened to be interested in listening to me, but my ploy worked, and he never again leaned out while standing up. His new technique was to stay on all fours, crawl to the edge of the door, and flap his tongue in the wind. In Vietnam, new dog-training techniques sometimes happened on the fly.

Scout dog Clipper, ready for takeoff on his favorite ride, 1967
(author collection).

The chopper formation in the air was quite a sight: twenty or thirty ships clustered in small groups composed a large spread-out tactical flying formation, with gunship escorts flying below. On the ground, the enemy probably saw us and wondered where the hell we were going to land. Flying into our target area with such a formidable display of force gave me a feeling of tremendous confidence, almost of invincibility.

Through the open doors, I saw well-armed soldiers sitting inside the other ships flying alongside us. The door gunners' loaded M60s were pointed downward, but we were flying too high to be in any danger from ground fire. I was delighted that the VC didn't have surface-to-air missiles like those they used in North Vietnam to shoot down our fighter pilots and bombers.

Watching the huge, heavily armed armada in flight all around me, I was pumped with adrenaline. *With a force like this, how could the NVA and VC possibly whip us?*

The ships began their descent into a large LZ of flat ground with short vegetation. When we landed, I immediately jumped out and ran in a crouched position, Clipper beside me. To provide security for the ships, we headed to the tree line away from the landing area. With the choppers blowing any airborne scent away, the noise and movement made it impossible for Clipper to alert on anything in our immediate area. In that type of situation, a scout-dog team was neutralized and as vulnerable as everyone else.

We drew no enemy fire as we moved into the trees. Seeking cover, the soldiers spread out quickly and crept into the woods. Though we had made no contact with Charlie, the squad leaders directed their men to stay spread apart and keep their eyes open, weapons at the ready. We moved swiftly into a defensive position almost immediately after the entire platoon had gotten on the ground and under the cover of the surrounding forest.

The platoon leader quickly took control, assembling the lead squad, which included Clipper and me. Choppers made a lot of noise as they continued landing and dropping off troops in the clearing behind us. The platoon leader gave me a hand signal to point out the direction he wanted me to go. I told the two-man team assigned as my security to stay far enough behind us for Clipper to have full scent capability in the direction of travel. I instructed them not to get in front of the dog or me unless I signaled them, and that I'd turn periodically to check for their signals to direct my forward progress. I didn't want to get too far ahead or off track.

Clipper and I moved out through the stubbly vegetation and lightly wooded terrain. The rest of the platoon followed cautiously, eventually stretching out behind our lead. I stepped forward slowly, keeping my eyes on Clipper's head, ears, and body. Occasionally, I'd glance rearward to check my security team and get directions. Using hand signals, the troops behind me made sure I stayed on the compass heading. The farther we moved from the landing zone the quieter the surrounding jungle became.

During that initial penetration into enemy territory, Clipper didn't alert at all. I wondered whether his ears were still ringing from all the chopper noise or were distracted by the noise of the troops moving all around him. Since Clipper kept moving forward with what appeared to be little concern for his surroundings, I had to assume he wasn't sensing danger.

Before long, Clipper gave a mild alert by flicking his ears and canting his head ever so slightly. I stopped and knelt on one knee; everyone behind us stopped too. Listening closely, I heard nothing; looking at the area where Clipper had alerted, I saw nothing. Unsure whether Clipper's alert had been strong enough for me to signal for help, I got up and tugged his leash to tell him to move out again.

Clipper walked another hundred yards without alerting, and then his ears shot straight up and forward. I stopped, signaled one of the security guards behind me to come up, and told him that Clipper had alerted the same way twice, which was worth checking out. I couldn't say specifically what Clipper had sensed or how far away it might be. The soldier quietly moved back to confer with the platoon leader, who then came forward and signaled two men to cautiously sweep the front about fifty yards out and then report back.

When the soldiers returned, they reported seeing fresh footprints about forty yards directly ahead that didn't resemble GI jungle boots. Despite my confidence in a dog's ability to pick up a scent left behind by the enemy long after he was gone, I couldn't believe it: Clipper had alerted on an airborne scent! I immediately praised and hugged him for his alert.

The platoon leader's hand signal got me moving forward again. As Clipper approached the footprints, he sniffed the ground and moved in the direction of the scent. I followed him for several yards and then aborted. The footprints headed away from our direction of travel and we were getting too far away from the rest of the troops.

Standing in tall grass about fifty yards ahead of the rest of the platoon, I signaled the man behind me to come forward. While we knelt and talked about the situation, the platoon leader arrived. I whispered to him that Clipper was getting a fairly good scent and seemed to want to track the trail of footprints. The leader directed a squad of men to follow the fresh tracks for a short distance and report back. When the squad leader returned, he reported that there were footprints all over the place, but he'd seen nothing else. We stayed at a halt for a few minutes while the platoon leader got on the radio and made his report. Shortly afterward, we were ordered not to follow the trail of suspected enemy footprints but to continue the mission in the direction planned.

We moved out of the grassy area and into the woods. Several hours into our mission, it was fairly quiet except for the everyday murmur of birds and insects. Clipper, head rising above the vegetation, moved forward into the jungle easily, even though the low vegetation and vines got thicker. So far, navigating that part of the jungle wasn't proving difficult.

In pursuit of the enemy, Clipper, mouth closed, paused for a moment and lifted his head high as if sniffing something directly in front of us. I stopped, dropping to one knee to scan and listen for anything unusual; I even sniffed the air. Again, I neither saw, heard, nor smelled anything out of the ordinary. Even so, I motioned the closest man behind me to come up, and told him that Clipper's alert was fairly strong and straight ahead.

The platoon leader assembled a rifle team to search the forward area. They reported a huge clearing about seventy-five yards through the jungle, but no sign of the enemy. Looking at his map, the platoon leader nodded and then hand signaled me to push on. I complimented Clipper for the alert, hugging him and telling him, "Good boy! Good boy!" Clipper had done a great job up to that point.

We moved ahead, but standard operating procedure (SOP) dictated that we stop before entering the clearing. When coming out of the jungle, no one was supposed to enter a clearing unless the platoon leader directed. He was responsible for assessing the situation and deciding how he wanted the platoon to maneuver across any open space.

Everyone stayed just inside the trees awaiting orders. I noticed that Clipper began sniffing a small pile of bamboo shavings a few feet away. I figured the enemy had probably made a bunch of punji stakes there. As I pondered the pile, Clipper alerted sharply to the rear. I quickly turned to find a tall man in clean jungle fatigues, whose only weapon was a holstered .45-caliber sidearm. He held a field map inside a plastic sleeve. I immediately recognized the two black stars sewn onto his camouflage-covered helmet. I couldn't believe my eyes — it was Major General Mearns, commanding officer of the 25th Infantry Division, the same officer who'd visited the K-9 compound after the VC mortar attack.

What the hell is he doing out here? I wondered. *Is he trying to earn his combat pay, or what? And how the hell did he get here in the first place?*

I rose to a standing position and, without saluting, nervously greeted him: "Good morning, sir." In a combat zone, it was forbidden to come to attention and salute, because Charlie might be watching; if he saw a telltale salute, the officer could get a bullet in the head.

The CG was out of view under the cover of vegetation. He smiled and asked me, "What's the name of your dog, soldier?"

"Clipper, sir!"

The general knelt on one knee and said, "He sure is frisky."

"Shake hands, Clipper!" I commanded softly. Clipper lifted his paw into the general's palm; the CG smiled and shook it. Then, while he examined his map and peered at the open clearing through the trees, he asked me several questions about how scouting worked.

The general's radio operator and several of his staff officers, all wearing clean jungle fatigues, surrounded him. They didn't say a word to me, but kept looking and smiling at Clipper.

I chatted with Major General Mearns for a few moments before he turned and headed back to the main element of the platoon. I looked down at my dog and said, "Clipper, you just met the CG of the 25th Infantry, the most powerful man in the division." Clipper didn't appear too impressed.

We were told during the mission briefing that there would be an entire battalion—several hundred troops—working the area. I figured the CG had landed with us on the choppers and had been beating the bush all morning. It was quite rare for a general to show up in the jungle and hump with his troops. Unlike World War II, Vietnam had no front lines, so danger was expected everywhere we traveled outside our base camp. I was impressed to see the commanding general walk in a combat zone with his men. It reminded me of seeing Lieutenant Colonel Hal Moore in the Ia Drang Valley during my first tour. I'd never forget that he gave me water and carried my pack when I dehydrated on my very first mission.

After Major General Mearns departed, we were given a short break in place. I poured some water into my steel pot for Clipper, and hugged him for doing such a terrific job. I was extremely happy with how we were working as a team. Even though I'd worked with him many times before, each mission was different and we learned new things every time we went out together. At this point in our relationship, our bond was very strong.

After a fifteen-minute break I heard some choppers overhead, flying just above the treetops. They landed in the clearing we were about to cross, picked up some soldiers, and took off. I figured that MG Mearns and his staff were the passengers. Clipper sat facing the clearing and watched everything take place. He moved his head back and forth as if searching the clearing, probing for clues as to what might be in the woods on the other side.

My friend Ed Hughes and his war-dog partner, Sergeant, were somewhere in this same area of operation. I recalled telling Ed that we'd trade stories when we got back to the K-9 Klub. *Oh, boy, have I got a tale to tell about how Major General Mearns came up to us and shook Clipper's paw!*

The platoon leader finally gave me the command to cross the clearing. Clipper and I slowly moved out, exposed to whatever might be waiting for us. I was tense looking at the other side of the clearing, several hundred yards away. As we walked farther, I glanced to my rear: my two bodyguards were spread out ten yards to my left and right rear. The rest of the platoon spaced themselves apart and cautiously moved forward. I could feel a light breeze, but had confidence that Clipper wouldn't miss a scent of danger.

As we moved deeper into enemy territory, my eyes stayed glued to Clipper's head and ears. Suddenly, his neck and head went rigid and his ears popped up, then he cocked his head to one side, his strongest alert of the day. I immediately got down on one knee. Crouching low, I looked and listened but couldn't see or hear anything unusual. I turned around and noticed that everyone behind us had also stopped and taken a knee.

My right knee was beginning to hurt from kneeling on the hard ground. A long time had passed since I'd jumped from that chopper in the central highlands and had a punji stake shoved through the knee — a hell of an aching memory indeed. Now I had to keep moving and deal with the lingering pain of that old injury.

I felt uncomfortable being so exposed in vegetation no higher than my boot tops, especially with fresh signs of the enemy all over the place. Clipper's ears and head remained erect, so I decided not to push our luck by proceeding. I turned and motioned to the man behind. The platoon leader moved up forty yards to join me. He asked for my thoughts, and I told him I had a bad feeling about going any farther.

The platoon leader wasted no time. He motioned for the nearest squad leader, who directed two fire teams of three men each, to move forward and sweep the area. After reconnoitering, both teams returned and reported having seen a long, wide, recently used trail about fifty yards off, but they'd made no contact with the enemy. The platoon leader signaled for me to lead on.

When Clipper and I reached the trail, which ran perpendicular to the mission's direction of travel, we saw fresh footprints and the tracks of wheeled carts and oxen leading into Vietnam from the direction of the Cambodian border. These certainly weren't the prints we'd expect of peasant farmers moving around. Besides, there were no farms or villages in the area.

John Burnam and scout dog Clipper.

The platoon leader figured the Cambodian border must be less than half a mile away. This trail had to be a branch leading off the main Ho Chi Minh Trail. Since the tracks were so fresh, he thought that a heavily armed battalion-sized NVA or VC force must have moved into South Vietnam from Cambodia within the past day or so. He used a grease pencil to mark the location of the enemy movement on his map.

I took the lead and crossed the trail, heading toward the facing wood line, less than seventy-five yards out. We were now traveling parallel to the Cambodian border. Before long, Clipper stopped and stood erect, ears pointed high and forward; the muscles in his shoulders grew tense and began to twitch.

When I looked back, my security guards motioned for me to keep going. The platoon leader must have decided to ignore Clipper's alert. I was puzzled, but got up and tugged on Clipper's leash. He started stepping side to side as if he didn't want to go forward. Then, several shots rang out over our heads. Instantly, we dropped to prone positions on the ground. Clipper was on his belly, his head up and pointing in the direction of the tree line ahead. I hugged him close and told him what a good dog he was. He licked my face.

There was a momentary silence as I strained to spot the shooter. I saw nothing but a wall of dark green vegetation ahead. Behind me, everyone lay in the short grass, trying to figure out where the shots had come from. Someone decided to fire an M16 over my head into the trees; right away everyone else started shooting.

I knew that if a sniper was hiding in a tree, the entire platoon was visible to him. From the direction of the shots, I thought that Clipper might have been Charlie's first target. We were definitely not out of a sniper's range of fire, because the rounds had cracked over our heads. Charlie was either a bad shot or Clipper and I had been mighty lucky.

The firing stopped when it became apparent that our side was doing all the shooting; then there was a lengthy silence. The platoon leader ordered two squads to fire and maneuver until they reached and secured a position at the edge of the trees ahead. As the squads tried to do so, several more shots came from the jungle. Voices behind Clipper and me were giving orders to get up and move out on line. I got to my feet and tugged Clipper to move forward along with everyone else.

Several more shots came from the jungle ahead. Again, the entire platoon dropped on their bellies and poured a deadly barrage of fire into the trees. Clipper didn't move while I placed several rounds where I thought the shooter was. I patted Clipper on the back and told him he was a good boy. Several men flanked us, taking up firing positions.

Directly behind me, a voice shouted, "Get up and move out on line, soldier!"

I wasn't about to move, because I didn't feel safe exposing myself to a sniper who I felt was zeroing in on Clipper and me, so I ignored the voice and remained flat on my belly in defensive firing position. When I looked up, a tall man with two black bars on his helmet was standing over me. It was the captain, the company commander I'd met that morning. I was startled to see him glaring down at me and ordering me to get up and assault the tree line.

I looked at him as if he were crazy and replied, "Sir, why don't you call for artillery or air strikes before we go into those trees?"

"Soldier, I said get up and assault!"

I finally obeyed and moved forward with the rest of the infantrymen. Charlie didn't fire a single round. When Clipper and I reached the edge of the wall of trees and joined a group of infantrymen, there was too much milling around and chatter for Clipper to be effective.

The platoon leader approached, and told me that one of his men had spotted a bunker not far from us. He asked if I'd use my dog to check it out. On other missions, Clipper had avoided going into bunkers, foxholes, and tunnels. I learned to never force a dog to do anything he didn't want to do, especially in enemy territory. I told the lieutenant, "Clipper doesn't like going into holes in the ground, but I'll go with you to see if he gets an alert."

The lieutenant immediately led the way, moving out at a quick pace; Clipper and I followed close behind. A few yards after we had passed the last infantrymen, Clipper raised his head and alerted up into the trees. I didn't give it a second thought because there was too much activity all around for the alert to be accurate.

It wasn't long before the three of us were by ourselves. The lieutenant snaked a path through the thick jungle vegetation. The nearest American was now at least twenty yards behind us. At point-blank range, muzzle flashes lit up in my face. The lieutenant's body slammed into my chest like a sack of rocks, knocking me onto my back and making my helmet fly off my head. Because I was still hanging onto his leash as I fell, Clipper rolled over on top of me.

Directly to my front, Charlie opened up with automatic rifle and machine-gun fire directly over me. Fortunately, I'd fallen near a small tree. I rolled behind it, Clipper at my side. American rifle and machine gun fire answered from behind. Clipper and I were caught in the crossfire between my platoon and the enemy. With an arm around Clipper, I hugged the ground. The firing from both sides got so intense that it chopped up the vegetation like the blades of a lawn mower. Charlie was dug in and shooting at us from camouflaged underground bunkers.

Clipper and I were trapped, unable to move. I knew that the lieutenant had absorbed the initial fusillade. He had to be close by, but I couldn't see him through the dense vegetation. He wasn't crying out in pain or shouting for a medic, so I assumed that he must be dead.

The exchange of fire was furious, back and forth, over our heads. *I guess Charlie doesn't see Clipper and me,* I thought. *Or maybe he thinks he's already killed us!* Because we were so close, I decided not to make any sudden moves and give Charlie a second chance. I slowly moved my rifle to a firing position. As I got the barrel up by my face, I noticed a plug of mud jammed inside the muzzle. *Must have happened when I fell onto the wet ground.* Trying to clear the muzzle with my finger only pushed the mud in deeper. I thought of tossing grenades, but then remembered that I hadn't packed any.

Under those circumstances, it would have been suicide to break down my weapon and run a cleaning rod through the bore and chamber to clear the plug. It was more important for me to stay alive than to figure out a way to shoot. If I absolutely had to, I could risk firing my weapon, but the round in the chamber might explode in my face.

Clipper and I lay only fifteen feet or so from Charlie's entrenched positions. Between the exchanges of small-arms fire, I could hear

Vietnamese voices whispering from their foxholes. I knew Clipper heard them too, but he didn't make a move or a sound. My dog and I were in deep shit with no way out. My adrenaline spiked and my heart pounded so loud I could hear it.

This was a much different situation from that of the APC ambush: This time I was closer to the enemy, had no helmet, no functional rifle or grenades, and could be killed by either side. I didn't dare make the slightest movement or noise that would draw attention to my location. I was grateful to be with Clipper who, unlike the frightened Timber, wasn't jumping around and trying to get away.

I prayed, "God, please get us out of this deathtrap."

Minutes felt like hours. I thought my time on earth was running out. I wanted to melt into the dirt to get away from it all. I was scared, and so was Clipper — I could feel him shivering underneath my arm as his own heart thumped against it.

I found it peculiar that I could simultaneously hear Charlie whispering in Vietnamese and my comrades shouting in English. Not long into the firefight, I heard the deafening sound of artillery rounds exploding behind Charlie's positions. Shrapnel splintered the trees and shredded the vegetation all around us. The Americans were walking the artillery closer and closer to our positions. Between volleys, the exchange of small arms and machine-gun fire continued.

I lay silently holding Clipper and trying not to move a muscle. To my surprise, something touched my foot. I spun my head around and saw an American soldier, one of my designated security guards. We made eye contact but exchanged no words. He gave me a thumbs-up and motioned me to move back to the rear.

As quietly as I could, I slowly turned around on my belly. Clipper followed. When I tried to crawl away from the tree, my backpack caught in some vines and moved them. Charlie must have spotted the movement. Rifle fire erupted again. Somehow, I broke free and crawled away with Clipper at my side. I anticipated feeling the agony of a bullet entering my body or hearing Clipper groan from being shot as we crawled.

Charlie was either shooting too high or we were as flat as the rotting leaves on the jungle floor — and lucky!

To my rear, the distinct sound of an M16 echoed — the soldier who'd relieved me was providing cover for our escape. I flinched at the sound of a grenade exploding behind me. I hesitated briefly but didn't turn to look.

As I crawled, an American soldier appeared before me and motioned me to stay down. He fired over my head. As Clipper and I passed, I saw a dead Vietnamese in khaki clothes dangling from a tree by one bare foot. His arms hung down below his head, fingers almost touching the pool of blood that dripped from his body and soaked into the earth. I quickly moved Clipper around the body and took cover behind a nearby tree inside the American perimeter.

Behind the American lines, there were dead and wounded on the ground everywhere. I broke down my CAR-15, ran a cleaning rod through the bore to release the clump of mud, and took up a defensive firing position next to an infantryman on the perimeter. I quickly checked Clipper's entire body, feeling for holes and looking for blood. Clipper didn't wince in pain as I touched him. He was okay. It wasn't long before the artillery barrages halted and the shooting trickled to a stop.

That was the way such firefights usually began and ended. Charlie had either been eradicated or had decided to break contact — it was hard to tell. Reinforcements from another platoon reached the perimeter and took up firing positions. Nearby, a medic worked on a wounded soldier who screamed that he was going to die. The medic tried to calm the wounded man, stop the bleeding, and patch him up, but to no avail; the soldier died, and the medic quickly moved on to tend another.

I saw the lieutenant's lifeless body being carried in a poncho. The platoon sergeant, now in charge, told me that, after the captain had been shot, the company commander had killed a VC who was in a tree. I remembered that, before the firing started, Clipper had alerted up in the trees and I had disregarded it. I now realized that Clipper might have sensed the danger there. Guilt pierced my heart for the lieutenant who'd paid the price for my mistake. The platoon sergeant also informed me that the soldier who'd come to rescue us while we were trapped in that crossfire had also been killed. Instead of Clipper saving lives with his alerts of danger, this time it was an infantryman who gave his life to save our lives.

It was easy to figure that most of the American casualties had happened during the first few seconds of fighting, while everyone was standing and waiting for the lieutenant to check out the bunker. Baiting us with the sniper, Charlie had sucked us right into his death trap.

The sounds of helicopters, small arms, and machine-gun fire echoed in the distance, signaling that someone else was getting into the shit. The entire area must have been loaded with pockets of hardcore NVA troops protecting the exit paths of the Ho Chi Minh Trail. The reconnaissance team who'd scouted that area before our mission had done a good intelligence job. Now it was up to the infantry to fight smarter and defeat the bastards. Even though there was fighting going on nearby, we were ordered to stay in place. I rested under a tree with Clipper and gave him some water. I listened to the squawking of a nearby field radio, the distant noise of a firefight, and watched my fellow soldiers receive medical attention.

A soldier came up to me and asked, "Is your name Burnam?"

"Yes!" I answered.

The soldier handed me a helmet with my name written on the headband inside. He said it had been lying near a bunker next to the bodies of the lieutenant and another soldier. He couldn't understand how my dog and I had survived without a scratch. Before I put on the helmet, I checked it over. There wasn't a mark on it. Clipper didn't have a scratch either, and appeared to be dealing with the whole situation better than I was.

*Scout dog Clipper taking a well earned nap after a hard day's work, 1967
(author collection).*

Clipper had been a brave and competent soldier that day, alerting us to danger and then showing courage under extreme circumstances. Many of the troops came by to pet him for good luck. One called Clipper "the invincible scout dog." I chuckled at that. I hugged Clipper and told him what a brave dog he was. We must have had a guardian angel watching over us that day — I just hoped our angel would stick around.

Later, I heard that the platoon's casualties during that skirmish were considered light. It was decided that we hadn't suffered enough losses to be relieved of our mission. I joined the rest of the company to set up a defensive perimeter for the evening in the very field we'd crossed. The next day, the company would continue its mission, hunting NVA troops along the Cambodian border.

Clipper and I took up a firing position behind a bush well inside the perimeter, where I felt a little more secure. It was late afternoon when a helicopter appeared overhead and landed under the green smoke signal inside the large perimeter. I figured it was a supply ship and, not needing any supplies, I paid little attention to it. A few minutes after the chopper took off, I recognized a fellow dog handler, Sergeant Durbach of the 44th Scout Dog Platoon. I wondered what Durbach was doing out here without his dog. As Durbach approached me, I noticed that he looked fresh and clean-shaven, and his jungle fatigues weren't dirty like mine.

The sergeant carried a CAR-15 and had a light pack strapped to his back. We greeted one another with smiles and a handshake. As we sat on the ground, Durbach stroked Clipper's head and back, but he appeared nervous, his face conveying that something was bothering him. He forced a smile and asked me how I was doing.

"John," he said, "Ed Hughes and his dog, Sergeant, were killed today."

I couldn't believe what I was hearing. I was stunned.

Durbach filled me in on what had happened. After Ed's chopper had landed, he and Sergeant ran for cover along with the rest of the troops. When Ed reached the jungle wall, he moved inside to seek cover and was shot at point-blank range. The VC then shot Sergeant and hacked him to death with a machete. Taken by surprise, the pair probably never knew what hit them.

Durbach said that the NVA had overwhelmed the rest of Ed's platoon and forced them into a hasty retreat back across the landing zone, where they set up a defensive position and held off an assault. The NVA then retreated into the jungle where Ed and his dog lay dead.

I asked Sergeant Durbach how he knew so much if he hadn't been there. He said Lieutenant Fenner had received a call from 3rd Brigade headquarters in Dau Tieng. They told him that a dog handler and his dog were killed in action while on patrol near the Cambodian border. All the casualties, they said, except for the handler and his dog, had been recovered. It was apparently too risky to try to recover Ed and Sergeant at that time, so they'd left them behind.

"What a bunch of bullshit!" I said. "Those fuckers can't leave Ed and Sergeant out there alone all night. So, they sent you to get me to help recover Ed and Sergeant? Well, I'm ready. Let's go get some more men and fucking do it!"

Sergeant Durbach put his hand on my shoulder and said, "John, sit down and let me finish."

Then he told me that Lieutenant Fenner had sent him out about three hours earlier to size up the situation and report back. Since the attack, Ed's platoon had been reinforced with two more platoons. They set up in defensive position not far from Ed and Sergeant.

The company commander assembled two squads to go out and recover the bodies. Durbach arrived in time to accompany the patrol. When they'd found Ed and his dog, the NVA were long gone. Ed had been stripped of his weapon and gear, including his boots and his scout-dog patch. Sergeant's body lay near him, his left ear missing, as were his leash and harness. Both bodies were recovered without incident and sent home to Dau Tieng. Durbach's next task had been to locate me.

I was less than a mile from where Ed and Sergeant had died. I told Durbach that I'd heard a firefight in the distance after our battle, but it hadn't occurred to me that it might have been Ed's unit under attack.

Ed and Sergeant were killed on Monday, November 27, 1967, five days after Thanksgiving. The incident between Ed and Eply at the K-9 Klub had led to the two of them switching places for that mission; now Ed's comment played over and over in my head: *"Eply, if I get killed out there tomorrow, I'm gonna come back here and kick your fuckin' ass!"*

No one in the platoon could believe Ed and Sergeant were dead. Of course, every dog handler wanted to hear about it. I must have repeated the story twenty times that day. I didn't talk to Eply, but I could imagine how he must have felt.

The entire 44th assembled at a field chapel not far from the kennel compound to pay their last respects to Ed and Sergeant. The chapel was a large green tent with several rows of folding chairs and a makeshift altar. We held a memorial service without bodies — by now, Ed was in a morgue somewhere in Saigon.

To my distaste, the chaplain's sermon was filled with military jargon. He said something like, "Ed hasn't left us. He's gone on to serve a higher commander, the celestial six."

That term "six" was used in common military radio jargon as part of a commanding officer's call sign. I wasn't the only one to cringe at the eulogy: Dan Scott and many of the other handlers were livid about the chaplain's choice of lingo. We wanted to hear something beautiful and poetic from the Bible, not language that sounded like a military mission in the afterlife. I vowed that that would be the last time I'd ever attend a formal religious service for a fallen comrade in Vietnam. I'd deal with it in my own way instead.

Edward Coward Hughes, killed in action along with his faithful scout dog, Sergeant, near the Cambodian Border on November 27, 1967. I was working Clipper in the same area, ducking for cover during an ambush when Ed Hughes was killed (author collection).

A few days after Ed's death, Lieutenant Fenner asked me to join Sergeant Durbach to escort Ed's dog, Sergeant, to a military morgue in Saigon. Veterinarians wanted to complete an autopsy on the dog, and Saigon certainly had more extensive veterinary facilities than our field hospital. The second part of my mission would be to positively identify Ed's body in the morgue.

Edward Cowart Hughes III, nineteen years old, now rested in peace. He would soon be going home to his grieving family in Garden Grove, California.

I would continue with Clipper on missions yet to come against the same enemy that had taken the lives of Ed and his best friend Sergeant.

Chapter 17

Booby Traps

DENSE FOREST SURROUNDED the Ben Cui and Michelin rubber plantations that stretched several miles around Dau Tieng. North of the dirt airstrip stood a small range of steep foothills covered by a thick canopy of jungle foliage. Resident Vietnamese workers lived in the many small hamlets scattered throughout the rubber-tree plantations. A combination of numbers and letters — such as AP 2, AP 12, and AP 13 — was used to mark the location of each hamlet on our tactical grid maps.

Every so often, a blue-and-white civilian helicopter flew into base camp. It would stick out like a sore thumb, since all the military aircraft and equipment were painted olive drab or camouflage. The civilian choppers belonged to business partners of the Michelin and Ben Cui plantations. Scuttlebutt had it that these companies were concerned that the U.S. Army was destroying too many of the precious rubber trees to build its base camp. They apparently wanted payment for each tree we damaged or destroyed. They were also unhappy that we tied our dogs to the trees, because the chains rubbed the bark raw and the dogs dug holes around the roots. They complained about all the wooden hooches that the dog handlers had built between the rows of rubber trees.

I never learned whether the army ever paid for damaged and destroyed rubber trees. In the K-9 platoon, "Fuck 'em all" was how we felt about their complaints. As grunts, we didn't care and we didn't want foreign civilians snooping around the K-9 compound. I reflected on what my former first sergeant had warned me of in Okinawa: "*There are spies out there. They want classified information about what we do. Don't talk or try to figure them out; they're professionals. Report everything to your security officer immediately. Do you understand, soldier?*"

It was common knowledge that booby traps were expected in the rubber trees away from base camp. Clipper could see, hear, smell, and sense danger from great distances and with accuracy. I knew Clipper was bright, a proven combat veteran war dog, and a great partner. I didn't think he'd ever intentionally walk through a trip wire stretched between two trees. I assumed Clipper would avoid that type of danger, but I had to learn what alert he'd give when he came near a trip wire.

One morning before I cleaned Clipper's run, I walked to the rubber trees behind the hooches. I had a roll of regular olive drab (OD) trip wire — thin, fairly strong, and pliable, which I'd taken from a trip-flare. I tied a strand knee-high between two rubber trees and twanged it with my finger to assure that the wire was as tight as a guitar string.

After I cleaned the kennel and played with Clipper, I put him on leash and choke chain for training. We headed in the direction of the trip wire. Clipper walked ahead without pulling, just as he did when working on a mission. We went to an area of short grass that was clear of obstacles. The trip wire was set up about seventy-five yards away. I didn't want to walk a straight line to the target, so I tugged the leash left or right to direct Clipper through the rubber trees. As we moved deeper into the trees, Clipper didn't alert. We came closer to the trip wire, but I still saw no sign of an alert from him. When he was about fifty yards away from the target, Clipper gave a weak alert with a slight movement of his ears but he didn't stop walking.

When the wire touched his head, he ducked under it, so I jerked the leash and said, "No Clipper! No!"

Clipper turned and looked at me as if to say, "What did I do wrong?"

I moved Clipper's head close to the wire and clutched it in my hand. I got down on one knee, looked Clipper in the eye, and showed him the thin green wire. Then I gently tapped the wire on the black tip of his nose. Each time I tapped Clipper's nose, I raised the tone of my voice and said, "No Clipper! No!"

I talked to him as if he were a trainee. I said, "Clipper, that, my friend, is a fucking trip wire. Do not cross it. Do you understand? Do you have any idea what might happen to us if you crossed it? Boom! That's right, BOOM!"

Clipper responded to the word "no," but I doubt he'd understood anything else.

I walked Clipper around a bit to calm him, and then let him approach the wire again. Clipper gave a weak alert and, as before, walked under the wire. We continued to practice, but Clipper did the same thing each time. He surely must have tired of hearing me say, "No, Clipper! No."

Finally, I decided to add a blasting cap to the end of the trip wire, so that if Clipper tripped the wire, the POP! it made would get his attention.

The first time Clipper went through the wire, it triggered the blasting cap, startling him. I quickly went to one knee and said, "Clipper, that's what I'm talking about. You just killed us!" Clipper just looked at me with a blank expression.

After we practiced with a loaded trip wire several times, Clipper finally decided to stop and sit a few feet in front of the trip wire. I was so excited and proud of him that I hugged him and said, "You're the best scout dog in the platoon — the greatest fucking dog in the world! Good boy, Clipper! Good boy!"

We had actually accomplished a new trick! I made Clipper repeat the exercise day after day until I was sure his behavior hadn't been a fluke and that we were on the same wavelength. Sure enough, Clipper had really learned not to go through the trip wire. He would either sit in front of it or avoid it entirely and go around it.

To make the training tougher, I put several wires in different locations to see how Clipper would negotiate more than one obstacle. I learned that if Clipper came directly upon a trip wire, he'd sit in front of it more often than he'd go around. Also, I learned that if he sensed the wire from a distance, he'd go around it. I was quite pleased to have made so much progress with Clipper in just a few weeks' training.

I still had no idea how effective the trip-wire training would be when Clipper worked in thick brush or moved across wooded terrain, down trails, or among the rubber trees. I dreaded trails and always tried to avoid them, especially in very remote jungle. Dirt pathways around populated areas weren't as hard to negotiate. Common sense dictated that staying in the bush was safer than walking on smooth dirt trails, which were perfect for the enemy to stage ambushes and hide punji pits and explosive booby traps.

The Vietcong were smarter in the bush than Americans, because the bush was their home turf. Most of us teenage American grunts had never traveled outside the States, let alone seen a jungle. The closest I'd ever come was thumbing through a *National Geographic* magazine. The NVA had mastered guerrilla warfare tactics long before I was born. We young Americans were infants, still learning how to walk and talk our way through that kind of war.

By conducting these training sessions, I hoped I had learned one more way to keep us alive while we walked point. Still, I didn't intend to volunteer our services as an expert booby-trap-detection team. No way!

The day came when my name appeared on the rotation schedule for another mission. I'd be working with the 2nd Battalion, 12th Infantry (White Warriors), whose motto was "Led by Love of Country." That unit was organized back in 1861 during the Indian Wars.

The "2/12" consisted primarily of foot soldiers who were sometimes transported in trucks or chopper air assaults into enemy territory. I preferred working with foot soldiers, especially after my ambush experience with a sister battalion of armored personnel carriers (APCs). Working with the mechanized infantry had become one of my greatest fears.

I reported to the 2/12 down the road from the K-9 compound. I thought, *There's one good thing about living in a small base camp: everything's within walking distance.* Brigade G2 (military intelligence) had information concerning a VC buildup around Dau Tieng. The enemy was reported to be operating out of hidden base camps in the nearby jungles surrounding the rubber plantations. At night, VC were infiltrating the hamlets and reconnoitering our camp's perimeter to assess our strengths and weaknesses. They knew a lot about our capabilities, such as how many helicopters we had, when they flew in and out, the locations of our ammunition dumps, where our main communications bunkers were, and how many troops were inside.

At least twice a week they attacked our airstrip with mortars, wreaking havoc on our aircraft operations. The mortars were mainly coming from the foothills north of Dau Tieng and east from somewhere in the rubber trees and surrounding jungle. Retaliatory artillery and air strikes on the suspected locations didn't fix the problem. Helicopter gunships weren't effective enough without someone on the ground to help them pinpoint their strikes.

Now, infantry foot soldiers and scout-dog teams were deployed to search out and destroy those VC and their hidden base camps. Someone once told me that the infantry was called the Queen of Battle. When no one else could get the desired results, the Queen of Battle was sent in to finish the job. I thought army should have called the infantry the manlier King of Battle, but that title was already taken by the artillerymen. Go figure!

Clipper and I were going on a two-day mission with the 2/12 infantry. My assigned platoon would be flown by helicopter several miles east of Dau Tieng and dropped off in a clearing to conduct our search for the enemy. On day one, our job was to patrol the jungles east of the Michelin plantation. On day two, we were to sweep west through the rubber plantation and march back to our base camp.

Another company of the 2/12 had the job of conducting search-and-destroy operations in the northern mountain sector of the rugged foothills where most of the VC mortar attacks had been coming from.

Charlie's weapons consisted of an 81mm mortar tube, base plate, sighting mechanism, and a bunch of mortar rounds. Charlie could quickly and easily assemble the weapon, fire, disassemble, and move off before a retaliatory strike arrived. These highly mobile mortar squads were deadly accurate and difficult to detect unless flushed out by ground troops.

The American infantry had similar capabilities in its arsenal, but American artillery required vehicular or aircraft transportation. The smallest artillery pieces, 105mm howitzers, fired explosive shells that were much bigger and deadlier than mortar rounds. Charlie wasn't equipped with such large artillery; he carried all his weapons on his back.

The 2/12 was given the order to hunt down and eliminate Charlie's mortar teams. To get to the mission site, we flew east by chopper, escorted by gunships. Clipper and I were in the lead formation's second troopship. The door gunners' post-mounted M60 machine guns were loaded and ready for firing. It was a short ride over the rubber trees to the nearby jungle. The choppers descended into a small clearing and landed under the green all-clear smoke signal.

Clipper and I jumped out and darted toward the jungle wall to our front. Its outer skirt was too thick to get through without a machete. The platoon leader ordered one of his men to take point and cut a path. Clipper and I followed the machete man as he hacked his way forward.

With such thick vegetation, the platoon leader had to pull in the flank guards. He tightened up the column to maintain tighter control and accountability. It reminded me of the thick vegetation in the central highlands during my first tour with the 7th Cavalry. I had no dog back then, but we sure could have used a great one like Clipper.

We pushed deeper into the thick, dark vegetation. Thunderclaps roared overhead. It soon began to rain, and drops of water made their way through the dense canopy and down onto the platoon. Millions of raindrops splashing on the leaves and branches helped muffle the sounds of our movement. The man with the machete kept switching it from hand to hand so we could walk at a steady pace through the rain-soaked jungle. The pace man walked behind Clipper and me. His job was to count the number of steps we'd traveled. Periodically, the lieutenant halted our progress to get the pace man's count and to use map and compass to check our distance and direction of travel.

Our jungle fatigues and boots were sopping wet from the heavy rain and tromping through the soaked and rotting debris. That trail we had forged with machete and boots would disappear in a few days; that was how fast it could repair itself after being cut and mashed by boots. That made it all the more important to have a radio and map. However, the radioman and platoon leader were the primary targets of the enemy. If just the radio took a bullet, we'd be in deep shit, cut off from any immediate support.

Then there was the unavoidable thorny vegetation we called wait-a-minute-vines, which scratched deep into our exposed wet arms and hands and tore holes in our fatigues. When a grunt rolled up his sleeves, cuts, scratches, and thin scars could be seen running up and down both arms. The wounds immediately distinguished an experienced infantry-man from a crowd of new men or REMFs (rear-echelon motherfuckers). It was east to figure how much time a grunt had spent in the bush by the number and age of the scars on his body from his grind in the bush.

The jungle was alive with insects, spiders, snakes, and other weird-looking critters crawling on the ground or sitting on the leaves and branches around us. The rain made it easy to spot the huge spider webs. When someone spotted a snake, each man quickly passed on the word "Snake!" I don't think any of us youngsters knew a poisonous snake from a nonpoisonous one — we feared them all.

As we moved forward, Clipper started jumping up and down like crazy as if he had stepped on hot coals. I looked down at him dancing around, groaning, and furiously biting at his paws. The point man had apparently stepped on a decaying log, crushing it open, and hundreds of large wingless insects swarmed out. Clipper had stepped right on them and they attacked. I leaped over the log, pulling Clipper away and brushed off as many bugs as I could, stomping on the ground to keep the disturbed insects from climbing up my boots and pant legs.

I moved to the side and let the others pass. A soldier stopped to help me get the bugs off Clipper. Eventually, Clipper calmed down, so we moved on to catch up to the man with the machete. I'm sure that if Clipper could talk, he'd have asked me for some boots to wear and a soothing chopper ride back home.

The rain had finally stopped. There was still no sign of Charlie. All I heard were birds and flying insects and the sounds of grunts slapping exposed skin to kill mosquitoes and other bugs. The sound of the machete cutting through vegetation became less frequent as the jungle thinned out. The platoon leader decided to halt so we could take a brief lunch break. Flank guards were posted, and machine guns were manned to the front and rear of the column.

Scout dog Clipper being playful after a job well done, 1967
(author collection).

I sat on the wet jungle floor, my back against a big tree. Clipper didn't seem to mind my examining him for bugs and bites. He had lots of bite marks on the tender areas of his paws. I took out Clipper's steel comb and ran it through his furry back and neck, which helped clear off the bugs. Clipper enjoyed being groomed. I found some bloated, peanut-sized purple wood ticks attached to his skin. I lit a cigarette and used its red-hot tip to burn them off. Clipper was happy to be rid of those little pests. He would get a dip in a vat of medicine when we got home.

I expressed my love for Clipper by hugging him and telling him that he was doing a good job and was very brave. I gave him fresh water and a package of dog food. He showed his appreciation by licking all over my filthy, sweaty face. After nourishing himself, he lay down on his side, leaning against me, and licked his sore paws. I ate a jungle-temperature can of ham and lima beans and washed it down with some cool water. The smell of American cigarette smoke filled the air.

Glancing around, I saw steam rising from damp jungle fatigues. Squad leaders quietly moved about, making sure that we were all okay and that we buried our trash. All too soon, the order was given to saddle up. I spotted the radioman next to a tree, the lieutenant at his side talking into the handset.

A West Point graduate, the lieutenant possessed impressive leadership skills. He walked and talked with the confidence of an organized and well-trained officer. When he spoke, his squad leaders listened and obeyed his instructions. I preferred being with a unit that had that kind of discipline. As a "scout-dog team for hire," it was the nature of our job to work with many units. I found that the organizational structure was pretty much the same from unit to unit, but the leadership and discipline ranged from poor to outstanding.

As a scout-dog handler it was hard for me to get to know anyone in the field very well, and working with that platoon was no different; names just didn't seem to stick in my head for long. But one thing that made me welcome was that the grunts loved to see and pet my dog. Clipper gave them some comfort by offering up his paw when they'd say, "Shake!"

Kenny Mook had been my first best buddy in Vietnam with the 7th Cavalry. Now Clipper was my new best friend during my second tour.

Since the vegetation was easy enough to navigate without a machete man, I took the position of point man with Clipper in the lead. I directed the flank guards not to get ahead of Clipper, explaining that they would diminish his scouting effectiveness. Clipper slowly picked his way through the jungle as I watched his head and ears for any sign of an alert.

Clipper alerted and stopped moving; his ears were up high. As the rest of the platoon got down, the platoon leader sent a fire team to investigate. They returned with a negative report. As Clipper and I continued forward, he alerted a second time. Suddenly, something came dashing and crashing low in the brush a few feet in front of us. Clipper quickly jumped to one side and I flinched with surprise. Before I knew it, whatever had crossed our path had disappeared into the jungle.

After Clipper's next alert, the platoon leader decided to send out a patrol to sweep a wider area to the front. The fire team returned and reported finding the edge of a base camp with well-worn trails directly ahead. The platoon leader came up to my position, said I was doing a good job, and gave Clipper a pat on the head. I followed the men cautiously stepping through the jungle at the edge of the base camp. The second squad was right behind us; the rest of the platoon remained in reserve.

I had a flashback to the time I had followed the platoon leader to check out a bunker along the Cambodian border. He had been killed directly in front of me. That wasn't such a good memory to dwell on at the moment, so I tried to erase it from my mind.

A soldier signaled me to move up. Clipper led the way. We were now a few short steps inside the edge of a Vietcong base camp. Weapons at the ready, the first squad spread out and carefully penetrated its interior.

Enemy base camps varied in size depending on their purpose and how much of a force they housed. Some camps were used as training sites for local guerrillas, while others were fortresses. For the most part, VC camps were underground, and few exposed signs betrayed their existence. The vegetation was carefully cleared away, leaving a few paths. The jungle floor of the camp we now explored had recently been disturbed, but there were no occupants.

Clipper alerted wildly, but there were too many soldiers moving all around for me to get too excited. The VC base camp appeared to be about one acre in size, and could probably accommodate a company-sized unit of fifty to a hundred soldiers. It had "spider holes" — tiny bunkers — all around and well-trodden paths throughout. Even though it appeared empty, it was much used. Charlie could spring up at any time. Clipper and I continued the search; two other soldiers followed us for security.

A soldier found a pile of Chinese grenades inside one of the bunkers. I knew from experience never to touch an isolated pile of enemy grenades because it could be the last thing you ever touched. Someone used C-Ration toilet paper to mark that bunker, warning others to leave the grenades alone. Those primitive black-powder grenades had cast-iron heads, shaped like tiny pineapples, attached to hollow bamboo handles with strings hanging out of them. Pull the string, toss the grenade by the handle, and — BOOM! These grenades worked well enough, but American grenades had a more complex design and were much deadlier.

Clipper alerted to something on the ground and started sniffing at a clump of cut branches. I recognized it as a cover for something hidden below. I pulled Clipper away in case it was booby trapped. I motioned everyone nearby to seek cover. From behind a tree, I used a bamboo stick to move the brush away, and was thankful not to trigger an explosion. As I peered from behind the tree I realized that what Clipper had found was a buried fifty-gallon drum full of what looked like crushed green weeds. As I approached it, I smelled marijuana. I couldn't believe it — Clipper had discovered Charlie's pot stash!

Word quickly spread throughout the platoon about a cache of marijuana. No one said anything when some of the grunts grabbed handfuls of weed and stuffed their pockets. Everybody who came by wanted to know who had found the stash. Well, Clipper was the hero once again. It really didn't take much to excite a bunch of grunts.

The platoon leader got on the radio, reported the findings through the camp, and then ordered the marijuana destroyed. One squad leader stuck a flare down inside the drum of weed and ignited it. The scent of pot smoke carried all through the base camp. I got out of there before it could get me high, and I wasn't sure how Clipper's senses would be affected if he got loaded.

After we completed our search, we moved a safe distance from the base camp. The bunkers containing war supplies were blown up with C-4 (plastic explosive). The force of the explosions scattered dirt and debris all around us, but no one got hurt.

The lieutenant called for a spotter round of artillery so he could pinpoint our location. A bit later an artillery round whistled through the air and exploded a few hundred yards away. Satisfied, the platoon leader marked his map; the coordinates could be used later to destroy the VC base camp with an artillery barrage or a bombing run.

The vegetation thinned as Clipper and I moved out on point. Flank guards were posted about ten yards on either side of the column. We departed without incident and soon reached a small clearing. It was getting too late to travel, so the lieutenant decided we should set up camp there for the evening. Clipper and I took up a position inside the perimeter near the platoon leader's CP (command post).

Half the platoon had to be awake through the night. The lieutenant was hoping the VC would pass our way on their return to their base camp. Clipper remained alert, but nothing out of the ordinary happened that night.

In the morning, Clipper and I assumed the point position and slowly moved through a heavily wooded area with knee-high undergrowth. Clipper stopped at the edge of a tiny clearing with ankle-high grass and a small tree near its center. I followed Clipper as he edged forward. When he reached the tree, his sprang up and over me as if he had been launched from a catapult. He let out a loud yelp. I hit the ground, thinking that Clipper must have been hit.

As I lay there, Clipper stood on his hind legs, his right forepaw stretched high above him. He twisted and turned, trying to get loose from something that was suspending him. No shots had been fired. I was totally confused, but soon realized that Clipper had been caught in an animal snare. I released his right paw and checked him; he was shaken but not injured.

Turning around, I saw two soldiers lying on the ground, shaking their heads in laughter. I was totally embarrassed for Clipper's misstep and hurried to the other side of the clearing to continue the mission. As we walked, I kept wondering what had happened back there. *How could Clipper step into an animal snare? We had so much trip-wire training. Did the pot smoke impair his senses?*

Clipper had just made a mistake, I thought *So what? It happens to everyone. What about me and that after-shave lotion in the Ia Drang Valley, or the time I almost killed the squad leaders by accidentally discharging my M16 on full auto? Besides, Clipper's a dog, not a robot.*

Most important, no one had been hurt. I realized that I couldn't blame Clipper. I needed to clear my mind of such thoughts and stay focused. A lot of people were depending on us.

The platoon leader stopped us at the edge of a rubber plantation and reset the tactical formation for movement through the wide rows of trees. I felt relieved when no one said anything to me about what had happened with Clipper and the animal trap. The squad leaders spread their men out and moved flank guards to the far right and left wings of the main body.

Continuing to walk point, Clipper and I passed row after row of rubber trees. It was quiet and there were no Vietnamese working that sector of trees. We knew that all hamlets had to be approached with caution, but we were under orders not to fire inside a hamlet for fear of wounding or killing noncombatants.

About a hundred yards into our advance, there were several explosions in the near distance, followed by small-arms fire. The platoon leader halted us. I looked back and saw him talking on the radio; then he started running and passed me. He pumped his fist up and down over his head and yelled, "Double-time! Double-time!"

The entire platoon started running to keep up. That pace didn't last long, because the weight of our heavy packs forced us to slow somewhat. Squad leaders shouted to their troops to stay alert.

When Clipper came upon a steep ravine with a creek running below, we abruptly halted. A narrow footpath led to a log that bridged the creek. The platoon leader directed two riflemen to cross the log first and provide cover while the rest of us crossed.

Clipper cautiously stepped onto the log, and crouched low as he stepped forward across it. I gave him enough slack in the leash and followed close behind. It took us a little longer than the others to inch across, but we made it. I was so glad that I had Clipper in a harness. If he'd slipped and fallen, I could easily have hoisted him back up, but if I'd had a choke chain around his neck and he fell, it could have snapped his neck. When we got to the other side, I gave Clipper a big hug and praised him for a job well done. There was no doubt that training Clipper on the log crossing in base camp had helped.

Clipper and I assumed the point position, with the platoon leader, his RTO, and two riflemen directly behind us. The rest of the platoon spread out in a tactical formation to the left, right, and rear. Clipper gave a strong alert to our right front, then stopped and stood rigid, head and ears pointing to the right. I quickly took a knee, looked in that direction, and spotted troop movement about a hundred yards away through the rubber trees. Immediately, I praised Clipper, "Good boy, Clipper! Good boy!"

The platoon leader got on the radio and we learned that our sister platoon was in the near distance to our front. Clipper had spotted the troop movement. I tapped the bottom of the twenty-round magazine to ensure it was properly seated in my CAR-15, and yanked Clipper's leash to motion him to move out.

It was quiet as we penetrated deeper into the trees. When I reached the rear guard of our sister platoon, the platoon leader stopped me from going any farther. We'd arrived twenty minutes after first hearing the sound of shooting; crossing the creek had taken most of that time. We stayed put while the platoon leader headed in search of the platoon's command post.

I sat next to an infantryman from the other platoon and asked what had happened. He told me that his platoon had been moving through the rubber trees when they unknowingly entered a kill zone of concealed VC who had triggered command-detonated mines. The blast had killed several of their troops instantly and wounded several others. He said the rest of the platoon had fired in the direction of the explosions, but Charlie never returned fire. The platoon's advance was halted while they awaited medevac and reinforcements.

I saw gunships and slicks in the air. Several landed on a road not far from us to pick up the dead and wounded. When the platoon leader returned, he changed our mission, ordering us to merge with another platoon and sweep through the hamlet ahead. There was a possibility that the VC who had detonated those mines might still be hiding among the women and children who lived in the hamlet. We were not to shoot while inside the village unless we had a clear target of aggression. I noticed that the nearby area of rubber trees had been well worked by the Vietnamese; there was little or no grass or weeds between the rows.

Weapons at the ready, we moved cautiously through the tress, scanning for signs of danger. I stepped on something that felt weird and rubbery under my boot. I looked down and saw a human hand, but didn't stop to think about it. I had to keep moving until I reached the outer perimeter of the lead platoon.

The infantrymen were spread throughout the trees. We weren't far from the hamlet. Clipper's ears perked up when a soldier to my right yelled, "Hey, dog-man, check out the bomb lying against the trunk of that rubber tree."

I glanced at the tree trunk and saw a huge warhead at its base. The soldier told me that his platoon had discovered it after having been hit by the mines. He explained that the VC probably hadn't had time to rig it as a booby trap or they'd have already detonated it. Instead, an American soldier had booby-trapped it for the VC. If anyone tried to move it or tamper with it, that bomb would explode. Clipper couldn't stop alerting on that booby trap until he'd completely lost sight of it as we moved away.

When we arrived at the hamlet, Vietnamese women and children quickly came out of their straw-roofed huts to greet us. Clipper became agitated; he growled as they approached. I held him back as the other soldiers entered the village. I held my finger on the safety lever of my weapon just in case I had to flick the switch. More soldiers arrived and began a search for the VC who'd detonated the mines. As they searched, I heard someone inside one of the huts shout, "You VC? You kill Americans? Where VC? Bullshit! You lie!"

A thorough search revealed only the hiding places of women, children, and old men. We couldn't figure out where the VC hid — it was like trying to track a ghost. Maybe it was one of the women or old men who had detonated the mines. I trusted no one!

The residents of the hamlet were confused and afraid of what we might do to them. The Vietnamese were scared of Clipper, so I stayed a safe distance away and didn't participate in the search for fear that Clipper might bite someone. I decided to take advantage of Clipper's aggressive behavior and use him as a guard against anyone trying to leave the village.

Several of the Vietnamese women and old men were taken into custody and loaded into choppers for further interrogation in Dau Tieng.

When the village situation calmed down, a few Vietnamese women with baskets of bananas moved quickly past Clipper and me and offered the fruit to the American troops.

I was among the first group of soldiers ordered to leave the village and move across the dirt road and into the rubber trees for our final push to Dau Tieng. Once in the trees, the troops were spread out in a sweeping formation to cover a lot of ground in our hunt for the enemy. After Clipper and I moved past a few rows of trees, we were ordered to stop and hold our position.

We waited several minutes while the rest of the platoon departed the hamlet to join us. Finally, the signal was given to move out again. Clipper and I slowly moved between the rows of rubber trees; troops spread out to our left, right, and rear.

As Clipper and I passed between two trees, there was a shattering explosion to our immediate right. I hit the ground and dragged Clipper down beside me. We didn't hear any shots being fired, but then I heard the sounds of a hurt soldier not far from me. I quickly crawled over to him. He lay on his back, rocking in pain, his legs and boots covered with blood.

I yelled, "Medic! Medic!"

When the medic arrived, he cut the young black soldier's boots off and treated the wounds on his legs and feet. Looking around on the ground, I discovered a broken tripwire attached to a short stick stuck in the ground. The other end of the wire was tied to a rubber tree. I immediately thought, *That could have been me if I;d moved one more tree over. Would Clipper have alerted on that booby trap?"* I'd never know the answer.

After the helicopter had evacuated the injured soldier, I told the platoon leader that I'd take the lead. I asked him to move the rest of the platoon into a column and follow behind my dog's lead. I didn't give the platoon leader a chance to respond as I quickly turned and took the lead. Clipper had demonstrated that he could detect trip-wired booby traps in a mock training situation. Now, he'd be tested to detect them here or more of these men would be injured or killed.

I glanced behind and noticed that the platoon leader had ordered the troops to form a single column behind us.

I thought, *Clipper's in charge now, even if he doesn't realize it. If anyone can do it, Clipper can get us through this area and safely home.*

With the outer perimeter of the Dau Tieng base camp less than a half-mile ahead, I kept my attention glued to Clipper's head and ears while he guided me forward. Clipper gave a faint alert to the left, briefly hesitated, and then moved right. I glanced in that direction and saw nothing, so I didn't stop. I had to trust Clipper's movements through the overgrown knee-high weeds and thick grass below his head. It was easy to walk through, and Clipper had no problem negotiating a path.

Clipper gave another weak alert to his right and then moved left. He performed that maneuver again and again without much hesitation or stopping. A short time later a voice from behind ordered me to halt. As

I looked back, I saw a long column of American troops snaked through the rubber trees behind me. We stopped just briefly and then moved out again. That stop-and-go situation occurred several times during the journey. I wasn't sure why we were stopping. No one behind me said anything, and I didn't ask. They could have been checking something out or reviewing the map for direction of travel or someone may have spotted tripwires or booby traps.

I didn't think Clipper's alerts were strong enough for me to stop and worry about danger. The way he was moving was deliberate and I saw nothing out of the ordinary. I decided to keep my eyes on Clipper instead of trying to figure out why he was walking the way he was. I was grateful that there had been no more explosions. So far, Clipper had led us on a safe path.

We finally reached the outskirts of Dau Tieng's base camp. I stopped short of the concertina wire and spotted soldiers staring at us from the other side standing next to their bunkers. I dropped to one knee and waited for the rest of the platoon to catch up. My right knee was aching again, but I knew that I'd soon be safe inside the K-9 compound.

While I rubbed my right knee, several soldiers caught up with us. One of them stopped and told me to wait for the platoon leader. Another soldier smiled as he passed by. The soldiers moved along the fence of concertina wire in a column toward the base camp's entrance gate.

The lieutenant I had worked with throughout the mission had finally showed up. I stood up to greet him. He smiled and thanked me for getting his men through all the other booby traps. Then he knelt and gave Clipper a hug and told him what a great dog he was.

I was puzzled, so I asked, "What other booby traps, sir?"

The platoon leader looked at me as though I should have known the answer to that question. He told me that when Clipper had changed directions for the first time, one of his men had spotted a grenade tied to the base of a rubber tree with a wire leading to another tree.

He stated, "After you and your dog changed directions several times, my men got wise to what was going on so they started searching for booby traps. The times we had stopped were used to mark the booby traps Clipper had avoided." He explained that the marked booby traps would be detonated after the entire company was safely through the area.

I finally realized that Clipper's deliberate changes in direction were to avoid the booby traps and tripwires. I hadn't seen any of them because I didn't stop to search. Then I remembered that Clipper had performed that maneuver of going around the tripwires when he didn't feel like sitting in front of them during our training session.

The platoon leader told me that it was brave to take the lead when I didn't have to. He said, "If it hadn't been for Clipper some of my men could have been wounded or killed. I'm going to recommend you and Clipper for the Bronze Star." The lieutenant shook my hand and as he walked away, turned to me and said, "I'm going to ask for you and Clipper the next time I need a scout."

That was the finest compliment Clipper and I ever received for doing our job.

I smiled, waved, and gave the lieutenant a thumbs-up. I looked down at Clipper and tapped my chest. Clipper jumped up and rested his front paws on my shoulders. I looked into his big brown eyes and gave him a strong bear hug. I told him what a great warrior he was and how proud I felt to have him as my friend and scout.

I thought about the lieutenant's words. That was the first time anyone had ever wanted to recommend me for a medal. I felt honored but knew that all the credit belonged to Clipper. He'd been the hero that day. I was the lucky guy behind the leash and grateful to have such a wonderful companion to lead us to safety. I felt that there was nothing more valuable or rewarding than knowing that others had lived because of my dog. My trust and confidence in Clipper dramatically increased that day.

On the other hand, I knew the army didn't award medals or badges to war dogs for exceptional performance of duty or for bravery and heroism in combat. The army officially recognized scout dogs only as military combat equipment. In four months, I'd be rotating back to the

States. Clipper, on the other hand, didn't have a rotation date; his orders were to serve his country in Vietnam for the rest of the war. I didn't want to believe the naked truth about what Clipper's fate would be.

What the hell do army brass and politicians know about Clipper and how he's risked his life to save others? I thought. Clipper was a soldier, not a piece of equipment. He knew what he'd been trained to do, and he was a hell of a lot more responsive and trustworthy in carrying out his duties than many of the humans I'd met during the war.

How did the army know what my dog was mentally and physically capable of? How many lives would Clipper have to save to be recognized as something more than gear? I thought it was cruel and unjust to punish a dog by making him walk point for the entire war. The army had recruited and trained Clipper to save lives. Shouldn't they treat him with respect and give him a rotation date home too? These were questions I could never ask out loud. A lowly grunt, I had to follow orders and never question the decisions made by people at higher levels of authority. I pondered Clipper's fate.

"Thanks for another safe mission, Clipper!"

Chapter 18

The Capture

IT WAS EARLY in the morning when Clipper and I got an assignment to report to Company A, 2nd Battalion, 12th Infantry. Brigade intelligence had reported that an NVA courier routinely traveled, sometimes alone, between the provinces of Tay Ninh and Dau Tieng. They wanted him captured and brought back for interrogation.

I quickly got my stuff together and fetched Clipper from his run. When he saw that I had my field gear strapped on my back and my helmet on, he wagged his tail, ready to go. We reported to the mission patrol leader, a lieutenant, who showed me his field map marked with the most likely places to trap and bag our target without killing him. I thought it was the type of mission usually assigned to a long-range reconnaissance patrol (LRRP). Maybe they were busy with other missions, so the 2/12 infantry got the job. What did I know?

Choppers lifted us off at the crack of dawn, and we headed toward the majestic Black Virgin Mountain, an inactive volcano. *Nui Ba Den,* as the Vietnamese called it, jutted up from the ground about 3,000 feet, towering over Tay Ninh Province, about eighty miles west of Saigon. Its steep summit, capped with a dense green blanket of rugged jungle, was usually shrouded by clouds and mist. The highest peak in the area, Nui Ba Den was easily seen from miles around.

The majestic and massive Black Virgin Mountain (Nui Ba Dinh) seen from atop a lookout tower in base camp, 1967 (author collection).

The U.S. Army 5th Special Forces Group had captured the summit in 1964. When we flew close, we could see the 25th Infantry Signal Corp's VHF and FM relay-station towers and some other tall antennas atop the mountain. The signal corps relayed communications between units of the 25th Infantry Division located in Cu Chi, Tay Ninh, and Dau Tieng—the Iron Triangle. The summit of Nui Ba Den was heavily fortified and appeared nearly impossible to reach by foot from below. The VC used the lower slopes as observation posts and radio-relay positions, and constantly harassed the American troops stationed on top with sniper fire and mortar attacks, and fired on those in the jungle valley below as well.

Four combat infantry platoons were assigned to the mission to capture the enemy courier. Each had a separate area to reconnoiter for suitable ambush sites. I didn't know why I was the only dog handler assigned to the mission; we could have used four scout-dog teams, one attached to each combat platoon.

Green smoke signaled a safe landing in a small clearing less than a mile from the base of Nui Ba Den. We quickly moved away from the aircraft and under the cover of the jungle. The patrol leader motioned me to take the lead. Clipper and I moved into the jungle, which wasn't too dense to navigate, and were soon about a hundred feet ahead of everyone else.

The patrol leader frequently signaled me to stop while he checked the map for the location and distance to a trail we were trying to reach. For several hours we cautiously moved parallel to Nui Ba Den. Clipper eventually gave a strong alert, ears and head held high. I stopped, dropped to a knee, and motioned the nearest man forward. A three-man fire team was dispatched to check out the alert. On returning, they reported a well-used trail less than 200 feet ahead. The patrol leader moved up to my position and evaluated the map coordinates; according to his map we were on target.

Clipper and I quietly approached the trail under the cover of the surrounding vegetation. The platoon didn't yet want to risk exposure by getting on the trail, and I didn't want them to get ahead of me for fear that their scent and movement would reduce the effectiveness of Clipper's alerts. We moved quietly, using all the proper methods of a successful patrol: radio silence, camouflage, and concealment.

Eventually, we set up an ambush alongside a fork where two narrow trails intersected. The spot provided excellent concealment and lines of sight in either direction. The platoon leader strategically positioned each man about five feet inside the surrounding vegetation. Clipper and I were positioned at the end of the ambush, which gave Clipper the best chance to alert if any VC came down the trail.

The plan was to surprise and capture the courier. We sat silently waiting, swatting mosquitoes and killing bugs, ants, and spiders. It reminded me of a spider waiting in its web for prey. As the hours passed, the sky darkened until it was pitch-black. We stayed alert in stationary positions all night, but nothing happened.

John Burnam taking a break at the ambush site near
Black Virgin Mountain, 1967 (author collection).

As dawn chased the shadows away, the men stirred. No one was allowed to light cigarettes because the smoke might alert the enemy. Of course, we didn't really know whether Charlie had already located us, or whether we'd succeed in ambushing the courier.

As the light brightened, Clipper suddenly alerted toward the trail. I immediately informed the man next to me, who passed the warning down the line. I spotted the target of Clipper's alert: an NVA soldier in khaki uniform and straw hat, riding a bicycle, a rifle slung over his back.

I got a major adrenaline rush as I watched the enemy get closer and closer, realizing that I was the first man he'd reach. Clipper remained silent and fully alert on the target, ready to pounce. The enemy soldier appeared to be alone and relaxed. He had two canvas bags draped over his bike's rear fender. *This must be our man,* I thought.

When the courier was right in front of me, I turned Clipper loose; he darted into the road, lunged, and knocked the NVA soldier off his bike. The man landed on his back. I gave Clipper the command "Watch him!" Clipper growled and showed his teeth but didn't attack. The enemy soldier looked so completely surprised that I thought his eyeballs were going to pop out of his head. Immediately, the rest of the patrol surrounded the man, weapons pointed at him. Clipper's growling and barking kept the frightened man squirming on his back in the dirt. A soldier quickly stripped him of his rifle.

I handed my CAR-15 and Clipper's leash to the nearest soldier and told him to hold back the dog. Remembering my wrestling days, I was convinced that I could contain the prisoner without using a weapon. I reached down and rolled him onto his stomach, straddled his body, and spread his arms and legs. He was so scared that he pissed his pants while I searched him.

In one of his pockets I found a worn Zippo lighter engraved with the 1st Infantry Division shoulder patch and the slogan "Big Red One." As far as I knew, the Big Red One didn't operate near Tay Ninh province; I thought they were way up north. The canvas bags attached to the bicycle were filled with Vietnamese currency and documents. I was sure we had the NVA courier that army intelligence was so eager to get their hands on. I didn't want to think how this North Vietnamese soldier had gotten that lighter. *The bastard must have taken it off a dead American,* I thought.

We were expected to take weapons, ammunition, and military documents from the enemy wounded or killed. What was disgraceful to me was robbing a dead man of his personal effects to keep as souvenirs. Vietnam was a brutal and ugly war that destroyed thousands of human lives and left grieving families from both sides in its aftermath.

I was in complete control of the prisoner now. If he tried to escape, I'd tackle and pin him in a wrestling hold he couldn't wriggle out of, or I could command Clipper to attack. *There's no damn way that guy's getting away,* I thought, my blood boiling. I was hoping he'd try to resist or escape; if he did, I'd have an excuse to vent my rage thinking he had robbed a fallen American soldier, but the prisoner was too scared to move a muscle or show an expression of defiance.

After I completed the body search, two other soldiers took over. They tied the man's hands behind his back, taped his mouth shut, and blindfolded him. The patrol leader radioed for a chopper to get him out of the area immediately. Under cover of the jungle, we hustled to the pickup point. Several choppers arrived, and flew my platoon and our prisoner back to Dau Tieng.

I was grateful that Clipper and I had accomplished another mission and there'd been no American casualties. I hoped that all my future missions in Vietnam would be that successful, but I knew that was just wishful thinking.

Chapter 19

Beau, Ringo, and Base-camp Lore

RETURNING TO BASE CAMP after a mission was always a welcome comfort. Our K-9 Klub was the best place for everyone to unwind and try to have some peace from the war outside the wire.

Huddled within the wooden buildings of our sleeping area, the K-9 Klub served as mailroom and lounge. It was modestly furnished with tables, chairs, a refrigerator, a bar, and a portable air conditioner. Screened-in windows covered with sheets of clear plastic kept the cool air inside and the bugs out. The club was even wired for electricity to accommodate some modest but important morale-lifting conveniences.

Good and sad times about family, girlfriends, and activity back home were always hot topics of conversation. Some guys bragged about all the girls waiting for them; others talked of going to college, getting a job, and starting a business. Nobody voiced aspirations of making army life a career.

The *Stars and Stripes* newspaper reported the war's current events throughout Vietnam. Many of the dog handlers passed time reading books, outdated magazines, and hometown newspapers. We played cards and drank canned soda pop and Ballantine and Pabst Blue Ribbon beer. We especially enjoyed Kool-Aid, because it spiced up the nasty taste of the local water supply.

Sergeant Way, dog handler, 44th Scout Dogs, and an American Red Cross volunteer enter the K-9 Klub, 1967 (author collection).

News of our fellow dog handlers and friends who were in hospitals recovering from wounds was always a topic of major interest to everyone. Kentucky, wounded during the kennel attack, was wounded a second time, shot in the buttocks by a VC sniper during a search-and-destroy mission. Another dog handler, Randy Cox, was severely burned while he and his dog rode inside an armored personnel carrier that was hit by an enemy rocket. Randy's dog had died from his injuries. Randy was evacuated to a burn unit in the States and never returned to active military service.

Beau

In May 1967 there was a story in the 3rd Brigade's newspaper about fellow dog handler Mike Phillips and his scout dog Beau. Mike was a twenty-year-old, curly-haired redhead from Cleveland. Beau, his German shepherd partner, had an aggressive attitude. They trained together at the Scout Dog Training Center in Fort Benning, Georgia, and arrived in Vietnam with the original members of the 44th Scout Dog Platoon in January 1967. Both had tasted the bitterness of war.

According to the story, Beau had been wounded on two occasions, the first during a three-day mission. Phillips and Beau had been scouting for an infantry unit near a large clearing when Beau alerted. Phillips had immediately recognized the danger, signaled the men behind him, and dived for cover. The Vietcong opened fire, but Beau's alert had halted the American patrol short of the enemy's kill zone.

During the ensuing firefight, a round from an AK-47 struck Beau in the front leg. Phillips protected Beau by covering him with his body while returning fire. The Americans, who suffered only light casualties in that battle, defeated the enemy. If not for Beau's alert, American casualties could have been much greater. Beau's wound wasn't grave, and Doc Glydon patched him up.

Mike and Beau were back in action for Operation Junction City in a rugged area of War Zone C. Sitting in a clearing, the two were preparing to move out when enemy mortar rounds began exploding all around them. During the attack, Beau and Phillips were wounded. A piece of shrapnel passed completely through Beau's middle, breaking his backbone. Another piece of shrapnel pierced Phillips' right arm. Beau's wound was so serious that he was evacuated to a hospital in Saigon. In Dau Tieng a death certificate was filed because no one expected Beau to survive, let alone rejoin the 44th Scout Dog Platoon. Beau was a tough dog, however, and refused to give up. He made it through the surgery and was rehabilitated back to health. A month later, Beau returned to duty with the 44th. His death certificate was torn up and thrown away.

Ringo

I knew that Ollie and Mac and a few other dog handlers sometimes worked their dogs off leash without having any control problems in the field. Roger Jones also liked to work Ringo off leash on combat missions. In fact, Roger had won the Trainee-of-the-Cycle award at the scout-dog training school in Fort Benning in late 1966. Nonetheless, I preferred to work Timber and Clipper on leash during missions.

Official copy of a report of the 44th Scout Dogs Operations for Operations Diamondhead and Uniontown for the month of June 1967 (document courtesy of Mike McClellan).

In June 1967, Roger and Ringo were leading an infantry platoon on a combat mission. Ringo was working off leash ahead of Roger when he alerted and a firefight broke out. Startled by the close exchange of fire, Ringo bolted and disappeared into the jungle. Roger returned to base camp without him. Lieutenant Fenner and Bob "Doc" Glydon were accountable for every scout dog and handler, and were furious when Roger returned without Ringo. After a debriefing, a "Report of Survey" form was filed charging Roger with suspicion of negligence. It could have resulted in court-martial proceedings, but Roger was never punished because the incident was kept in-house.

A few weeks after Roger had lost Ringo in the field, the local *Stars and Stripes* paper carried the story of a wounded German shepherd who had followed an American combat patrol into the Cu Chi base camp According to the story, the dog—badly wounded in the jaw, dehydrated, and hungry—had survived several days on his own, hiding in the jungle. The dog had been taken for medical attention to the 38th Scout Dog Platoon, a sister dog platoon based at Cu Chi, about sixty miles from Ringo's home base in Dau Tieng. Because each dog had a serial number tattooed in the left ear, Doc Glydon was able to verify that the wounded dog was Ringo, Roger's missing scout dog.

Ringo had suffered a close-range gunshot wound in the face. The bullet entered one side of his jaw and exited the other. Ringo was evacuated to Saigon where he underwent a special operation performed by an expert military dental surgeon. Roger flew to Saigon to attend his dog through the successful surgery. A month later, Roger and Ringo returned home to the 44th. Ringo eventually recovered from his wounds, though missing a piece of his tongue.

For surviving his wound, evading the enemy by hiding in the bush, and then only showing himself to an American patrol that had passed close by, Ringo was our hero. We admired the courage and strength it had taken for Ringo to escape and evade being captured and killed.

Base-camp Lore

Staff Sergeant Barnett and Ringo after Ringo's return from surgery in Saigon. Note that part of Ringo's tongue is missing, 1967 (photo courtesy of Ban Barnett).

Dog handlers had unique ways of expressing their individuality. For example, my hooch-mate, Dan Scott, always had a book sticking out of his back pocket because he liked to read every chance he got. After dropping out of Officer Candidate School, Scott was reassigned to scout-dog training. Upon graduation, he was shipped to Vietnam and assigned to the 44th in March 1967, the same month that I returned to Vietnam for my second tour of duty.

Scott had somehow acquired a WWII relic: a twenty-five-inch-long 45-caliber machine gun commonly called a grease gun. Although .45-caliber ammunition was standard issue through our supply channels, Dan had also acquired several thirty-round clips to go along with his new weapon, which was designed to be slung from a shoulder strap and fired from the hip with one hand.

Lieutenant Fenner didn't seem to mind that some of his men preferred weapons other than the standard-issue CAR-15 or M16. Mac

McClellan insisted on carrying his M1 rifle in the field and wouldn't trade it for anything else. He said it was more reliable: it fired when needed and didn't jam like the M16.

Specialist Four Mike "Mac" McClellan and Achates
inside the 44th Scout Dogs kennel area, 1967
(photo courtesy of Mike McClellan).

Scott toted his grease gun on every mission, swearing that it never jammed. It didn't have a semiautomatic selector switch like the CAR-15 because it was designed to fire on full automatic. I didn't think that grease gun could hit the side of a barn beyond twenty feet, but everyone agreed that if the bullets didn't kill the enemy, the noise would scare them to death.

A sense of humor was not only a way of expressing one's personality but also of just having some fun. One day, Scott stood outside my hooch and called, "Hey, Burnam! Get out here. I have something to show you!"

Scott was holding two jars in his hands: In one was the largest centipede I'd ever seen; in the other was a monster scorpion. Before long, several other dog handlers gathered around while Scott placed the two jars on the ground. We started placing bets on which of the critters would survive in a fight. I put my money on the scorpion because it looked meaner. When all the bets were in — about fifty-fifty on scorpion and centipede — Scott emptied the jars and forced the critters into a fight. It didn't last long: Less than a minute into the first round, the centipede killed the scorpion. I lost my bet.

We all fantasized about girls, and fellow scout-dog handler Bill Zantos found a unique way of finding a girlfriend. Two local Vietnamese women, both of whom we referred to as Mama San, operated a laundry and boot-shine service in a large military canvas tent across the road from the K-9 compound. A chalkboard listed the prices they charged for each laundry item as well as the cost of boot polishing. We used Military Pay Currency, or paper money, to pay our laundry bills.

One of the older Vietnamese women who worked in the laundry tent took a shine to Bill Zantos. Compared to the rest of us, Bill had a robust body, which quickly earned him the nickname Heavy. When the dog handlers found out that Heavy was doing the boom-boom thing with one of the Mama Sans in the back of the laundry tent, they had a great time poking fun at him. Fortunately, Bill had a good sense of humor and laughed right along with us.

★

The 44th set up a volleyball net between two rubber trees inside the K-9 compound. The game gave us some exercise and helped take our minds off our troubles. There always seemed to be plenty of dog handlers who wanted to play, and we played for hours, shirtless, in the shade of the mature rubber trees.

About once a week, Charlie launched mortar rounds at the Dau Tieng airstrip, firing from the small mountains north of the K-9 compound. We quickly learned that the maximum range of these mortar rounds brought them about 200 yards short of the volleyball court, so whenever we heard mortars exploding on the airstrip, we'd stop the volleyball game and watch the fireworks.

Since the shrapnel from the mortar rounds never reached us during those random daytime attacks, we didn't need to run and seek shelter in the bunkers. Most of the shells exploded in and around the runway, sending the helicopters scrambling to get airborne. During each mortar attack, Dau Tieng sounded a siren like the one used for an air raid. The attacks never lasted long — they were just Charlie's way of saying hello!

Occasionally, Charlie would get lucky and blow up a helicopter or ground vehicle or hit a building near the runway. American retaliatory strikes were immediate: Our gunships were airborne instantly. With a vengeance, the Americans would fire volley after volley of artillery rounds. The infantry would patrol on foot to search the rugged mountain terrain. Scout-dog teams would also be sent out to locate Charlie's mortar squads. Once in a while we got lucky and surprised Charlie, killing him and capturing some of his mortar tubes. For the most part, however, that was a game of cat and mouse. Charlie was too smart and usually got away in time, only to return another day and launch more shells. We learned to respect those tenacious little bastards because they were so good at guerrilla warfare.

Fateful Road March for Prince

On September 2, 1967, a hot, humid morning with not a cloud in the sky, Lieutenant Fenner decided that we should go on a road march because he thought we weren't getting enough exercise in camp. He directed the entire platoon of fifteen or so scout-dog teams to assemble. We were to march around the entire perimeter of Dau Tieng. We decided to travel light, with only our helmets, weapons, one canteen of water each, and our dogs on leash. With the hot sun and balmy air, none of us was thrilled with the idea of a road march, but orders were orders, so, shortly after lunch, we formed up in single file.

Heading out of the compound, we must have been a magnificent sight: German shepherds and scout-dog handlers stretched out for a quarter mile. As the platoon moved along the shoulder of the road, I realized it was the first time I'd seen this type of organized activity since my assignment with the sentry-dog platoon in Okinawa, where it was routine to march around in formation. In Vietnam, emphasis wasn't placed on organized training activities; usually, we rested while in base camp and trained at our individual discretion.

Because our base camp wasn't very large, the dogs drew immediate attention as we passed infantry company areas, battalion and brigade headquarters, the field hospital, motor pools, the airstrip, maintenance hangers, and trucks and jeeps driving down the road. We figured we'd be gone just a short time. It must have been 110 degrees that afternoon, and the dusty road offered no cover to protect us from the sun and heat. We marched at a slow pace. In about two hours, the column of scout-dog teams had made a nonstop loop around the entire base camp. The dogs' tongues were just about dragging in the dirt. So were the handlers'.

We were within a few hundred yards of the entrance of our K-9 compound when the worst possible thing happened: Tony Pettingill's dog, Prince, gasped for air and collapsed near the gate. Doc Glydon was unable to revive Prince, who died of dehydration. I watched as Tony, sobbing, cradled Prince in his arms. There was nothing anyone could do for him. Prince was the only casualty of that road march, yet another tragic accident that took the life of a war dog.

We buried Prince in the cemetery inside the K-9 compound next to the dogs that had died before him: Erik, Shadow, Sergeant, 44, Hardcore, and others. The grave markers were starting to add up.

Prince, 44th Scout Dogs, after his handler,
Bob Pettingill, placed him on a stretcher, 1967
(photo courtesy of Ban Barnett).

Chapter 20

Rat Patrol

THE ARMY NEVER LET A GRUNT rest for very long. Even when we were back at base camp between combat missions, we had to pull duty with the 3rd Brigade, 25th Infantry Division's military police detachment. That served to keep us occupied and useful.

Responsible for law and order as well as a ton of other security jobs in and around the Dau Tieng base camp, the MPs also controlled the traffic in and out of the gates. The village of Dau Tieng was off-limits to American grunts at all times; liberty passes to enter the village were never issued (there was nothing to see and nothing worth buying there anyway). The MPs also patrolled inside the village at night.

The primary reason American troops occupied Dau Tieng was because the rubber plantations just happened to be strategically located for military use as a forward firebase and as a buffer between Cambodia and Saigon. It was the third arm of the Iron Triangle. The Song Saigon River, which ran right through the village, was used by the Vietnamese for commerce, fishing, bathing, and transport.

Somehow, the 44th got involved in supporting MP night patrols in Dau Tieng village. Lieutenant Fenner, who maintained the duty roster, made sure that every scout-dog handler was on his list. When we weren't in the field, dog handlers were expected to go on what we dubbed Rat Patrol.

Rat Patrol was never conducted during daylight hours. It started after midnight, and mainly served as a show of force. A scout-dog team would accompany a small detachment of MPs into the village several nights during the week. A dog handler traveled light, carrying a CAR-15, a bandoleer of ammunition, a flashlight, and a few canteens of water for his dog. Instead of steel pots we wore soft flop hats. The MPs carried M16s and .45-caliber pistols as side arms. One MP backpacked a PRC/25 field radio to relay situation reports or call for help if necessary.

The local whorehouse frequented by the Vietnamese soldiers was off-limits to Americans; however, it was one of our checkpoints. An ARVN and an American Military Assistance Command Vietnam (MACV) command post near the center of town was heavily guarded and surrounded by barbed wire and sandbags. The Rat Patrol used it as a pit stop for a cup of coffee and a place to hang out and talk with the American advisers on duty there.

Rat Patrol was conducted with clockwork precision and didn't surprise any of the locals. Every villager knew where we went and how many of us were on the team. The patrol walked the main road and the beaten paths of the village. Every now and then the patrol had to chase someone through the darkness, but the one being chased always seemed to get away.

The Rat Patrol never snuck up on an unsuspecting squad of North Vietnamese Regulars setting up a mortar tube or sitting around smoking pot. Charlie was too slick for that.

The village of Dau Tieng didn't have street lamps, traffic signals, or a town square with a huge lit-up clock. It was a poor town where people lived in small huts and mostly traveled on foot or on bicycles. In their dirt yards, chickens, oxen, pigs, and tiny dogs hung around. There were no paved roads. In fact, everything seemed to be dirt, including the floors inside the homes. Some of the businesses had a more enduring look, heavily influenced by French-style architecture, but there were few permanent-looking structures in Dau Tieng.

We enjoyed going on Rat Patrol for one reason: We could visit the local bakery. Dau Tieng's Vietnamese baker used a primitive brick oven with a cast-iron door to bake small narrow loaves of bread. What a treat it was to smell and taste hot baked rolls at 2:00 a.m. in the darkness. The baker gave us the hot bread; he never charged us for his goods, saying that the Rat Patrol kept the VC from stealing all his bread. Part of a scout-dog handler's mission on Rat Patrol was to bring back some bread for his friends.

I figured MPs were like the local cops back home, but instead of free donuts at the local all-night convenience store, we enjoyed free bread at the local Vietnamese bakery. The only redeeming value of Rat Patrol was bringing home the bread!

Soon, that old wounded knee of mine would force me to leave Clipper for some expert medical help in Cu Chi, which was far from Dau Tieng.

Chapter 21

Cu Chi – PX Driver – Short-Timers

On Christmas Day, 1967, the battalion mess hall served a big turkey lunch with all the trimmings. The past week had seen a major increase in incoming mail and packages from the States. For me, Christmas was another day off from the war, which was a good thing. Any day I didn't have to expose Clipper and me to the enemy was a good day.

I was only a few months away from ending my second tour of duty in Vietnam. I couldn't wait to be processed out when some personnel clerk announced my rotation date. My hope was that the army would get me home in time to celebrate my twenty-first birthday on March 16, 1968. Thinking about leaving Vietnam put me in a good mood that Christmas day.

For Clipper and his pals in the kennel, Christmas was a day like any other day in Vietnam — same old dog food, same old rubber tree, same old water pail, same old kennel run, same old mutts as neighbors. Clipper didn't even know that he had no chance in hell of ever going back to the States with me. That was too depressing a thought, so I didn't talk about it much. Neither did the other dog handlers.

The K-9 Klub was where we all shared care packages from home. Christmas was especially great because of the number of packages we received from the States. Some of them took a real beating during the long trip to Vietnam. The cookies packed in popcorn would arrive crumbled and the cakes mashed and the chocolate bars melted, but they still tasted great and we ate every crumb. We certainly got our share of fruitcakes too. I guess the folks back home figured that fruitcake wouldn't spoil on the long journey. I hated fruitcake, but we were all grateful to receive any care package from home.

✳

Rumor had it that if the United States declared war on North Vietnam, our tours of duty would be extended for the duration of the war. That would have been the biggest of all bummers. I didn't figure I'd last the duration of a full-blown war with North Vietnam. In my line of work, soldiers and dogs walking point and being the first exposed to the enemy got severely wounded or killed sooner or later.

I truly believed that the American ground and air forces could kick ass and take names all the way to Hanoi if they were unchained from all the political war restrictions and allowed to fight to victory. As it stood, our fighting was restricted to the borders of South Vietnam. We also had a fortress mentality, meaning that we operated out of fortified base camps, fought the enemy, and returned to base camps, only to go out another day to the same places and do the same things again and again. It was like continuously mopping up the water from a leaky pipe but never really fixing the plumbing problem.

The defensive perimeter circling the Dau Tieng base camp had to be manned round the clock, even on Christmas. Patrols were scheduled, as a minimum security, to probe right outside the perimeter. This was our only insurance against Charlie surprising us on Christmas. We didn't want to get caught with our pants down, and even though the 3rd Brigade's infantry units were standing down, they remained on one-hour alert status.

Old Knee Injury

Combat missions, combined with walking, running, jumping, and carrying a loaded backpack, had taken a heavy toll on my right knee. After a mission, it stayed inflamed, puffy, and red for a few days before it felt better. I finally got to the point where I began walking with a noticeable limp.

When I talked to Lieutenant Fenner about my knee, he agreed that I should see a doctor. After an initial evaluation at the local field hospital, the news the doctor gave me wasn't good: I'd damaged the ligaments around the fleshy area of my old punji-stake wound, and the beginnings of degenerative arthritis were developing in the joint. The doctor told me that this condition could worsen with age.

Age? I thought. *I'm only twenty years old!* I wondered what my knee would be like when I became an old man of thirty.

The doctor said that further aggravation of the knee would cause even more discomfort or permanent damage, and then I'd need another surgical repair. For at least a year since my surgery, I'd been pounding hard on that knee. I didn't want to go under the knife again; the recuperation period was too long and I was almost through with my second tour. I knew I just had to hang in there for a few more months before I went home.

The doctor at the Dau Tieng field hospital scheduled a mandatory appointment for me to see an orthopedic specialist in Cu Chi, home of the 25th Infantry Division. The 3rd Brigade in Dau Tieng was a subordinate brigade of the 25th Infantry. The medical facility at Cu Chi was better staffed and had more sophisticated equipment than the small field hospital in dusty old Dau Tieng.

Cu Chi Base Camp

In the middle of January 1968, a supply chopper flew me to Cu Chi for my appointment with the orthopedist. I expected to be away from Clipper for only a few days.

Boy, was I wrong!

When I met with the doctor, I underwent another complete medical examination, including a blood workup. The doctor told me he was going to put a cast on my leg to immobilize it for a month. He asked how much time I had left in Vietnam, and I told him I was scheduled to rotate back to the States in two months. Based on the condition of my knee, he said I wouldn't be leaving Cu Chi. He placed me under the medical care and observation of the Cu Chi hospital for my remaining time in Vietnam.

I thought this news was fine and dandy, but I really needed to get back to Dau Tieng to collect my personal effects and see Clipper. I'd always been bothered by this kind of quick decision making that was so typical of the army.

The hospital issued me a temporary physical profile document signed by the doctor. I was restricted from running, jumping, crawling, prolonged standing, and marching for three months, which would carry past my March rotation date to the States.

The doctor told me he was obligated to ensure my health and welfare. My knee would get better only if I quit abusing it. In his eyes, I was "just a kid," and he told me so. I decided to educate the doctor on my idea of a man.

I said, "I resent being called a kid or a boy. If I'm old enough to fight a war and spill blood for my country, I'm old enough to be called a man."

The graying old doctor smiled and told me that he had sons my age, but they were in college. My initial thought was that if the war continued, his sons would probably be drafted for Vietnam duty. I also had the impression that the doctor was trying to give me the gift of a valid medical reason for staying out of combat. My health was important to me, and though I might have been a little crazy to return to Vietnam for more punishment, I sure as hell wasn't so stupid as to pass up this opportunity not to get shot at anymore.

I remembered the kindness of Dr. George Bogumill, the surgeon in Japan who had repaired my knee back in 1966. Unlike a field commander in constant need of fresh healthy bodies to fight the enemy, he wasn't motivated by the war. Field commanders expected a certain amount of casualties and considered infantrymen replaceable. I'd experienced that attitude many times during my military service. Doctors, on the other hand, had more caring and sensitive natures. They didn't see or experience battle, but dealt with the aftermath. They helped mend the bloody young bodies toted in dirty plastic ponchos or carried on stretchers from the battlefield. Sadly, a doctor and his medical staff were unable to save everyone from dying. The doctors were truly a breed apart from the world of warfare in which I lived and breathed.

I didn't like being in a field hospital because it meant having to watch my fellow soldiers suffering from their wounds. Hanging around the tents of Cu Chi hospital, I saw naked men sitting in ice-filled metal tubs on dirt floors. Those men were burning up with fever caused by malaria, and the sight of them made me glad I'd taken my malaria pills regularly. Some of those men would die if the doctors couldn't break their fever in time. What a way to leave that lousy war—high fever, shaking all over, sitting in cold water, and then dying. I could sense the pain those young guys were going through, but I could only observe and hope they'd survive.

The most depressing aspect of being a patient in a large field hospital was that I wouldn't get a chance to say goodbye to Clipper or my dog-handler friends. Because of the distance between base camps, communication required some kind of radio patching system. I felt uncomfortable going into some unit's headquarters and asking if I could make a long-distance call to check on my dog. They'd look at me like I was nuts and show me the door. Since I was a stranger in these new surroundings, I felt powerless to do anything out of the ordinary. The hospital personnel clerk advised me that he'd contact the 44th Scout

Dog Platoon and forward the paperwork authorizing my reassignment to Cu Chi field hospital.

The doctor decided not to put my leg in a cast after all; instead, he wrapped it in a large flexible bandage. He advised me not to overdo physical activity, and told me to see him for checkups every few days until the swelling went down. If my knee continued to swell with fluid, it would have to be drained with a syringe.

I had hated needles ever since a doctor back in Littleton, Colorado, had stuck one in my left ear to drain fluid that had accumulated from the punishment of high school wrestling. That ear had frequently puffed up with fluid as a result of my not wearing protective ear guards. After having drained the ear with a needle a few times, the doctor decided to lance it with a scalpel and squeeze the fluid out — a little procedure that hurt like hell. After that visit I never went back. Over time, the fluid hardened and my left ear became deformed — but it didn't hurt anymore. Wrestlers called this condition cauliflower ear.

✸

I was assigned living quarters at Headquarters Company, 25th Supply and Transportation Battalion (S&T). I reported to First Sergeant Milanowski. When he noticed the CIB (Combat Infantry Badge) and paratrooper wings sewn above my left breast pocket, he smiled and said, "Welcome, Sergeant Burnam!" I had finally been promoted to sergeant, E5 in December 1967. My scout-dog platoon sergeant had pinned the stripes on me in the K-9 Klub just after I had returned from a mission with Clipper. Rear-echelon troops couldn't earn a CIB unless they were assigned as infantrymen in an infantry unit, but they respected anyone who wore it. The CIB is the highest honor earned by an infantryman outside medals for individual heroism.

My promotion came a few weeks after Private First Class Ed Hughes was killed in action. Unlike "blood stripes" — the stripes of a sergeant killed in battle given to the next person in line for promotion — my stripes were merit-based, so I wore the new three-stripe chevrons on my sleeve proudly. I also got an increase in my monthly paycheck. I felt pretty cool and cocky to be a sergeant — equivalent to a squad leader in rank and authority — especially when I was addressed as "Sarge."

"Top," the First Sergeant, was trim, with a build and height about my size. He sported a typical military haircut, and kept his head covered in a clean military OD baseball cap. He wore properly fitting pressed jungle fatigues and brush-shined jungle boots. Top was the perfect example of a professional career soldier. My first impression was that I liked him, and he seemed to like me too.

Since I was a sergeant, Top assigned me to the noncommissioned officers' (NCO) quarters, which was just a green canvas tent with no special trappings. I'd had better quarters in Dau Tieng. No one below the rank of sergeant was allowed to live in the NCO quarters; NCOs were separated from the low-ranked enlisted men and not allowed to fraternize.

PX Truck Driver

After I settled into my new digs, a runner came by to tell me to report to First Sergeant Milanowski. I hustled my butt over to Top's office in the "head shed" — the headquarters building. Top informed me that I'd been assigned to work at the Post Exchange (PX) and was to report to Sergeant Major Kelly who ran the place. With a smile, Top told me that it was the best job he could find for me, and I believed him. I thanked him and headed out in search of SGM Kelly. SGM (E9) was the highest enlisted rank in the army. High-ranking soldiers always made me nervous.

The PX was about a mile away from the 25th S&T. I walked along a dirt road that wound its way around the entire inner perimeter of Cu Chi with exit roads leading to places inside the perimeter. My knee wrapped tightly, I limped a little, but at least I no longer had to carry a sixty-pound pack and rifle.

I found SGM Kelly's office in a detached small building behind the huge PX store where everyone on base shopped. I spotted him through the screen door, sitting by himself at a desk, his back to the door. I knocked lightly. He didn't look up, but his deep voice told me to enter. I walked in, removed my headgear, stood at attention behind him, and announced myself: "Sergeant Burnam reporting as directed, Sergeant Major!"

The SGM swiveled his chair around and faced me. "Do you have any experience working in a store, Buck Sergeant?" (A common nickname for a three-striper.)

"No, Sergeant Major!"

"Well, you'll learn."

He told me to stand at ease and tell him about myself.

I noticed that the SGM had a Combat Infantry Badge with two stars connecting the top of the wreath, which meant that he'd been award-ed the CIB three times — in WWII, Korea, and Vietnam. He had deep wrinkles around his eyes and cheeks, and looked much traveled in the army. I couldn't imagine serving as an infantryman in three wars. That old soldier must have been born with army blood in his veins or else was just plain crazy, but he deserved my unconditional respect. I surely wasn't about to ask him how he'd ended up as SGM for the PX.

SGM Kelly assigned me to new quarters near the PX; he told me that he didn't like waiting when he needed someone. My new accommoda-tions were in a wooden building with a wooden floor. I had a metal bunk bed with a mosquito net rigged above it. The hooch was equipped with a refrigerator stocked with food, soft drinks, and beer. It had tables, floor lamps, chairs, and a small bookshelf stocked with paperbacks and magazines — the nicest place I'd lived in since entering the army!

By that time, I'd been in Cu Chi a few weeks. When I asked the SGM for a chance to visit Clipper in Dau Tieng, he denied my request. Offi-cially, I was no longer a scout-dog handler assigned to the 44th. The SGM told me that I hadn't worked long enough to earn time off, but he promised me a convoy trip or chopper ride to Dau Tieng before I left Vietnam in March. I'd heard army promises before, so I wasn't sure his would be kept either, but I hoped it would because I missed Clipper and my buddies.

My new job was driving a tractor-trailer rig to the infantry units throughout the base camp. The fully enclosed trailer was stocked with sundries such as candy, peanuts, canned finger foods, canned soda and beer, cigarettes, and Zippo lighters. I had to manage the cash register for all sales.

What a job! I thought. *My own store stocked full of all the food and drink I can handle.*

When I pulled up to an infantry company area and opened the doors for business, I had no problem selling the sundries and collecting the money, which I had to turn in to SGM Kelly at the end of each day's work. He didn't require an inventory of stock; he left that to me. My job was to keep the truck re-supplied. Occasionally, I was tempted to take whatever I wanted, but if I were ever caught stealing, I'd likely end up in LBJ (Long Bin Jail). I wasn't a thief, especially with just a month and a half left to serve in Vietnam. I knew I could do this PX truck-driving job standing on my head. Any infantry grunt would have loved to trade places with me.

When I parked the rig in an infantry company's compound, it was like the Good Humor Man had arrived. After I'd opened the large metal door and lowered the stairs for business, a line of soldiers would quickly form. I'd position myself at the small cash register near the entrance, which was also the exit. Due to the cramped space inside, I could let in only a handful of soldiers at a time. Their eyes would light up when they saw the rows of metal baskets hanging on the walls filled with packaged candy, canned food, and drinks.

Infantrymen were very special to me; I knew how hard they worked in South Vietnam, and I would always smile and welcome each of them as they entered my store. I had even made up my own rules: when I serviced an infantry unit smelling of fresh muck from the field, I'd yell, "Two-for-one sale today, guys!" They'd smile and go crazy, buying all they could carry. Many of those young guys looked new to Vietnam. They reminded me of myself when I first got to Vietnam almost two years earlier. I knew that some of them would never make it home alive.

Short-Timers

When I earned a day off, I'd hang out with the other soldiers who worked inside the PX store as cashiers or shelf stockers or in the store's warehouses. Many were former infantrymen recovering from wounds, or soldiers with thirty days or less to serve in Vietnam. They were called short-timers. Some field commanders did their best to keep short-timers out of harm's way for their last thirty days in-country, but a good number of short-timers still humped the boonies, and some even got killed or wounded weeks or even days before their scheduled departure from Vietnam.

The goal of an infantry short-timer was to become an REMF (rear-echelon motherfucker). They sought jobs like truck driver, supply clerk, vehicle mechanic, hospital helper, personnel and finance clerk, or cook helper. They would accept any job that would keep them away from combat until they left Vietnam. When the infantry was out in the jungle looking for a fight, the short-timers manned the base-camp perimeter defenses.

Once a guy reached short-timer status, it was also a tradition to carry around a short-timer-stick. Some guys carved tree branches into fancy sticks and notched them to show how many days they had left in Vietnam. As each day passed, they'd cut a notch off the stick until only a stub was left — hence "short-timer." A short-timer also marked a big "X" on his calendar at each day's end. Many of them spent much of their free time writing letters and sending stuff home.

I was surprised at some of the things I found out that short-timers tried to mail home as souvenirs. For example, there was a story of one soldier who sent home an M60 machine gun. He broke it down into little pieces and mailed each piece in a separate package. The recipient wrote back to report what had arrived and what hadn't. The operation took several months, but the man apparently succeeded. At least that's what I heard. The military postal system had so many packages coming in and out of Vietnam that it must have been impossible for them to check each one for illegal contents.

Some short-timers got superstitious; they did only what they believed wouldn't put them in any danger. They'd avoid walking close to the perimeter for fear of getting shot by a sniper. Walking around base camp with several other men, they'd refuse to take the lead or bring up the rear. They ate with their backs to the wall so they could keep an eye on everything. Some wore their flak vests every day while in base camp; others had been known to live and sleep inside a bunker during their last thirty days. The list of odd and superstitious behavior went on and on.

One short-timer told me, "I'm so short and bold that I can look a fire ant in the eye and still kick his ass!"

No one wanted to hang around short-timers, especially FNGs (fucking new guys) who had twelve months' service ahead of them. It was tough enough for *veterans* to have to listen to short-timer bullshit. I hoped I wouldn't develop any superstitions when I had only thirty days left to serve in Vietnam — I believed that if it was my time to meet my maker, nothing on earth was going to save me.

I also knew this to be true: somehow, I had to find a way to see Clipper and my fellow scout-dog handlers before I left Vietnam.

Chapter 22

TET Offensive and Convoy to Saigon

IT WAS TET, the Vietnamese New Year, January 28, 1968, and a temporary ceasefire was in place to observe the holiday. American forces were on stand-down. To everyone's surprise, the North Vietnamese Army had rudely violated the ceasefire and launched an all-out assault on Saigon's military district, the U.S. embassy, and almost every military firebase throughout South Vietnam. The history books would call this massive attack the Tet Offensive.

It was early morning when I heard mortar rounds and rockets whistling overhead and exploding not far from my hooch, which was located deep inside the camp perimeter. I immediately grabbed my M16 and a bandoleer of magazines, and headed to the nearest bunker. Several others were already inside. The sounds and number of incoming rockets grew intense. The best we could do was to stay inside the bunker and scan through the portholes for VC who might have breached our defensive perimeter. It reminded me of the mortar attack on the kennel a few months back.

As the minutes passed, all I heard was explosion after explosion. The sandbags stacked around the bunker were absorbing shrapnel, as were our wooden hooches. At one point, a huge blast rocked the walls and gray-black smoke filled the air outside. My ears were ringing. Having no radio in the bunker, we couldn't contact anyone to get a status report or call for help if we needed it. Helicopters were in the air, and machine guns and American artillery fired in the distance.

A nearby ammunition dump took a direct hit. As each wooden crate of rockets, artillery rounds, grenades, and bullets exploded, it set off another crate, until the entire stockpile of munitions was destroyed. There was no way to contain it.

When the incoming rockets suddenly stopped, we all left the bunker to check the damage to the surrounding hooches. None of them had been destroyed, but some were splintered with shrapnel. There were no human casualties in the area.

As the evening progressed into darkness, American artillery batteries launched lots of flares into the air, lighting up the sky and allowing some visibility in our vicinity. The parachuted flares slowly descended to the ground and burned out. The sounds of war were far off in the distance.

That next morning the entire base camp buzzed with activity. I reported to work as usual, except I had my M16 and bandoleer of magazines with me. The PX and the nearby buildings had sustained only minor damage.

SGM Kelly summoned me. He told me that General William Westmoreland, commanding general of the military forces in Vietnam, was scheduled to give a speech to be broadcast over the armed forces radio network to all the troops stationed throughout South Vietnam.

General Westmoreland's broadcast reported that the Tet Offensive, with an estimated 70,000 enemy troops involved in the attacks throughout the country, had been a major military defeat for the Vietcong and the NVA. Friendly forces had repelled them overwhelmingly. The American embassy had been secured, and law and order was restored on the streets of Saigon, the capital city. Of all the military base camps throughout Vietnam that had been attacked simultaneously, none has fallen into enemy hands.

American casualties were reported as minimal, but the VC and North Vietnamese Army had suffered thousands of dead and wounded.

General Westmoreland called the Tet Offensive a great victory for South Vietnam and the American and allied forces. The general's lengthy speech was motivational, and at the end, I waited for him to announce that all orders to leave for the States were canceled — but he didn't. I breathed a huge sigh of relief, since I had only two months left in Vietnam.

My mind had turned to Dau Tieng. I worried about how Clipper and the rest of my pals had handled the attack. Getting news from Dau Tieng was especially difficult from Cu Chi, so I went to SGM Kelly and pleaded with him to find out what was going on there. He put me in contact with a SGM buddy of his who worked at the division tactical operations center. The SGM took me to the communications shed — a well-fortified and heavily guarded bunker with a bunch of antennas sticking out of it. The head-shed buzzed with radio communications. The SGM got on a radio and eventually patched me through to the 44th Scout Dog Platoon's landline.

Through the static, I could hear Sergeant Dan Barnett on the other end. To my relief, he told me that everything was okay; there'd been no dog or handler casualties. The VC had hit Dau Tieng hard but apparently unaware that most of the combat infantry units were in base camp at the time of their attack. The Americans had easily driven back Charlie's attempt to penetrate the perimeter wire. Sergeant Barnett told me that Lieutenant Fenner and the original group of dog handlers had already rotated back to the States, but that he himself had extended his tour of duty six more months.

After he asked how my knee was doing, Sergeant Barnett explained that most of the dog teams were out on patrol supporting Tet counteroffensive ops. He told me that Clipper had not been assigned to another handler, and assured me that Clipper was my dog until I left Vietnam. Sergeant Barnett asked if I was going to get a chance to come back to Dau Tieng before rotating to the States in March. I told him how hard I was trying and not to give up on my return. After that, the transmission ended and the line was static.

Convoy to Saigon

In mid-February 1968 I was ordered to report to Sergeant Major Kelly. I heard he was furious about something, and I had an uncomfortable feeling that I was in for a butt reaming, but didn't know why. Instead, the SGM told me that with all the hell of the Tet Offensive going on, he needed experienced combat infantrymen to ride shotgun on his re-supply convoy to Saigon. He had requested support from the infantry units, but they told him to go blow. It pissed him off that they couldn't spare infantry troops for his convoy. He was advised to use REMFs (rear-echelon motherfuckers) for the job: cooks, mechanics, supply clerks, and administrative personnel. Considering the circumstances outside the wire with Charlie running all over the place, SGM Kelly was uncomfortable with that idea. In the past, he had always gotten veteran infantry support to ride his convoys to Saigon. Several infantry combat veterans were already assigned to PX jobs, but they were all wounded short-timers, including me.

John Burnam and Tom Fagen at Cu Chi Base Camp, February 1968. Tom, an infantryman "short-timer," was wounded and then reassigned as a convoy truck driver.

SGM Kelly said that he needed a good sergeant like me — one with combat experience — to help the MPs honcho an empty convoy into Saigon and Bien Hoa to pick up badly needed supplies for the division. If I accepted the mission, SGM Kelly promised that when I returned he'd make sure I got a chopper ride to Dau Tieng to see my dog.

Those were exactly the words I wanted to hear; the rest of his speech about needing *me* was bullshit. The clever old sergeant had hooked me with the dangling carrot, so I volunteered. I figured that to see Clipper and Timber again outweighed the risks of the mission. Despite my previous experience with army promises, I had a good feeling that the SGM wouldn't screw me over on his personal promise.

What I missed most about Clipper was his loving companionship and how he got excited when I called his name. I wanted to roll around in the dirt with him one more time. I longed to have him sit next to me and lean against my leg like he always did. I missed the simple pleasure of having Clipper at my side. It was torment not to be able to see my dog one last time.

When I accepted the mission, SGM Kelly leaned close to my face, looked me in the eye, smiled, and told me that I had just separated myself from all the boys in Vietnam. I figured that was a compliment from a man who had earned three Combat Infantryman Badges (WWII, Korean War, and Vietnam War).

My orders were to leave at first light. The convoy would be fueled, engines running, and waiting at the staging area on the roadside near the PX. That night, some new pals I had met — Freddie and a soldier I'll call "Red" — paid me a visit. Both worked for SGM Kelly in the PX. Red volunteered to ride shotgun in one of the convoy trucks. I soon learned that Red had another reason for wanting to go to Saigon; he said he needed to see his Vietnamese dentist about a tooth problem.

I liked Red and Freddie, but Freddie refused to volunteer to ride shotgun, so he stayed behind. We could only travel during daylight hours, so the trip was to be a three-day mission: one day to get there, one day to load up, and one to get back.

The next morning, I was assigned to ride in a jeep at the head of the convoy, which was escorted by MPs in several other jeeps. If we needed help, gunships, artillery, and infantry troops were within striking distance of our route to Saigon.

My jeep was equipped with a driver, a gunner behind a mounted M60 machine gun, several thousand rounds of ammunition, two radios, and a radio operator who could communicate with SGM Kelly and the airstrike support. I was responsible for coordinating all tactical decisions with the experienced MP escorts, who were ultimately in charge. I had worked with the MPs on Rat Patrol in Dau Tieng, and had developed respect for them.

SGM Kelly issued me the Signal Operating Instructions (SOI) — a tiny booklet with the word "SECRET" printed on each page. The SOI contained all the radio call signs and frequencies for getting military support. It was attached to a chain around my neck and hidden inside my shirt. I was responsible for this highly classified military document; if in imminent danger of capture by the enemy, destroying that booklet was my highest priority.

The daylong drive to Saigon put us on a road that went through the middle of the fiercest fighting in our province. Cu Chi was near Hobo Woods where the Vietcong were heavily concentrated. Charlie fought like hell to keep Hobo Woods to himself, and many Americans and some of the 38th scout-dog teams had lost their lives in that awful place.

Highway 13 from Cu Chi to Saigon was damaged with deep potholes and blown bridges, but was clear enough for our seventy-mile trip. Mechanized and armored tank squadrons and infantrymen on foot had secured the most dangerous sections of the road, which was a vital link in our supply lines and had to stay open and secure for business during all daylight hours. For obvious reasons, during the Tet counteroffensives, no convoys traveled outside base camp at night.

By the time the convoy of empty flatbed trailers attached to diesel tractors was assembled and prepared to roll, I was ready to go. I didn't have enough time to check over everything carefully, but what the hell — I'd learned to live without ever having enough time. I relied on the drivers to ensure that their vehicles were serviceable enough to make the three-day journey.

I put my M16 and backpack behind my seat. Each truck had one man who rode shotgun inside the canvas-covered cab. One MP jeep rode ahead of me, another brought up the rear. I was assigned the second vehicle behind the lead jeep. I walked down the line of ten flatbeds, their smokestacks filling the air with diesel exhaust. Not knowing what kind of road conditions we'd encounter, we planned to keep the moving column as close together as possible.

I hopped into my jeep and waited for the MPs to signal "Start rolling." The machine gunner handed me a set of goggles to keep the dust out of my eyes. Red rode shotgun in the first truck behind my jeep. My radio squawked with call signs for radio checks. After we were assured that everyone was on the radio net and on the right frequency, it was time to go. One by one, we rolled out of the gate and into Charlie's territory.

I remembered that President Roosevelt said, "The only thing we have to fear is fear itself." Well, I was definitely feeling fear at first, but my stomach soon settled down as the slow and bumpy ride continued.

Several miles into the trip, I saw a few burned-out military trucks tipped over on the edge of the road, apparently pushed there by bulldozers. Helicopters followed overhead, and infantry troops were positioned near the tree lines at various vantage points along the route. It looked as if the Americans had broken Charlie's back when he'd tried his maximum offensive a few weeks earlier. I figured that he was probably licking his wounds and regrouping, so we had timed this convoy run well. So far, I felt okay about the mission.

A few hours and twenty miles out, the convoy hadn't been attacked; not a shot had been fired and all the trucks were accounted for. We were going at a snail's pace, but our progress was steady, and it looked like we'd reach Saigon before dark.

Every bridge we needed to cross had been damaged, but the engineers had made usable paths around them. During some stretches, thick jungle closed in on the road. If Charlie decided to hit us, that would have been where we'd be most vulnerable. Maybe Charlie had already seen us and decided not to attack, thinking the convoy was empty — or maybe it was just our lucky day in the sunshine.

Sections of the road were dry and dusty. The goggles came in handy as dust caked in the sweat on my face. It was a long, hot ride, but I still had plenty of water and snacks. The radios stayed on but remained silent except for the occasional situation report.

At last, the convoy approached the outskirts of Saigon and headed for a secure staging area within the Cholon District. There we were scheduled to park in a fenced and guarded compound and spend the night in a hotel across the street. The next morning the convoy was to roll from the city of Saigon and into the Bien Hoa beer-and-soda yard.

As we entered the Cholon District, I could see that some fighting had occurred there. Direct hits from tank and artillery rounds had made gaping holes in some of the buildings, and war debris littered the roadsides. Several civilian cars were burned and overturned on the shoulders of the road. Martial law had been declared, roadblocks were all over the place, and very few pedestrians walked the streets. It looked like a ghost town. The MP jeep ahead of mine was doing a good job of navigating us through the area. So far, we'd kept all the trucks intact and hadn't had to stop along the way for emergencies or maintenance problems.

At six o'clock in the evening, the convoy reached a large dirt parking lot surrounded by a ten-foot-high triple barbed-wire fence. South Vietnamese Army troops wearing burgundy berets opened the gate to let us through. All the trucks and jeeps fit inside with plenty of room to spare. The South Vietnamese military would handle vehicle security, and our hotel expenses had already been paid. We had only to check in and get our rooms for the night.

Carrying our M16s, bandoleers of fully loaded magazines, lightly packed backpacks, and .45-caliber pistols, we descended from our vehicles and headed for the hotel across the narrow street. I wanted one of those burgundy berets for a souvenir, so I approached a Vietnamese guard and offered a trade. He couldn't speak English, so I took a dollar out of my pocket and used hand gestures to bargain for his headgear.

The soldier smiled, took the buck, and gave me his beret. I didn't realize it would be so easy; I'd been prepared to give more if he'd demanded it.

I stashed the beret, and Red and I walked to the hotel. The trucks and jeeps were now under the full protection of the South Vietnamese Army and the American MPs.

The hotel's Mama San greeted us and assigned us rooms. She recognized my stripes and said she had a special room for me. The hotel was three stories high and not fancy by any stretch of the imagination. My room had only a single metal-frame bed and a beat-up dresser with a small dirty mirror. The window afforded a view of our vehicles parked across the street. I noticed that a few Vietnamese troops were guarding them and patrolling the street. Curfew was in effect for everyone but the military.

Later that night, Red came to my room to talk. I knew from previous conversations that he had attended an American linguistic school somewhere in the States. He spoke excellent Vietnamese and had been an interpreter for military intelligence in Saigon before being transferred to Cu Chi several months previous to this mission. Red had less than thirty days before he'd be going home. When he became a short-timer, he'd talked his way into a rear-area job in the PX where we had met.

Red showed me his back tooth, which had broken two days earlier, and the red infected area around it. When he heard about the convoy to Saigon, he volunteered to ride shotgun because he refused to see an army doctor or dentist. Instead, he insisted on seeing his Vietnamese dentist in Saigon. Because he spoke fluent Vietnamese and had been well established in Saigon's intelligence network before coming to Cu Chi, he had a lot of acquaintances he called friends in Saigon. He had no approval from any military medical personnel to see a dentist there, but I could see that Red intended to pursue his dental preference and that he was kind of asking my permission to leave the hotel to have his tooth fixed.

Red told me so many stories about Saigon life and cultural activities that I trusted him to know how to get around the city, but I felt the need to remind him that we were restricted to the hotel for the night, that the city was under martial law, and that he was out of his fucking mind to leave the safety of the guarded hotel. We were safer in numbers and weapons.

Red argued that there was nothing to worry about: his dentist worked just a few blocks from the hotel. He had to at least get some painkillers, and would be back before I could miss him. With those words, Red headed downstairs. After he left, I paced for a few seconds, thinking that if something happened to him, it would be my ass in trouble. *Aw, shit,* I thought. *I can't let him go by himself and I can't keep his fucking bonehead ass here either.*

I grabbed my rifle and bandoleer of ammunition and followed after Red. I spotted him just as he was about to climb into a covered horse-drawn rickshaw.

"Red!" I yelled.

Red turned around, grinned ear to ear, waved, and told me to hurry. I caught up with him and climbed into the black rickshaw, which was driven by a smiling Vietnamese. Red gave him directions to the dentist's office in Vietnamese. I looked at him, shook my head, and told him that I couldn't let him go alone, so off we went like a couple of war-zone tourists.

The driver headed toward the first Vietnamese-manned roadblock where soldiers holding machine guns stood behind waist-high sandbag walls. At the roadblock, Red spoke Vietnamese to the guards, who immediately smiled and let us through.

"Shit, Red, your dentist isn't down the street from our hotel, is he? Do you know where the fuck you're going?"

"Sure, I do. We're almost there," he assured me with a grin.

We turned down some empty side streets and eventually pulled over in front of a row of small buildings. Several Vietnamese citizens were milling around, and I noticed that there were no military personnel in sight. I checked my watch and saw that it was a little after seven. I advised Red that if his dentist wasn't there, we were heading back to the hotel before it got dark. Red said nothing as he stepped out of the rickshaw, walked to the entrance of a building, and knocked on the door.

A Vietnamese woman opened it, smiled, and greeted Red as if he were a long-lost friend. They talked in Vietnamese and she laughed when Red showed her his tooth.

I was getting nervous sitting outside in the rickshaw. Red finally came back to tell me that his doctor had left but would be back at six the next morning. He also said that we had plenty of time for him to get his tooth fixed and get back to lead the convoy by nine in the morning.

"Trust me," Red said. "The beer-and-soda yard at Bien Hoa is less than an hour away."

Why did I let myself get into this shit? I asked myself.

Red told me that the building was a hotel and a dental office. After I climbed out of the rickshaw, the well-dressed Vietnamese woman, who spoke broken English, greeted me with a smile as she bowed and motioned me inside. I smiled back, but gave Red a dirty look. I told him to call our hotel and let a member of our convoy team know where we were and when we'd be back. Using the Vietnamese woman's phone, Red made the call and spoke in Vietnamese to someone back at our hotel.

Then he looked at me and said, "John, we're set. They expect us back by nine o'clock tomorrow morning. Hey, buddy, I'll take care of you. Isn't this a nicer place to sleep than that rat hole we were in?"

"Uh-huh, this is great!" I agreed. "But we're the only two people here, and there's safety in numbers — especially American numbers."

Red was right about one thing, though: the inside of this hotel was upscale compared to where we'd been assigned to spend the night. Aside from the Vietnamese woman and her family, no one else appeared to be staying there, which I thought a little too strange. Also, the dentist's office was locked. I wondered how Red would get the painkillers he said he needed, unless he planned to break in.

The Vietnamese woman asked if we were hungry. She said that the recent fighting in the streets had chased away her customers. She gave us bowls of steamed rice with chunks of meat mixed in.

"Hey, Red, this is pretty good," I said. "It's the first hot meal we've had. The meat tastes a little like beef. Ask her what kind it is."

Red looked at me and said, "Its dog! That's a delicacy in the Vietnamese culture."

I spat out a mouthful on the table. "Man, I can't eat this shit if its dog. Why the hell didn't you tell me that before? You know I'm a dog handler, you asshole! What the fuck is wrong with you?"

Red smiled and said, "I think it tastes great!"

After he finished eating, Red decided that he wanted to visit a friend he used to stay with when he lived in Saigon. He told me that she was a beautiful Vietnamese/French girl with round eyes. I immediately opposed the idea of his leaving the hotel, especially to see a woman. Red was really pushing his luck with me, but before I knew it, a small black car pulled up in front of the hotel. Red already had a plan, which he was now putting into action. He told me to bring my weapons and get into the car for a short ride. We were going to pick up the woman and we'd be back in a half hour.

I wasn't thrilled about a car ride in the dark of night. Red, on the other hand, was totally relaxed, as if there were no martial law or war going on in Vietnam. When he walked to the car, I couldn't see staying behind by myself, so I followed. Splitting up now would be an even worse idea. I didn't like it that Red had put me in a totally reactive mode since our arrival. His utter disregard for all the danger signs around us was driving me nuts. Although we hadn't heard any shooting since we'd entered Saigon, we had no way of knowing what might happen.

We sat in the back seat of the little car. Red spoke Vietnamese to the driver, and off we went. Heading down a dark, quiet side road several blocks from the hotel/dental office, the driver turned left onto another side street, which looked more like an alleyway. Red looked nervous and spoke to the driver in a louder than normal tone. The driver turned his lights off and kept driving slowly down the alley while he talked with Red. Up ahead, several black-clothed figures suddenly appeared out of the darkness and slowly approached the front of the car. It looked like they were armed with rifles. Quickly jumping into the front seat, Red pointed his .45 at the driver's temple and spoke fast in Vietnamese. The car screeched to a sudden stop.

The armed men continued moving in our direction, their weapons at the ready. From a distance, I assumed that they weren't friendly, so I chambered a round into my M16 and quickly rolled down the car window. I stuck the barrel out and awkwardly pointed it in the direction of the approaching figures. Red screamed in Vietnamese at the driver. All of a sudden, Red's pistol went off. I flinched and ducked, ears ringing like crazy. I looked up to see what had happened; Red had intentionally missed the driver and had blown out the driver's-side window.

The driver slammed the car into reverse and turned the headlights back on. The men started shooting at us. Several bullets hit the front of the car. I returned fire with my M16. The car's jerking made my aim terrible, but I squeezed off round after round.

Finally, we backed out of the alleyway. The car screeched on the pavement as the driver spun the wheel to straighten it out. Red was still pointing the barrel of the .45 at the driver's temple. We sped down the street and made a sharp turn onto a different road. I didn't know where the hell we were. My heart thumped hard, but I was relieved that we weren't being chased or fired at anymore.

Red's face dripped sweat and his eyes bulged out of their sockets — he looked like an enraged madman. He kept talking to the driver, who answered him in a terrified voice. To my surprise, the man suddenly stopped the car. I was scared. All I could think was that we needed to get the hell out of there! The city of Saigon at night was an unfamiliar battleground. We had to make it back to our hotel as soon as possible. The Tet Offensive had brought the war to every nook and cranny throughout Vietnam; we weren't safe anywhere.

Red shouted, "John! Get the fuck out!"

I didn't hesitate or question. Once I was outside the car, I nervously looked up and down the street but saw only darkness. Red scooted over to the door. I pointed my weapon through the windshield at the driver, who froze, both hands on the wheel. Red frantically shouted at him in Vietnamese and then leapt out the door and told me to follow him and not look back.

My heart was in my throat as we ran through the darkness. We turned the corner and ran across the street. To my amazement, we were only a block from the dental office/hotel. The streets were bare and totally dark. Red suddenly stopped, turned, and banged a clenched fist on the hotel door, which opened to let us inside. By that time, we were completely out of breath.

The nicely dressed Vietnamese woman looked bewildered as she and Red chattered in Vietnamese. After they finished, Red told me the woman wouldn't be letting anyone else into the hotel that evening. Of course, she'd said more than that. Red wasn't telling me the whole story, but it was late and I was upset and not interested in asking questions. One thing was certain: My right knee was killing me. I hoped it wouldn't swell up.

We locked our room door and barricaded ourselves inside. Red and I took turns pulling guard duty until the sun came up. Throughout the night, I heard vehicle noises and voices on the street outside. I was sweating at the thought that some enemy might have spotted us and knew where we were. I was scared to death and felt trapped.

Neither Red nor I caught a wink of sleep. At first light, I heard a man's voice downstairs. Red quickly sat up and smiled. He told me the voice was that of his Vietnamese dentist. I looked at my watch and saw that the dentist had arrived promptly at six o'clock. Red moved the barricade, unlocked the door, and went downstairs. I was still stunned from the events of the night before. I stayed behind the dresser, M16 at the ready. From downstairs, I heard laughter and friendly voices. I cautiously made my way to the bottom of the carpeted stairwell. Red was already sitting in the dentist's chair, getting his tooth examined.

When the dentist finished, Red got up from the chair, pocketed some pills, and paid the man. All I wanted to do was to get the fuck out of there and safely back to the hotel where we were supposed to be staying. As we left, I saw few people on the street outside. Red flagged a rickshaw and we headed to our hotel. As we approached the first manned roadblock, I got really nervous. Red instructed me not to say anything, but to look tough and hold my weapon where the Vietnamese could see it. I did as instructed and, to my surprise, the soldiers lifted the arm of the roadblock and let us pass. We crossed three more roadblocks without incident before reaching the hotel.

We made it back before 9:00 a.m. Neither of us talked about our near-fatal encounter with the enemy or whoever the hell it was. I grabbed a can of spaghetti and meatballs from my pack and gulped it down, washed my face, and shaved. Through the window, I saw our troops milling around the parked trucks inside the fenced yard. Grabbing my gear, I walked out of the hotel to my jeep. Red was already sitting inside the first truck behind my jeep. He waved at me with that wide grin on his face.

I was fuming. *How can that fucker smile at me after putting us through all that shit? The bastard's got a death wish, and I can only blame myself for becoming part of it.*

I walked past each vehicle and checked inside for a head count of drivers and shotguns. Every man was accounted for and ready to go. After a radio check, the MP jeep slowly led us into the street. The convoy wound its way through Saigon and headed to the Bien Hoa beer-and-soda yard.

I noted that Red had been right about one thing: Bien Hoa was only an hour from the hotel. And what an incredible sight it was to see so many stacked pallets of beer and soda and a warehouse full of supplies. Vietnamese civilians operated forklifts, lifting pallet after pallet onto the flatbed trucks. They tied down the pallets with handheld metal banding machines while the Americans watched and directed the loading procedure. It took about five hours to fully load the trucks. Then the convoy maneuvered back through the streets of Saigon without incident, pulling into the staging area at Cholon before six o'clock that evening. We stayed at the same hotel across the street for our last night in Saigon. The second leg of the trip was over.

Back in the same hotel room, Red and I had a long talk over a few beers. We discussed the details of the incident that we'd barely survived the night before. According to Red, the Vietnamese driver had been a North Vietnamese officer posing as a cab driver, and was trained to capture unsuspecting Americans. He had not expected to encounter an

American who spoke fluent Vietnamese. A serious look on his face, Red blurted out, "If not for my background in military intelligence and the fact that I speak Vietnamese, we'd both be prisoners of war right now."

I responded angrily, "You're full of shit! You almost got us both captured and killed."

I wasn't too happy with myself because I could have prevented the whole situation. I had made two very bad decisions: First, I let Red leave the hotel; second, I foolishly went with him. How stupid could I have been to take such risks with only one lousy month left to serve in Vietnam!

The next morning, we fired up the engines and headed down the road for the long trip back to Cu Chi base camp. When we arrived, SGM Kelly was standing at the roadside, watching his convoy roll up to the PX. After I reported to him that all the men and trucks were accounted for and all the goods intact, SGM smiled at me.

"Job well done, Buck Sergeant! Give me that SOI and I'll have those trucks unloaded. Did anything happen on the mission that I should know about?"

"No, Sergeant Major, nothing but the usual bullshit!"

I reminded Sergeant Major Kelly of his promise to let me go see Clipper in Dau Tieng.

Chapter 23

Goodbye, Clipper

SGM KELLY KEPT HIS END of the bargain and coordinated space for me on a re-supply chopper to Dau Tieng. I packed a bunch of goodies for my dog-handler friends. When I arrived, it was a ten-minute walk from the airstrip to the K-9 compound. Thinking of seeing Clipper again made the painful limp in my step seem unimportant. I first stopped at the kennel and met Dan Scott, who was standing at the entrance, shirt-less as usual. We shook hands and I gave him a bear hug. It had been a long time since we'd seen each other, and Dan knew I couldn't leave Vietnam without coming back to say goodbye.

It felt like Christmas when I handed him a brand-new Zippo lighter with a pack of flints and a can of lighter fluid. I showed him a copy of my orders to leave Vietnam, and he was really excited for me. He asked how my gimpy knee was healing and what Cu Chi was like. After a short bullshit session, I decided to walk to the kennel and spend some time with Clipper. Dan and I planned to party in the K-9 Klub later that night.

When I got to the kennel Clipper wasn't in his run. I should have known that he'd be out under the shade of his tree during the day. As I walked through the kennel, it was great to see and smell all the other scout dogs and hear them barking for attention.

I walked outside to the rubber trees to find Clipper. In the distance, I spotted him lying on the ground taking a nap. I quietly whispered his name. Clipper's ears popped up and he canted his head. Looking in my direction, he rose to his feet, stretched out his legs and back, and turned his head slightly to the left and then to the right. I could tell that he was trying to figure out who had called him.

I walked closer without saying another word. When Clipper recognized me, he went crazy. He charged toward me until his leash fully extended and stopped him in his tracks. I rushed over to him and he jumped up and put his forepaws on my chest. Wagging his tail joyfully, he licked all over my face and, in his immense excitement, piddled on my leg and boots. It felt great being with him again. I hugged his soft furry body tightly.

What an exhilarating moment! Words can't begin to describe the emotions that poured out of me. That dog was my best friend and we were together again at last.

I fastened Clipper's choke chain to the leather leash and took him for a walk to calm us both down. I gave him no commands. He moved automatically to my left side and walked at a slow pace, constantly staring up at me with love and happiness in his eyes. He remembered exactly what my walking pace was and didn't once pull ahead or cross my path. After a while, I slowly worked him through some basic commands and scouting positions. It was as if we'd never been separated.

How am I ever going to leave this dog after seeing him again? I wondered. Clipper thought I was back to stay; he couldn't know that I'd only be visiting with him for a short time. We spent the entire afternoon together in the shade of the rubber trees.

Later that night, I joined the rest of the scout-dog handlers in the K-9 Klub. Some new guys had arrived since my departure. It was March 1968, and all my old friends from the original 44th had returned to the States. Their twelve-month tour of duty was over and I never got the chance to say goodbye. Dan Scott was also due for rotation in March, so he was a short-timer like me. After we said our farewells, I grabbed an empty cot in my old hooch for one last night's sleep in Dau Tieng.

I got up early the next morning to say my last goodbye to a dog who didn't deserve the fate in store for him. I walked into the kennel to see Clipper. When I opened his run, he ran off to wait under his tree until I caught up and hooked his collar to the twenty-five-foot leash. I filled his water bucket with fresh water and cleaned his run. Then I sat with him under his tree and stroked his head and back, recalling all the combat missions we had accomplished together, the many times Clipper had alerted me to danger, and the countless lives he had saved. It was hard to believe I was going to have to leave him behind. He was a real American hero, but he'd never get to go home and receive the hero's welcome he deserved.

Obviously unable to speak for himself, Clipper was at the mercy of people who had recruited him for military life, teamed him with a handler, trained him for war, and shipped him off to Vietnam. As Clipper's handler, I felt I was the only one who had truly developed an allegiance to him. Now, because our government had classified Clipper as expendable equipment, I had to leave him behind. I felt as if I were abandoning a brother who was condemned to the dangerous job of walking point for the rest of the war. *How can my country burden me with this lifelong memory?*

Clipper deserved to live the rest of his life in a peaceful environment away from that war. I wanted him to be given the same respect and dignity I expected for myself. He had earned it. Dogs who served during WWII were given discharge papers and adopted by their devoted handlers or sent home to their original owners after the war. That was not to be for the valiant war dogs of the Vietnam War. For their service, heroism, bravery under fire, and risking their lives to save others, the surviving dogs were given to the South Vietnamese Army or disposed of by other means. They lie buried in war-dog graveyards throughout South Vietnam that are all but forgotten except by those who buried them.

Since I had met Clipper, it had always been my dream to bring him home even though I knew it was not to be. Clipper had already served in Vietnam for fifteen months, and I wasn't sure how many more missions he would survive walking point. I feared that Clipper's death would be violent, especially after the Tet Offensive had ignited the war into such frenzy. I could only hope that when Clipper finally did fall, he would die quickly and painlessly. As I sat under that tree with him leaning against my leg, I knew that I would never see him again in this lifetime. The tragedy of it haunted me like a never-ending nightmare.

I noticed that the sign I had nailed above Clipper's tree ten months before was still there. WAR IS GOOD BUSINESS – INVEST YOUR DOG. That protest disgusted me now. I ripped the sign down and broke it into tiny pieces.

At last, the time had come for me to let go. I tried to hold back my tears. I didn't know how to say goodbye to my best friend, so I looked into his big brown eyes and gave him one last loving farewell hug. Then I turned and walked away, awash in the sad, bitter truth that Vietnam would become my dog's final resting place.

Clipper stood erect, ears pointed high, like the champion he was. I turned and slowly walked away, never looking back, but I felt him watching me. I vanished down the dirt road leading away from the 44th Scout Dog Platoon. I knew then that I truly had no more reason to stay in Vietnam, but every reason in the world to keep Clipper alive in my heart for the rest of my life.

Goodbye, Clipper, Tattoo 12X3, March 1968
(author collection).

Chapter 24

Leaving Vietnam

MY DEPARTURE COULDN'T have been scheduled at a worse time. I could easily have had my exit orders rescinded because the Americans were in the middle of a fierce counteroffensive against the North Vietnamese Army near Cu Chi and Tay Ninh Province.

Sergeant Major Kelly summoned me to his office. He promised me another stripe if I'd stay six more months. I declined his offer as politely as I could: "No, but thanks for the offer!"

I knew it was time for me to leave the war behind, go home to Littleton, Colorado, and have a big party with my family and friends. Two years was enough to spend fighting in Southeast Asia.

It was the second week of March 1968 when I made it out of Cu Chi base camp to Saigon in the back of a troop truck that was part of a heavily armed convoy escorted by tanks and helicopter gunships. The road to Saigon was still littered with burned-out vehicles pushed to the roadside. Along the way, infantry troops were positioned off the road to protect the convoy from attack and keep the road open. Without incident, the convoy reached the city limits of Saigon where the devastation had reached a new level since my last visit a month ago. The Tet counteroffensive operations had more deeply scarred an already beleaguered and battered city.

Saigon remained under martial law. Homeless pedestrians walked the roadways and filled crowded busses. Armed military police and South Vietnamese Army troops barricaded and manned the city's major intersections.

The convoy stopped along the road next to Camp Alpha, the U.S. Army Replacement Center where I'd first entered Vietnam. I climbed out of the truck, grabbed my duffel bag, and handed my M16 and bandoleer of ammunition to the sergeant who'd been riding shotgun. As I entered the gates of Camp Alpha, I handed a copy of my orders to a soldier who stood at the gate with a clipboard in hand. Each step was bringing me closer to returning to the world outside Vietnam.

I stayed in Camp Alpha for several days to out-process. My name was placed on a manifest and I was assigned a group number. When I heard my number called, I reported to a building where we all were strip-searched. The military police looked for and confiscated any pistols, grenades, knives, and other items that wouldn't be allowed aboard a commercial jetliner. I had nothing they were searching for. Clipper was all I had ever wanted to take home with me.

After being searched, I boarded a bus to Tan Son Nhut airfield. During the ride, I sat on a bench seat next to the window and thought about my Vietnam experience, Clipper, and the friends I was leaving behind. Before I realized it, the ride had ended and I was standing on the runway. Military guards in jeeps surrounded a commercial jetliner. In single file, we walked to the plane. A military attendant with a manifest checked off our names as we climbed aboard. I found an empty seat next to a window.

When everyone had boarded, the doors closed and the aircraft slowly moved down the runway. As soon as it lifted off, a resounding cheer filled the cabin. I settled back into the soft seat and looked out the window, watching the airfield and the city of Saigon grow smaller and smaller as the plane climbed. After several minutes, only the South China Sea was visible below.

Our next stop would be San Francisco, where we'd set foot once again on American soil. Despite the ongoing counteroffensives, the timing and process of getting everyone out of Vietnam had been impeccable.

Recent battles must have lit a spark under their butts; they wasted no time getting us out. In a matter of only twenty-four hours I was out of harm's way and leaving Vietnam forever. I only wished they'd apply this same sense of urgency to rescuing our four-legged brothers.

During the long flight, cute, round-eyed American stewardesses smiled as they waited on the passengers. They served coffee, tea, soda, snacks, and hot meals, but no alcohol. I had a lot of time on that flight to think about going home. I couldn't wait to be part of the American culture I'd left behind two years earlier.

My only fear was that I had heard some of the new guys who had recently arrived in South Vietnam say that people back at home were starting to actively protest America's involvement in the war. I didn't remember reading anything about this in letters from my family and friends. The folks writing the letters always wished me well and said they couldn't wait to see me again. I didn't understand how people who hadn't been in Vietnam could think they knew about what it was like there for an American soldier.

I thought about some of the first things I would do when I returned. I knew I wanted to get my very first new car. I had read that the 1968 Dodge Charger 440 RT had a 300-horsepower engine and ram-air and could clock a quarter mile in thirteen seconds. I had to have that car. I wanted to drive up to a lookout point in the Colorado Rockies and peer down on the city lights of Denver at night.

I still had my tiny red address book listing the names and addresses of family and friends with whom I had corresponded. I hoped they hadn't moved or changed their phone numbers, because I wanted to visit with them again. I couldn't wait to live halfway around the world from the sound of explosions, machine guns, helicopters, fighter jets, armored vehicles, C-rations, infantry talk, and the permanent stink of fish in the air.

As the wheels touched down at San Francisco International, a chorus of cheers reverberated through the cabin. When the bottoms of my shoes touched the runway, I was so grateful to be home that I bent down and kissed the ground.

Military policemen greeted us and escorted us to several military bus-es parked on the runway. They drove us past U.S. Customs and directly to Oakland Army Base where we were confined to a warehouse. It was a holding area for in-processing, reassigning, and discharging U.S. Army personnel. There was no marching band or welcome-home parade; we were, however, treated to steak dinners in the warehouse mess hall.

I was on American soil at last and that was all that mattered to me. During out-processing, I was paid in American greenbacks. I reached into my pocket and felt a coin. I pulled it out and saw that it was a South Vietnamese silver-plated five-dong coin dated 1968. I decided to hold on to it as a keepsake, a permanent reminder of the year I returned home from Vietnam.

Within eight hours of arriving in Oakland, I was released on furlough. The personnel sergeant told me that I would soon receive a stateside unit of assignment in the mail at my home of record in Littleton, Colo-rado. And that was it — I was free to leave Oakland Army Base.

Taxis lined up outside the gate to take us wherever we wanted to go. Several of us shared a ride to San Francisco International to continue our journeys east and home. When the cab pulled up in front of the airport, I hooked up with another infantryman, George Johnson, whom I'd met during out-processing at Camp Alpha. He was going home to New York.

George and I had a hard time believing that in just a day and a half we were out of the jungles of Vietnam and on the streets of San Fran-cisco. We agreed that things were happening a little too fast, so we decided not to book a flight home right away. We wanted to go into San Francisco, clear our heads a bit, and get used to American soil, so we put our baggage in lockers inside the terminal and headed downtown.

It was March 15, 1968, and we were proudly walking the sidewalks of San Francisco, wearing our Class-A khaki uniforms, Combat Infan-tryman Badges, and Vietnam combat ribbons. It felt so peaceful in downtown San Francisco.

George wanted to buy us our first beers in America, so we stopped at a bar and sat down to enjoy the scenery. I began to notice that we were the only soldiers in the place. It wasn't crowded, and the bartender was friendly. I ordered a bottle of Coors, but they didn't have any. I figured I'd have to wait till I got to Denver to get a cold Coors beer. We ended up ordering bottles of Pabst Blue Ribbon.

Suddenly, our uniforms became targets for some angry Americans who were protesting against the Vietnam War. One of the patrons blurted out, "Hey, baby killers, did you enjoy burning down villages?"

I was outraged by the man's taunt, but held back my anger. Having gone through what I had in Vietnam taught me how to control my emotions in a heated situation. I realized that getting into a bar fight would mean police and jail time.

I didn't understand why this man was so fired up against soldiers he didn't know. George rose up from his barstool, but I put my hand on his shoulder and told him that fighting this guy wouldn't be worth the consequences. George agreed and we ignored the remarks. A few other men sitting in the joint started to let us know that we weren't welcome there. This surprised and confused us; we didn't know what to think or say. The longer we stayed in the bar, the more uncomfortable and upset we became. We decided to keep our mouths shut and just get the hell out of there. George paid the tab and we walked out without finishing our beers.

George suggested it would be a good idea to get out of our uniforms. We found the closest men's clothing store, bought civilian clothes and shoes, changed in the dressing room, and walked out carrying our uniforms in paper bags. Only our military haircuts still distinguished us from the rest of the American male public. God, how we wished we had long hair so we could blend into the civilian crowd. I felt totally depressed and self-conscious, trying not to appear so military. My dream of coming home and feeling welcome had been shattered in just one afternoon.

I wondered if the people who had been writing to me while I was in Vietnam had held back the truth about what was really going on back home. I suddenly felt the need to be more observant and guarded around civilians and to expect more of the same when I got to Littleton, Colorado.

Chapter 25

Life After Vietnam

My flight from San Francisco to Denver's Stapleton International Airport was uneventful. When we landed, my brother Tom met me at the gate. He was happy to see me and we talked nonstop all the way home. It was good to see my family again. Everyone was happy that I was finally safely home. I was treated to a feast of food, laughter, and attention. I felt loved and appreciated for my service and survival in Vietnam. Everyone wanted to hear my stories and asked lots of questions about Kenny Mook and the Bong Son battle and my dogs Clipper, Timber, and Hans. I shared what photos I had.

My father wanted me to get out of the army and get a job or go to college. Dad had served as a U.S. Army medic in WWII in Europe, and was awarded a Silver Star for valor. He rarely spoke of his service.

Most of my high school friends were away at college. The others had fulltime jobs, and some were even married and had little children. I spent several weeks driving the hell out of my new 1968 Dodge Charger 440 RT and visiting friends attending the University of Colorado and Colorado State University. My college friends treated me well, but we were in different places mentally and heading in different directions both academically and professionally. I enjoyed listening to their intellectual perspectives on subjects other than Vietnam.

John Burnam, home from Vietnam, with
1968 Dodge Charger 440RT, March 1968.

There were so many changes since I had left home in September 1965. The Vietnam War was on TV every night and there were protests going on around the country against America's involvement. The narrative saddened me and I was certainly not interested in going out on the streets to protest against those people protesting against me. It was a no-win situation, like what I had experienced in San Francisco.

I wanted to believe that that had been an isolated incident, but it wasn't. Protesters were everywhere, flower power was in, draft dodging was acceptable, and "Hell, no, we won't go!" was the chant of the day. Hippies, drugs, and sex appeared to be prevalent wherever people my age gathered across the country. I did not fit into that subculture. The America I came home to was now angry and fractured into many differing opinions and political beliefs. It became a war of words with people who had no idea of and couldn't care less about my views on Vietnam. Occasionally, I got pushed around and wound up in a fistfight.

I tried to appreciate the fact that we all had freedom of speech, and I tried to overcome my fear of having some protester bust my head open someday.

It'll be a cold day in hell, I thought, *before I let anyone drive me out of my country or deprive me of the freedom I bled for and will defend until the day I breathe no more.*

I endured many nightmares about my war experiences. I couldn't get my mind to rest, and would stay up late staring into the darkness of my room. I worried about my ability to adjust to a mental state of peace and happiness with my surroundings, my future, and myself. Mentally, I worked hard to re-acclimate myself to the American way of life that I'd once known.

I spent a lot of time riding around in the mountains on a few dates with girls I knew, watched lots of TV, and went to the movies. I enjoyed the film *2001: A Space Odyssey.* TV shows I liked were *Hawaii Five-O, The Lucy Show, Peyton Place, Hogan's Heroes, Star Trek, The Andy Griffith Show, Lost in Space, Dark Shadows,* and *Rowan & Martin's Laugh-In.*

On April 4, 1968, a few weeks after I returned home, Dr. Martin Luther King was assassinated at the Lorraine Motel in Memphis, Tennessee. He was only thirty-nine years old. Flags were lowered to half-mast and the country mourned an American hero of the Civil Rights Movement. Before this news aired on TV and radio, I had no idea who this man was or what to think of all that was happening because of his death. It was another eye opener about the cultural problems, disruption, and unrest happening in the country.

Lyndon Baines Johnson (LBJ) was president. He looked tired during his TV appearances as he tried to defend the war in Vietnam and calm the country at the same time. I was confused and started to ignore the nonstop TV coverage about Vietnam. I also stopped reading the *Rocky Mountain News* and the *Denver Post,* except for the sports pages and the entertainment sections.

I waited anxiously for my next military assignment. My hopes were that the army would station me close to home at Fort Carson, Colorado. One afternoon, the mailman delivered a large yellow envelope addressed to Sergeant John C. Burnam. It contained a stack of official orders directing me to report to the 2nd Battalion, 54th Infantry in Bamberg, West Germany.

My heart sunk. *No way! This can't be right!* The next day I drove to the nearest army installation, Fitzsimons Army Medical Center in Denver. When I discussed my orders with the personnel sergeant, it was déjà vu all over again. I was informed that I still belonged to Uncle Sam, and based on my recent combat experience in Vietnam, I was desperately needed in Europe to balance the ranks of those without combat experience facing the Cold War with Russia.

I decided to fight the assignment, so I wrote to my district's representative, the Honorable Donald G. Brotzman, 2nd District of Colorado. He wrote back saying he couldn't do anything to have me assigned to Fort Carson, Colorado, and wished me luck in my new assignment in West Germany. The only luck I had was having survived combat in Vietnam. Other than that, I was powerless to influence my situation, no matter how hard I tried. I was deeply depressed.

It was late April 1968 when I said goodbye to my family and friends, headed to the Denver airport, and boarded a commercial airplane for New York and then another to Munich, Germany. When we landed, I followed the signs in English directing me to the military liaison office in the airport. There I was greeted by military personnel and processed for my assignment and trip to Bamberg. I climbed aboard a troop truck for the long ride. It was spring, and the German countryside and towns we passed through were absolutely beautiful and peaceful.

When we finally arrived at the military base of Bamberg, I was immediately assigned to Company A, 2nd Battalion, 54th Infantry. The infantry battalion was billeted in a quadrangle of old brick buildings. After greeting me, the company clerk escorted me to the office of the company commander. Then it was off to meet the company 1st Sergeant. Everyone was pleasant and interested in my combat experience in Vietnam. It turned out that none of my fellow infantrymen, from the company commander down to the lowest ranking man in the outfit, had served in Vietnam. I was treated with respect for having earned a Combat Infantry Badge, paratrooper wings, Bronze Star, Purple Heart, and Vietnam Cross of Gallantry medals and ribbons.

Sergeant John Burnam, commander of M114 reconnaissance vehicle.
Driver: Private First Class Eubanks from Georgia (July 1968).

The company commander assigned me to the reconnaissance platoon, which comprised a bunch of three-man M114 armored reconnaissance vehicles. Though small in size, each was equipped with a .50-caliber machine gun on a turret and an M60 machine gun attached to the rear. I was assigned as squad leader of six men and two armored carriers. Our job was to reconnoiter ahead of the infantry and report enemy positions and strength. It was like being a point man in Vietnam, except I got to ride and command two mechanized vehicles positioned ahead of the infantry's advance.

In August 1968, Soviet tanks rolled into Czechoslovakia. The invasion sparked civil unrest and resistance against the occupation. There were fears of escalation into a full-blown war. We were placed on alert and sent to reinforce the border between Germany and Czechoslovakia.

There I was on the border looking across an open field of hidden mines and booby traps, expecting jet fighters to speed across the border and knock us out in the first wave. From the Vietnam War to a conventional war with Russia scared the hell out of me, especially being part of the first line of defense. The last thing I wanted was to face Russian tanks, artillery, and jet fighters followed by a conventional infantry ground attack. Yikes!

As it turned out, the expected border invasion of West Germany never happened; I breathed a sigh of relief as we headed back to Bamberg in our little armored vehicles. While resting in the barracks, I was shocked when I learned from a news report that American infantry troops had massacred hundreds of unarmed Vietnamese civilian women and children at My Lai, South Vietnam. It took place on my birthday, March 16, 1968. It boggled my mind how such an atrocity could have happened, but it really had. Some of the infantrymen in my squad asked if I had killed any civilians or witnessed such incidents in Vietnam. I told them that I had not!

During my time with the mechanized infantry, I was selected for and completed formal training courses such as the Noncommissioned Officer Academy, Demolitions Training Course, Vehicular Mounted Weapons Training Course, Ranger Tactical Training Course, Escape and Evasion Course, and a very difficult Mechanized Infantry Scout Squad Proficiency Course. I was one highly trained infantry squad leader!

John Burnam at the .50-caliber machine-gun range,
West Germany, 1969.

When off duty, I frequented the German pubs in Bamberg and Nuremberg and drank lots of great German beer. I attended the Oktoberfest celebrations and ate lots of strudel, bratwurst, and schnitzel. I even learned a bit of the German language to better communicate.

I got excited when I saw the movie poster at the base theater promoting *The Green Berets,* starring John Wayne, David Janssen, Jim Hutton, and Aldo Ray. I had always wanted to wear the Green Beret, but it was no longer possible because of my knee injury and other circumstances affecting my military assignments. The film was about the Vietnam War and I enjoyed it because it mainly supported the soldiers' involvement in Vietnam instead of protesting it. Afterward, my fellow infantrymen asked me a lot of questions about the film's authenticity and about how it related to my own experience in combat. I found it difficult to explain the differences between movie entertainment and real war, but I tried.

Bamberg, Germany, was a great assignment, but it ended in January 1970. I went on leave back to Littleton, Colorado before heading to my next assignment with the 1st Battalion, 5th Infantry, 25th Infantry Division (Bobcats), Schofield Barracks in Oahu, Hawaii.

After I was promoted to Staff Sergeant, my right knee finally gave out. I had punished it with too many rigorous infantry tactical exercises and with carrying heavy loads of combat gear and weapons. I underwent another major knee reconstruction, and the army then reclassified my career field from infantry to personnel and administration — a desk job.

It was a difficult transition from infantry tactics and weapons to sitting behind a desk inside a building, processing personnel data and paperwork all day. It took me a while to learn the office language, fill out forms, operate a typewriter, and generate reports using other machines. Processing administrative data within a complex personnel-management and force-structure system was a huge mental challenge. Over time, I learned to be an effective communicator and leader of a small staff of personnel clerks.

In 1974, I was transferred from Hawaii to the Presidio of San Francisco, California. There I was assigned to the Standard Installation/Division Personnel Systems (SIDPERS) branch of the Military Personnel Office (MILPO). My job was to train personnel clerks on a new personnel system of submitting, processing, and managing personnel and organizational data. In the process, I created a unique computer-based training program that successfully taught hundreds of unit personnel clerks how to do their jobs more efficiently and in less time. My training program improved data accuracy, data compatibility, and timeliness of data submission.

An inspector from the Army Military Personnel Center in Washington, D.C., visited to examine our personnel operations. They evaluated my training program as exceptional. I was promoted to Sergeant First Class and awarded a Meritorious Service Medal.

THE WHITE HOUSE

WASHINGTON

January 6, 1981

To Sergeant John Burnam

I have recently learned of the substantial contribution you have made toward improving government operations. The more than $5.6 million in benefits to our government that result from your achievement help to realize one of our Administration's most important goals.

Improved productivity is vital to the social and economic well-being of our Nation. Contributions such as you have made support my conviction that Federal personnel constitute a major role in improving government service.

Please accept my personal thanks and congratulations. I hope you will continue to look for ways to better our government, while at the same time reducing costs to the American taxpayer.

Sincerely,

Jimmy Carter

SFC John C. Burnam, USA
SIDPERS Training
U.S. Army Military Personnel Center
200 Stovall Street
Alexandria, Virginia 22332

*Letter to John Burnam from
President Jimmy Carter, January 6, 1981.*

In 1978, I was recruited by the Military Personnel Center in Washington, D.C. My job was to proliferate my training program throughout the army's personnel offices around the world. The office of the secretary of the army's awards program recognized my work. I was awarded the "1980 Suggestion of the Year" during a Pentagon ceremony and given a $10,000 check for my training idea. The U.S. Army Training and Doctrine Command created a new formal Specialty Training Course for personnel clerks based largely on my direct input. I had also received a thank-you letter from President Jimmy Carter for saving the government 5.6 million in taxpayer dollars. The army awarded me the Legion of Merit medal for my accomplishments and I was promoted to Master Sergeant.

In 1984, I retired from military service and immediately went to work for General Research Corporation as a systems analyst, training developer, and technical writer. My career in IT (information technology) continued with Unisys Corporation and Bart and Associates, Inc.

On Memorial Day 1991, I had a life-changing experience: I was reunited with my Vietnam buddy, Kenney L. Mook, in Saegertown, Pennsylvania. Our reunion inspired me to write *Dog Tags of Courage* and then embark on the difficult journey to establish the National Monument for America's Military Working Dogs and Dog Handlers.

Chapter 26

National Monument Public Plea

IN EARLY MAY 1991, my friend Mark Hart invited me to spend the Memorial Day weekend at his family's retreat near Pymatuning State Park in northern Pennsylvania. I had told Mark that I had a Vietnam War buddy by the name of Kenny Mook who I thought lived in Meadville, Pennsylvania. Mark said that Meadville was near their summer retreat and that they would try to find Kenny. I didn't really give it a second thought. After all, it had been twenty-five years since I had last seen Kenny, severely wounded, on the battlefield in South Vietnam. I didn't even know whether he still lived in Meadville.

After our arrival, Mark's sister started making phone calls, and sure enough, she located Kenny Mook. Wow! I was totally surprised and excited to talk with him after all those years. We arranged to meet the very next day, Sunday, Memorial Day 1991.

After our reunion, Kenny and I decided to meet again for a longer period of time at his dairy farm in Saegertown, Pennsylvania. During that weeklong visit, I was up early every morning, helping to milk the cows, haul buckets of milk, and perform various other daily farm chores. I even got to watch a cow give birth to a calf in the barn, a fascinating experience for a guy who'd lived most of his life in large cities.

After each day's work, Kenny and I spent hours sitting at the kitchen table talking about where our lives had taken us the past twenty-five years. We also spoke of how we'd met and what we remembered about the battle of Bong Son where Kenny was wounded. I would say something about what I remembered and Kenny would finish the sentence; then he would say something and I'd fill in what I remembered. That exchange went on and on as if that battle had happened yesterday. I was astonished by our recollection of details. It was then that I decided to write it all down in a memoir for our families.

My reunion with Kenny is what really sparked my motivation to continue writing about the rest of my Vietnam experiences with the 44th Scout Dog Platoon. I took my time developing each story that had had an impact on my life in Vietnam. I finally completed the first rough draft in 1997. I had shared a few chapters with family and friends. They enjoyed the stories and thought that I should try to get my manuscript published, but I didn't take them seriously.

In early spring 1998, I read a brief advertisement about a Vietnam veteran dog-handlers' association in a magazine a neighbor had given me. After inquiring, I joined so I could start searching for dog handlers I had served with in the 44th Scout Dog Platoon. I located Dan Scott, Oliver Whetstone, Dan Barnett, and Mike McClellan, all key figures in some of the stories I had written. I met them all at different times and places, and each shared his memories, authentic documents, and photos, which added important detail to my stories.

Coincidentally, a documentary company was at that time searching for candidates to participate in the production of a TV documentary titled *War Dogs, America's Forgotten Heroes.* It was to be produced by GRB Entertainment in Hollywood. I volunteered and was interviewed over the phone. When I told the interviewer that I had an unpublished manuscript, he got excited and asked me to mail it to GRB for consideration. I decided to mail just few chapters. Before long, I got a call from the executive producer who was very excited about what I had written.

He offered me a free roundtrip plane ticket from Washington, D.C., to Los Angeles to be interviewed.

It was the first time I had ever been interviewed. I sat on a simple straight-back chair with the camera and interviewer at arm's length in front of me. I was instructed to relax and just look at and speak directly to the interviewer and not look into the camera. I was stiff and very nervous until I got past the warm-up questions and into storytelling mode. The interviewer's questions probed deep into my recollection of the details I had written about in chapters titled "Death in the Kennel," "Timber," "Trapped," Trip Wires," and "Goodbye, Clipper." I broke down emotionally several times throughout the long and intense interview. When it was over, the lights came on. I was exhausted—and the onlookers nearby were in tears.

✳

After returning home, I received a phone call from a GRB executive producer asking me to be a technical consultant for development and production of the live reenactment scenes for the documentary. I flew back to California and spent a week in a mobile trailer on the set. Each morning and throughout the day and night, I'd advise the producers, director, actors, and set construction crew on appearance, uniforms, dog-handler language, and staging the action scenes. I asked many of the participants to write a comment in my journal, which they did, and I still have it on my bookshelf as a memento.

Segments of my interview were selected as part of the promotional clip of the documentary prior to its airing on national TV. Subsequently, I traveled to New York in February 1999 and spoke at a fundraising dinner after the annual Westminster Dog Show. Then I was interviewed at CBS by nationally syndicated radio host Charles Osgood; the interview aired on *The Osgood File*. I was given a copy of the interview as a keepsake.

The finished documentary *War Dogs, America's Forgotten Heroes*, aired nationally on the Discovery Channel in 1999. The producers chose me to answer questions from the public, via telephone, immediately after the broadcast. The questions were screened by a moderator and passed to me. That was my first live exposure and interaction with a national audience, albeit telephonically. The documentary was a huge success for GRB Entertainment and for all the Vietnam veteran dog handlers who participated. Sadly, some of them have since passed away.

GRB
ENTERTAINMENT

November 11, 1998

Mr. John Burnam
4807 Executive Drive
Gainesville, VA 20155

Dear John:

I wanted to thank you for the relentless expertise, concern, and creativity you've brought in your role as Technical Advisor to our production of WAR DOGS. I know I speak for everyone at the Discovery Network as well.

When we invited you to play this special role, we knew we were getting someone who could ensure verisimilitude in myriad ways. What we didn't fully appreciate is how compassionately you would guide all of us -- the director, writer, actors, and crew -- to a deep and resonant understanding of the bond between animal and man, and the experience of being a young soldier in Vietnam.

Thank you for entrusting us with your story -- and helping us to tell it.

With great appreciation!

John Drimmer
Supervising Producer

cc: Tim Prokop

12001 Ventura Place, Sixth Floor, Studio City, CA 91604   (818) 753-3400   FAX: (818) 753-3401

Letter to John Burnam from GRB Entertainment.

By the spring of 1999, I had written many literary agents and mainstream publishers asking for a review of my manuscript for publication. Most never replied, and those who did liked the war-dog angle but rejected the manuscript on the grounds that Vietnam was a saturated subject, that my story would appeal to a small niche audience and was too risky an investment. I was disheartened after having been so optimistic, but I kept my chin up and contacted Cynthia Frank, president of Cypress House in Fort Bragg, California. What an incredible process that turned out to be. I was directly involved in all the decisions throughout the process: editing, layout, photo selection and placement, cover design, acquiring endorsements, printing, and marketing. Cynthia gave me an invaluable education in the business of publishing, and I thoroughly enjoyed the experience.

The first edition of *Dog Tags of Courage* was released in late 1999 after the TV premier of the documentary. I was so excited to hold the first copy in my hands and examine every page with a smile on my face. It was exhilarating to see what I'd begun as a brief memoir in 1991 become a salable hardcover book like the many others on my bookshelf. I mailed autographed copies to Kenny Mook and his family, my family, and those close friends who were directly involved with motivating me to never give up.

Not long afterward I got requests for book signings at Books-a-Million, Barnes and Noble, and Borders Books. The audiences were small but eager to hear what I had to say about what war dogs did in Vietnam. As time passed, I was invited to speak to veterans' organizations, dog-rescue organizations, police canine associations, dog-related businesses, middle schools, high schools, colleges, and universities.

John Burnam Fox News TV interview about Dog Tags of Courage.

I was even invited to ride in Veterans Day parades in the cities of Cleveland, Ohio, Birmingham, Alabama, and Phoenix, Arizona. No matter what part of the country I traveled, I got the same comment over and over again: "I didn't know we had dogs in Vietnam."

My book and storytelling success was gaining traction, so much so that I got a call from Hollywood's Lawrence Gordon Productions. I was so excited that I about fell out of my chair. They wanted permission to write a screenplay for Universal Studios based on *Dog Tags of Courage.* We agreed to a three-year contract, and I worked via phone as the technical consultant with screenwriters throughout the development of the screenplay. When it was completed in 2003, Universal Studios decided not to fund production of the film. Again, I was deeply disappointed. The screenplay still sits on my bookshelf.

After that discouraging news from Universal Studios, Marnie Wooding, an independent screenwriter and author, contacted me in 2003.

Marnie established Crooked Door Entertainment and wrote a screenplay titled "Moe." Moe was a fictional heroic German shepherd scout dog in Vietnam. The screenplay was for a PG-rated film loosely based on the stories in *Dog Tags of Courage*. Marnie and I worked together for three years creating and updating the screenplay, and Marnie worked tirelessly to attract investors for producing "Moe" as an independent film. She even met with some Hollywood production studios that expressed interest. "Moe" never got funded for production, however, and Marnie and I parted ways. "Moe" too sits on my bookshelf.

In 2004, TV documentarist for the History Channel called me to request an interview about my experiences as a scout-dog handler in Vietnam. I agreed to be their primary candidate for the documentary titled *Hero Dogs*. I was interviewed at several locations in northern Virginia and assisted with staging the reenactment scenes also filmed in northern Virginia. *Hero Dogs* aired on national TV on the History Channel and got excellent reviews.

In 2005, the film producers of the TV series *Dogs with Jobs* called me. They wanted to interview me as the primary story for a new episode. I agreed not to accept payment except for travel expenses, which was expected of primary participants in documentaries. The interview took place in my home in Fairfax, Virginia, and at the historic Hartsdale Pet Cemetery in New York. The documentary was titled *Clipper – War Dog*, and aired many times on various cable TV stations over several years.

I continued to receive requests for interviews from newspapers and magazines, especially for Memorial Day and Veteran's Day articles. I had also written several articles and was interviewed by writers of feature articles that appeared in *Vietnam Magazine, Northern Virginia Magazine, Spirit* magazine, *Dog Fancy, Northwoods, Korean War Veterans Association* magazine, *American Working Dog* magazine, *Military Police Regimental Association* magazine, and others.

John Burnam and reporter supporting pet
adoptions outside a pet-supply store.

In the process of having my name, books, and documentaries represented in the public eye, I received requests from budding authors who picked my brain on how they could get started writing their own stories and screenplays about war dogs of the various wars.

I had immersed myself in the subject matter of war dog stories of all wars since WWII. My work drew many letters and emails from people of all ages. I was thrilled by the number of people who had read my articles and wanted to hear me tell war-dog stories. It became quite evident that the war dogs, not so much the wars, were the key focus.

The most important book endorsements I received came from other veteran war-dog handlers who told me that my story was their story — we'd just had different dogs in Vietnam. I also received heartening letters from families who had lost loved ones who were dog handlers in Vietnam. They thanked me for writing *Dog Tags of Courage,* saying that they now knew a little more about what it must have been like for their loved one who was killed in action.

One of the surprise compliments I received was from Jennifer Mackler, who said that my war-dog stories had inspired her to become a veterinarian. Jennifer was also a member of a Colorado search-and-rescue dog club. She invited me to go on a training mission with her club members in the mountains of northern Colorado. I had a great time watching the German shepherd dog teams work out various search-and-rescue scenarios.

Upon graduating from the College of Veterinary Medicine at Colorado State University, Fort Collins, Colorado, Jennifer entered the U.S. Army as a veterinarian with the rank of captain. After completing her military service obligation, Jennifer started her own private practice.

✸

Wherever I traveled to speak, people would pull me aside to share personal stories of their family's pet dog. Over the years, I've received thousands of emails, including some from Poland, Israel, Germany, Canada, Australia, Mexico, Thailand, the UK, South Africa, and elsewhere.

As time passed, I continued to receive requests for interviews from national and local newspapers, dog and history magazines, TV news shows, and radio shows. I had become a de facto public advocate for the war dogs of all wars since WWII. My involvement over the years became a life-changing pursuit that I never envisioned influencing my life the way it has.

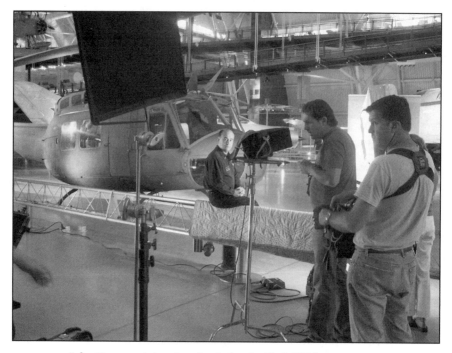

John Burnam interview for Animals Aloft *TV documentary.*

The one question I started to hear most often was "Why don't we have a national memorial for war dogs?" Great question. I had no answer, but the question stuck in my head — I too needed to know why.

Chapter 27

National Monument Legislation

I HAD BECOME ONE of the subjects of an article, "Let Us Remember Our Forgotten Heroes," in the April 1, 2001 issue of *PARADE* magazine. Pulitzer Prize-winning journalist Richard Ben Cramer wrote the article. Mr. Cramer contacted me and asked if I had any plans to establish a national memorial in Washington, D.C. I told him that that was the dream of every military dog handler I knew.

Mr. Cramer was on a short deadline and gave me just a few days to make a decision. Thirty-three million copies circulated across America — with a huge front-page photo of Stubby, WWI canine hero and a full feature article on war dogs — was difficult to pass up, so I launched the idea for a national war dogs' memorial and became its point of contact.

Military dog handlers across the country were pleasantly surprised when they got their copies of *PARADE* magazine in the Sunday papers. Based on the emails I had received, the general public's response was also supportive. I saw this as an opportunity for *all* military dog handlers to get behind a purpose larger than ourselves.

I realized that a national memorial would be a formidable task and that failure was certainly a real possibility, but to accept fear of failure before even trying was ridiculous. I had no experience with national memorials other than visiting them. After reading and listening to arguments on both sides of the issue, I decided to find out where this idea might take me.

As I dug deeper into the subject, I knew I was going to need help, so I contacted several veteran dog handlers who supported my idea. We formed a small ad hoc committee to discuss how to proceed. We all lived in different parts of the country, so communication was via email and phone. Face-to-face meetings were out of the question at the time because the cost would have had to come out of the family budget and no one was ready to take that step. However, they were all passionate and enthusiastic about taking the memory of the beloved war dogs to the highest level of recognition — a national memorial. Of course they all looked at little ol' me as the point man to lead the effort, and I was okay with that.

Our first specific task was to develop a brief mission statement of exactly what we wanted to accomplish. The general tasks included a design concept, a place to build the memorial, and the money to pay for it. Each of these elements presented more head-scratching questions, because no one had a clue about the process required to get there. We needed to dig into each task separately before outlining any kind of plan. It was a tall order with a lot of unknowns. It was also impossible to establish any reasonable timeline to complete any task.

I spent many hours and long nights thinking and researching in books, on the Internet, and in the library for anything about the U.S. military war-dog story. I did all this after my daytime job as a senior technical writer/editor at Bart and Associates, Inc. I learned that the official start of the U.S. military war-dog program was in 1942 and that dogs had been used in every war since. The idea popped into my head that a national memorial should probably represent all the war dogs and handlers who'd served in WWII, the Korean War, the Vietnam War, the Gulf War, and the wars in Afghanistan and Iraq. Everyone agreed.

The project came to a dead stop on September 11, 2001 when an airplane crashed into the World Trade Center in New York City. I was at my desk at work when an associate summoned me to the conference room to show me the TV news coverage. I stood there silently watching the smoke rise from the top of the building and listening to the nonstop chatter of the news reporters on every station describing all that they were learning minute by minute. I didn't know what to expect next.

I was stunned when a second plane crashed into the Pentagon and a third crashed into the second World Trade Center tower and a fourth crashed in a field in Pennsylvania. I had friends who worked in the Pentagon, which was not far from my office building. America was under attack, and I decided to leave the office and head home to start making phone calls to check on family and friends.

It was reported that the attacks were carried out by the Islamic terrorist group al-Qaeda. The United States was in a frenzy of confusion, yet swelling with patriotism I hadn't seen before. It was the beginning of the "War on Terror," and I fully immersed myself in the news stories. I had supported the decisions by President George W. Bush and the U.S. Congress to deploy American troops to Afghanistan and Iraq to take the fight to the terrorists' homelands. Americans from all walks of life were volunteering for military service to join the fight against the terrorists.

A friend in New York City informed me that a Vietnam veteran scout-dog handler, Robert B. Nagel, had died in the collapse of the World Trade Center. Robert was a lieutenant with the New York City Fire Department responding to the call of duty. I flew to New York to attend Mr. Nagel's memorial service and had a chance to meet his family. Afterward, I was given an escort to "Ground Zero" to view the aftermath. I had entered through the security gate and the aproned fence that surrounded the entire site. The incredible sight and smell of huge piles of burnt debris brought tears to my eyes. I stood there in silence watching the many workers and vehicles moving about the wreckage. It was a sad and mesmerizing experience, one I will never forget.

Robert B. Nagel and his scout dog, Prince, 59th Scout Dog Platoon, Vietnam (1969–1970). Lt. Nagel died in the line of duty, saving lives at the World Trade Center on September 11, 2001.

After the Iraq War dubbed Operation Iraqi Freedom was well under-way in 2004, I got back to my involvement with the monument project. Research had led me to the National Parks Service headquartered in Washington, D.C. NPS was a significant government agency directly involved in the approval process. They had records of a few public inquiries over the years asking the government to establish a national memorial for the war dogs; however, building national memorials was not part of their congressional mandate. Most interesting was that none of the folks behind the public inquiries ever followed through to pursue establishing a national memorial once they'd learned that NPS was not in the business of building them.

I learned from NPS that any proposal for a national memorial required the support of a U.S. senator or representative to sponsor leg-islation. In other words, approval of a national memorial would have to become a law enacted by Congress and signed by the President of the

United States. The process of enacting a new law could take years, and there was no guarantee of approval. The idea for a national memorial was shaping up to be a marathon of time and effort.

Committing several years to this project with no guarantee of the outcome doused the once fiery enthusiasm of many of the volunteers I had recruited. One by one, they dropped out to watch from the sidelines or just move on in their lives. I wasn't about to join them because I had just begun to scratch the surface of what I needed to find out. I had no idea just how far we could get before being officially rejected by the bureaucrats in Washington.

A major task I took on was to find and persuade a U.S. senator or representative to sponsor the needed legislation on Capitol Hill. This was difficult and very time consuming; for each appointment I had to take time off work to travel to Washington during normal business hours. I was fortunate to get appointments and sometimes met with the senator or representative. On other visits I had met only with their legislative assistants.

I showed up for each appointment dressed in a business suit and tie and polished shoes. My well-rehearsed sales presentation was short and to the point. The idea for a national memorial was always well received, but in the end they all said no. Their greatest concerns were that it could potentially take years to get through all the legislative gates and they couldn't possibly add another demanding task to their growing list of commitments to their constituents. However, each representative I met stated that he or she would vote for the bill if it ever got to the floor of the Senate or the House.

I had worn out my dress shoes walking the corridors of the Russell Senate Office Building, Dirksen Senate Office Building, Hart Senate Office Building, Cannon House Office Building, Longworth House Office Building, and the Rayburn House Office Building. I had learned exactly where the government was on Capitol Hill, and learned to use a taxi because there was no parking near any of the buildings. I also got more efficient at adding effective talking points to my oral and written presentations each time I met with someone new. The entire effort was evolving but funded out-of-pocket, and used all of my earned vacation time from my day job at Bart and Associates, Inc.

John Burnam and U.S. Representative Walter B. Jones,
3rd District, North Carolina.

I got lucky In February 2005, when I met with Representative Walter B. Jones, 3rd District of North Carolina. We first met in his office, which was then in the Cannon House Office Building in Washington, D.C. We had a long and productive conversation about the use of dogs to save lives in every war since WWII and the importance of recognizing them with their own national memorial. When our conversation ended, Congressman Jones smiled and thanked me for my military service and passionate commitment to the project. As I got up to leave, we shook hands and he looked me in the eye and said he would be honored to sponsor the legislation in Congress. I was ecstatic to have finally gotten a yes after so many failures!

Congressman Jones had asked if we were seeking government funding. "Absolutely not," I said. "Our plan is to seek public funding because the national memorial would belong to the American people, and we're confident that they will fund it."

At the time, I had no idea how much money we would need, especially since we hadn't progressed to an approved design or cost estimate. My presentation was about why America needed a national memorial, not its design and cost. Congressman Jones smiled and said that we would have a better chance of getting congressional support if we didn't ask the government for taxpayer money. He also said that we needed to be patient because it would take time to get things moving.

Every little success reenergized my enthusiasm and motivation to keep going with the dream of a national memorial. The day came when I got a call from Congressman Jones about drafting the bill of resolution with his legislative assistant, Joshua Bowlen. We worked closely on the language. A key element I fought for was language that would allow public access to people and their dogs, and it made it into the final bill.

During a subsequent meeting with Congressman Jones, he invited representatives of the National Park Service: the Deputy Associate Regional Director of Lands, Resources and Planning; the Assistant Director, Office of Legislative & Congressional Affairs; and the Legislative Liaison of the National Capital Region. After my formal presentation, NPS agreed to move our proposal for a national memorial into the formal congressional subcommittee process. This was a huge step forward!

There were many reasons for establishing the memorial on the National Mall in Washington, D.C. The primary one was that tens of thousands of war dogs and handlers had been trained and deployed with

American ground forces in every war memorialized on the National Mall. Many thousands were wounded, maimed, and killed defending and saving American men and women on battlefields of every war since WWII. They had earned the right to be recognized and honored alongside the other memorials on the National Mall.

John Burnam and U.S. Representative Roscoe Bartlett of Maryland at Civil War Festival Event next to Antietam Civil War Battlefield, Sharpsburg, Maryland. Congressman Bartlett sponsored the legislation that authorized the Department of Defense to allow public adoption of military working dogs retired from military service. President Bill Clinton signed the legislation into law on November 6, 2001.

Living in the metro area of Washington, D.C., I had visited the National Mall many times. I had attended the official dedication ceremonies of the Vietnam Veterans Memorial on November 13, 1982 and the WWII Memorial on May 29, 2004. They were once-in-a-lifetime historical events that swelled my American pride. On Memorial Day in 2007, I was invited to give a speech about the use of dogs during the Vietnam War at the Vietnam Women's Memorial. It was a clear, sunny day and many people gathered to listen. The media roamed the hallowed grounds interviewing people. It was easy to envision the national memorial for the war dogs there on the National Mall where every military dog handler thought it should be.

In June 2006, Congressman Jones introduced H.R. 5145 to the U.S. House Committee on Resources of the 109th Congress. The committee consisted of representatives from the Republican and Democratic parties. A Republican chaired the committee since they were the majority party at the time. The Committee on Resources is directly responsible for the nation's natural resources, which includes national parks. H.R. 5145 was the first bill of legislation ever proposed for a national monument for military working dogs and handlers on the National Mall in Washington, D.C., which is classified as national park land.

I was the only veteran war-dog handler summoned by official letter from Richard Pombo, Republican from California and Chairman of the committee, to appear at a hearing and give oral and written testimony. The letter read in part: "I cordially invite you to testify before the Subcommittee on National Parks on Thursday, June 28, 2006, at 10 a.m. in 1334 Longworth House Office Building. The subcommittee will conduct a legislative hearing on H.R. 5145, to authorize the National War Dogs Monument."

I was seated at a small table behind a microphone and timer as the chairman introduced me. I gave a passionate ten-minute speech for the congressional record.

John Burnam (center) testifying before the
U.S. House Committee on Resources.

Chairman Pombo and the other committee members thanked me for my enthusiasm. Mr. Pombo then reflected on the Commemorative Works Act of 1986, stating portions of the law that restricted our unit-type memorial from being approved for placement on National Park Service land and the National Mall. The Chairman stated that if H.R. 5145 were to be amended to say "on military property," it would be in conformance with the nation's Commemorative Works Act of 1986.

He pointed out that there were legal aspects we needed to be conscious of before Congress passed the Commemorative Works Act in 1986. He pointed out that Congress was, at the time, concerned about two memorials that were already moving through the legislature. They were the Law Enforcement Officers Memorial and the Women in Military Service Memorial. The concern was that Congress was starting to allow the building of unit memorials to professions, and this could result in many more being commemorated on lands administered by the National Park Service.

It wasn't long after the Law Enforcement Officers Memorial was adopted and built that the Emergency Medical Technicians and the Teachers of America came to Congress with their proposals for national memorials on national park land. The solution was adoption of the Commemorative Works Act of 1986, which now restricts all other groups from being authorized to build national memorials to themselves. This, Mr. Pombo stated, applied to dog handlers wishing to commemorate not only themselves but also their canine companions on the National Mall. The Chairman's advice to Congressman Jones was to amend H.R. 5145 in such a way that the memorial could be placed on military property and then resubmit the bill to the committee for reconsideration.

The other military war memorials on the National Mall represented an entire war and all armed services, all occupations, and the men and women who had served. The monuments had also met the criterion of memorializing wars that had been over for twenty-five years or more. Lastly, there was a moratorium in place that prevented any more memorials on the National Mall. Future national memorials meeting the criteria of the Commemorative Works Act of 1986 would have to be placed on other National Park Service lands.

Shortly thereafter, I was summoned to appear before the National Capitol Memorial Advisory Commission. This congressionally mandated body comprised representatives from the National Park Service, General Services Administration, National Capitol Planning Commission, Commission of Fine Arts, District of Columbia, Architect of the Capitol, American Battle Monuments Commission, and the Department of Defense.

I sat before Chairman John G. Parsons and made my oral argument for passage of H.R. 5145. The members of the commission listened with interest. When I finished, they addressed the restrictions of the Commemorative Works Act of 1986 and the moratorium on the National Mall. They concluded that H.R. 5145 had merit as a national memorial if we would modify the legislation to accept a military installation. The Department of Defense representative suggested that the U.S. Army Museum being constructed at Fort Belvoir, Virginia could be a consideration with public access, and keep the monument in the Washington, D.C. metro area. I nodded my head in agreement with his suggestion.

*John Burnam testifying before the National
Capitol Memorial Advisory Commission.*

The General Services Administration representative said that he was very impressed with my presentation and thought I had made a strong case, especially with regard to what had happened to the war dogs in Vietnam. He was sorry that the law was written the way it was, preventing us from building the monument on the National Mall.

Not long after the committee's decisions, I met with Congressman Walter Jones and Department of Defense officials to discuss amending the language of H.R. 5145 by including Fort Belvoir, Virginia, as a potential site. After the midterm elections in November 2006, however, the Democrats had won the majority of the seats in the House of Representatives, and became the majority party.

The House Committee on Resources reorganized under the new Democratic leadership, and they purged all pending bills, which included H.R. 5145, from any further action. After having gotten so far in the process, we were all stunned by the setback.

Undiscouraged, Richard Deggans, Larry Chilcoat, and I (the committee of volunteer veteran dog handlers) dug into our family budgets and met in a hotel in Corpus Christie, Texas, on [insert date] to hammer out a plan to get better organized. Since Larry and his wife lived nearby, they made all the arrangements. Emails and phone calls were fine, but there was nothing more productive than a face-to-face meeting over two days to discuss ideas and tasks.

We had established the John Burnam Monument Foundation, Inc. Everyone felt that my name in the title would help promote the project, because I had already gained some national recognition and had a successful track record of accomplishments (point man on Capitol Hill, published author, subject of TV documentaries and interviews nationwide, speechmaker, author of articles, etc.). From my perspective, having my name in the title just put more pressure on *me* to succeed, so there was no way I could quit even if I'd wanted to!

I was voted president, Larry Chilcoat became treasurer, and Richard Deggans took the job of secretary of JBMF, Inc. We were all veteran dog handlers of the Vietnam War. Together, we had developed our bylaws and operational procedures. Richard prepared all the paperwork to register JBMF, Inc. as a corporation in the state of Texas. We received the Texas Certificate of Formation as a Domestic Nonprofit Corporation approved by the Office of the Secretary of State on June 2, 2008.

Richard also prepared the paperwork for establishing JBMF, Inc. as a 501(c)(3) tax-exempt charity with the Internal Revenue Service (IRS). The Department of the Treasury approved our tax-exempt status on June 2, 2008. We were issued an Employer Identification Number (EIN 30-0487417), which authorized us to operate as a tax-exempt public charity, and we opened a bank account with SunTrust Bank in Washington, D.C., to manage and account for all public donations and grants. We had about $10,000 in the fund at the time.

JBMF, Inc. original board of directors:
Richard Deggans, secretary; John Burnam, president;
Larry Chilcoat, treasurer (photo taken in John's private home office).

Richard was the technical website developer who established the JBMF domain name for our website: www.jbmf.us. Together we worked hard to gather information and artifacts to load the web pages of the new website.

I began work with Congressman Jones and his legislative staff on a new bill. In April 2007, Congressman Jones resubmitted the national monument through the House Armed Services Subcommittee as part of H.R. 4986 National Defense Authorizations Act for FY 2008.

I remember a reporter asking me, "*What will you do, Mr. Burnam, if Congress doesn't pass the legislation?*" I thought about it for a minute and then said, "*I guess I'll have to organize the million-dog march on Washington, D.C.!*" My reply always got a good laugh when I told other people about that reporter's question.

The question was answered on January 28, 2008, when President George W. Bush signed H.R. 4986 into law, authorizing a national monument for military working-dog teams. It was a day to celebrate the years of relentless hard work.

Subsequently, H.R. 4986 was amended by Congressman Jones to authorize the John Burnam Monument Foundation, Inc. to build and maintain the monument. The amendment passed the U.S. House and Senate and was signed into public law 110-181 by President Barack Obama on October 28, 2009. The bill reads:

H.R. 4986 National Defense Authorization Act, FY 2008

Amended by H.R. 2647 – October 28, 2009

(PUBLIC LAW 110-181)

SEC. 2877. Establishment of national military working dog teams monument on suitable military installation.

AUTHORITY TO ESTABLISH MONUMENT – The Secretary of Defense may permit the John Burnam Monument Foundation, Inc., to establish and maintain, at a suitable location at Fort Belvoir, Virginia, or another military installation in the United States, a national monument to honor the sacrifice and service of United States Armed Forces working dog teams that have participated in the military operations of the United States.

LOCATION AND DESIGN OF MONUMENT – The actual location and final design of the monument authorized by subsection (a) shall be subject to the approval of the Secretary. In selecting the military installation and site on such installation to serve as the location for the monument, the Secretary shall seek to maximize access to the resulting monument for both visitors and their dogs.

MAINTENANCE – The maintenance of the monument authorized by subsection (a) by the John Burnam Monument Foundation, Inc., shall be subject to such conditions

regarding access to the monument, and such other conditions, as the Secretary considers appropriate to protect
the interests of the United States.

LIMITATION ON PAYMENT OF EXPENSES – The United
States Government shall not pay any expense for the establishment or maintenance of the monument authorized by
subsection (a).

Chapter 28

Monument Design

Graphic rendering of national monument design.

THE MONUMENT'S DESIGN had to be simple to understand, mean-ingful, accurate in its military representation, and an eye magnet. We all agreed that its centerpiece should be dogs and dog handlers. Since the monument was conceived to incorporate all wars from WWII to the wars Afghanistan and Iraq, the question was: what dogs and what dog handlers should be represented?

After research and much deliberation, it became clear that only a few dog breeds were used more than others in each war. During WWII, the Doberman pinscher played a huge role in the Pacific theater as a scout and sentry dog. German shepherds performed primarily as sentries, scouts, and messengers in both the Pacific and European Theaters of WWII. On the home front, the Coast Guard deployed German shepherds to guard America's coastal waters, beaches, and the major river-ways during WWII.

During the Korean War, the German shepherd was the prominent breed used for scouting and sentry duty. During the Vietnam War, the German shepherd was the dominant breed for scouting, sentry, patrol, and mine and booby-trap detection. A small number of Labrador retrievers were introduced during the Vietnam War as trackers.

During the Gulf War, Afghanistan War, and Iraq War, the German shepherd, Labrador retriever, and the Belgian Malinois were extensively deployed to search for improvised explosive devices (IEDs), mine detection, patrolling, building search, drug detection, and cadaver search.

We narrowed the number of working dogs to those four breeds. We discussed adding to the design one dog handler for each dog; however, I thought that adding four dog handlers outfitted in different war-era combat gear wouldn't work unless we connected each one to a dog. If we did that, I felt, we would defeat Richard Deggan's idea to not place specific war equipment on each dog because dogs had served in more than one war. After much discussion, we decided on one dog handler to represent the handlers of all wars since WWII and to not place any equipment of the dogs.

I suggested using the image of a military working-dog handler of the wars in Iraq and Afghanistan to represent all military dog handlers past and present. All agreed. We also decided that the dog handler should be outfitted in full combat gear, with weapon at the ready, and standing in an alert position behind the four dogs fanned out to his front. Each dog breed would also stand facing out in an erect and alert position of strength and vigilance.

The question was: What size should the dogs and handler be? We settled on 1.5 times the life size of each dog breed and 1.5 times the life size of a six-foot dog handler. We also decided that the statues must be cast from the purest bronze we could find on the American market. We agreed that whenever we got enough donations, we would hire only American businesses to provide all the products and services needed to build the monument.

The board of directors gave me the lead role to develop and coordinate the design and architectural aspects of the monument. The conceptual narrative design and pencil sketch I had created was given to graphic designer Brian Rich to render the balance, proportion, size, and color scheme. Brian was the first graphic artist to help us. We worked together to develop the logos needed to identify and symbolize JBMF, Inc. and the national monument's theme. Brian did a terrific job of bringing the monument to life in colorful graphics.

Brian Rich was the uncle of U.S. Marine Corporal Dustin Lee, a dog handler who was killed in Iraq on March 21, 2007. I had met Brian as a result of helping his sister, Rachel Lee, in her family's efforts to get the Marine Corps to allow them to adopt Dustin's military working dog, Lex, who had been severely wounded by shrapnel but survived the enemy rocket blast that had killed Rachel's eldest son, Dustin. Lex was recovering from his wounds at Albany Marine Corps Logistics Base in Georgia, and had been assigned as a training dog for new dog handlers. His health restricted his physical performance as a training dog.

The family had tried in vain for months to adopt Lex from the Marine Corps after they buried Dustin in April 2007. It was October and still no word. Ms. Kelly Hooker, a friend of the Lee family, brought their story to my attention and asked for my help in October 2007. I agreed to do what I could to help. In early November, I brought the Lee family's story to the attention of U.S. Representative Walter B. Jones during a scheduled meeting about the national monument. After our meeting, I read him a short story I had written titled "My Partner Dustin." I wrote it to draw public attention to the Lees' quest to adopt Lex. It was also written from the dog's perspective, telling of what had happened to him during and after the attack that had killed his master, and how, all alone in his kennel, Lex grieved for his partner as the days and months passed by.

Congressman Jones was moved by the Lee family's story and agreed to help. We had appeared together on a few Albany, Georgia, radio shows in November 2007 to support Lex's adoption. Congressman Jones also worked directly with the Marine Corps at the Pentagon to secure their approval. On December 21, 2007, the U.S. Marine Corps officially retired Lex to the Lee family with full military honors. The event was recorded by local and national TV news (FOX, ABC, and CBS) at the Albany Marine Corps Logistics Base. After the adoption, I traveled to Quitman, Mississippi, in February 2008 to meet with the Lee family and Lex for the first time. I visited "Dustin's Place," as Mrs. Lee called Dustin's gravesite, which was within walking distance of Mrs. Lee's parents' home in Quitman, Mississippi.

Dustin's uncle, Brian Rich, offered to help me in any way he could. When I asked him what he did for a living, he said he was a professional graphics artist. I immediately saw a need for his skills. Bryan developed the first graphic rendering of my pencil sketches of the monument's design. We spent several months working out details, until Brian had developed the design into a rendering that I could use in presentations.

Our bank account had built up enough public donations that we were able to hire Paula Slater, a renowned master of bronze sculpting. Several other sculptors submitted proposals, but Paula's was the most complete and articulate proposal on how the process of sculpting big dogs and humans worked from sketch to foundry molds to polished bronze. We were all impressed with Paula's passion for dogs and patriotic support of our nation's armed services. Paula's collection of completed artwork demonstrated her skills and attention to detail, which had been honed over many years of sculpting bronze statues.

Paula's first task was to sculpt an eighteen-inch miniature clay model of the monument's pedestal figures of four dogs and one dog handler. We were captivated by Paula's first creation, which required only minimal modification by the Pentagon's Department of Defense Military Working Dog officials.

Paula's attention to the tiniest details of canine anatomy made her work incredibly lifelike. After the clay model had been modified to specifications, Paula was awarded a contract to sculpt the first 1.5-sized Doberman pinscher. Paula's Doberman turned out better than anyone had expected. We kept Paula busy with successive contracts for each of the other three dogs

Twelve-inch bronze model sculpted by Paula Slater and bronzed by Mussi Artworks Foundry, Berkeley, Calif.

John Burnam and Artist Paula Slater with nine-foot bronze military dog handler at Mussi Artworks Foundry, December 2012.

When all the dogs were finished in bronze, we awarded Paula the contract to sculpt the nine-foot military dog handler. It too turned out to be an exceptional work of art. It took Paula three years to complete the entire effort and deliver five bronze statues in December 2012. Everyone was extremely impressed with each bronze figure.

I had the idea of adding a granite history wall behind the pedestal of the bronze statues. The wall would reflect a narrative of the service and sacrifice of dogs and handlers. All the granite was to come from the same quarry in Vermont. I also added a statement of recognition about the military veterinary corps. The following is the final narrative that was approved for engraving on the granite history wall's three panels (16' × 9' × 1.5'):

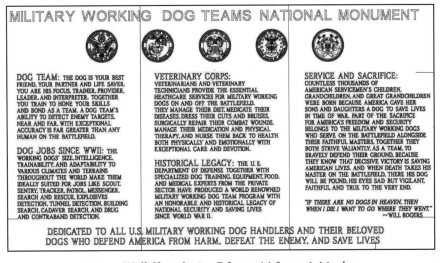

History Wall (front), size 7 feet × 14 feet × 1.4 inches;
narrative by John Burnam.

Since the back of the History Wall was blank, we developed the idea of adding laser-etched images of authentic photos of the military working-dog teams in action for each of the wars they had served in since WWII. I felt that the photos should represent the same dog breeds sculpted in bronze on the large granite pedestal of the monument. Our team accepted the idea. To assist in the research, I hired a professional National Archives researcher in Washington, D.C.

The task was to search the National Archives for archived photos depicting each dog breed in action scenes with their handler for each war since WWII. The researcher retrieved exactly the types of action photos I had requested. I carefully sorted through copies of the photos and chose those that fit the theme of the monument's design. Jim Smith, president of Laser Imaging and Design, Inc., expertly integrated the photos into a superb collage.

Laser-etched authentic photos on black granite (14 feet x 7 feet) attached to
back of History Wall. Design concept and photo selection by John Burnam;
artwork by Jim Smith, Laser Imaging Co.

The monument's components started to come to life as we added benches around the edge of the plaza. Larry Chilcoat had the idea to situate flagpoles — one for each of America's armed forces (Army, Marine Corps, Navy, Air Force, and Coast Guard) — behind the history wall.

We decided to use granite pavers for the entire walk-around area of the monument's 3,000 square-foot plaza. We added in-ground lighting for the bronze statues, the history wall, a dog water fountain, and flagpoles.

I wanted to add a functional dog water fountain so visiting dogs could have a drink. What I found on the Internet and elsewhere didn't fit the design or theme of the monument. For months, I struggled to come up with a design. One day, I recalled how I used to give water to my thirsty scout dogs, Clipper and Timber, in Vietnam. I would sit on the ground in the shade of a tree, remove my steel helmet from my head, place it on the ground, and pour water into it from my canteen. I passed a detailed written concept to Paula Slater, and she drew a pencil sketch.

Dave and Cheryl Duffield, founders of Maddie's Fund, a JBMF corporate sponsor, improved on the design by adding a circular granite pedestal with two curved granite benches, and a water trench carved into the granite, so that more than one dog could drink at the same time. Paula Slater used the Duffields' German shepherd, Sadie, as the model for the sculpture. The dog handler was sculpted in the image of a Vietnam War dog handler.

The sculpture was titled *Not Forgotten Fountain,* with the legend *"In everlasting memory of all the hero dogs that served, died, and were left behind in the Vietnam War."* — *John Burnam, Vietnam Scout Dog Handler*

Clay rendering of "Not Forgotten Fountain." Conceptual design by John Burnam. Sculptor, Paula Slater. Additional Design of German shepherd dog by Dave and Cheryl Duffield of Maddie's Fund.

After an exhausting compilation of every product and service and their purchase prices, I generated an itemized list of cost estimates (e.g., bronze sculptures of five dogs and two dog handlers, tons of granite, engraving, laser etching, construction of foundation, in-ground lighting units, flagpoles, landscaping, sprinkler system, contracts and contractors, attorney, accountant, operations, maintenance, etc.). The 5,000 square feet of space needed to assemble everything in was meticulously sized and measured. This included adding grass and an apron of indigenous vegetation to dress up the perimeter of the entire plaza. It looked very impressive in a graphic rendering on paper. Equally impressive was the estimated price tag of $2million.

Now, where exactly to build it?

Chapter 29

Monument Site Selection

IN OCTOBER 2010, the secretary of defense officially delegated the Department of the Army to establish the national monument at Fort Belvoir, Virginia, or another suitable installation under the jurisdiction of the secretary of the army. Fort Belvoir is less than thirty minutes south of our nation's capital, and appeared to be a promising location to build the monument.

Mr. Russell Santella, Environment and Installations, Office of the Assistant Secretary of the Army, Pentagon, was assigned to coordinate the meetings at Fort Belvoir. We met with the National U.S. Army Museum, Chief of Staff, Director Programs & Education, Acting Director, Exhibits/Collections, and the Civil Engineers. They had ninety acres of land that would be accessible to the public from a major road. Construction of the $200 million museum site had not started primarily due to a lack of funds.

The footprint of the monument was estimated at 5,000 square feet. Since construction of the National Army Museum hadn't yet begun, no one was sure where the monument would fit within the available land or even when we could start construction.

During one meeting, we were informed that the government had significantly reduced the museum's budget and available land from ninety acres to forty-one acres. As a result, I was informed that we had to reduce our monument's footprint to a simple pedestal of a dog and handler. Secondly, we couldn't start construction until after the museum was built in 2015. The idea of reducing the footprint and having to wait until 2015 to start construction, with no guarantee of that date, was distressing.

On October 6, 2011, I received a letter from the Department of the Army, Office of the Assistant Secretary of the Army, Installations, Energy and Environment. It read, in part:

> Thank you for your interest in the National Museum of the United States Army (NMUSA). The NMUSA staff has reviewed the information that you have provided and raises significant concerns about our ability to support the establishment of the Military Working Dog Teams National Monument on the grounds of the NMUSA. Due to site constraints and emerging guidelines for the allowable size of external monuments, there is no suitable location on the current site plan to accommodate the proposed 5,000 square feet required for the national monument.

The rejection letter was another devastating blow, and everyone felt very frustrated. We'd gotten used to telling people about Fort Belvoir and its amenities and the close proximity of Washington, D.C. Now we had to tell everyone that we had to find another place to build the monument. I kept telling myself, *"Patience, John, patience. We can work through this!"*

We wanted the monument to stay in the metropolitan area of Washington. I related our desires to Congressman Walter Jones and to Mr. Russ Santella, our contact at the Pentagon. Russ said that Fort Myer, Virginia, was interested in meeting with us. Fort Myer is the home of the Army's Old Guard and infantry regiment. It is a small historic army post established in 1887. The soldiers of the Old Guard were responsible for guarding the Tomb of the Unknown Soldier on the hallowed grounds of Arlington National Cemetery. The Old Guard also performed many other official and formal ceremonial details.

I met with the Fort Myer civil engineers and public affairs officer. We toured a few locations they felt could work for the monument. The immediate problems were a lack of available open spaces, very limited public parking, and restricted public access. In Fort Myer's favor were its historic buildings and easy access to the Arlington Memorial Bridge, which crosses over the scenic Potomac River into Washington, and the picturesque National Mall. After a careful evaluation, we decided to find another place.

As it turned out, there was nothing inside Washington suitable or available at the time. Security of the monument was a big issue for a Washington location. Our next opportunity was the National Museum of the Marine Corps situated next to the Marine Corps base in Quantico, Virginia. After a short meeting with the president of the board, the size of our monument's footprint was rejected as requiring too much land. It was suggested that if we were to reduce the space needed to a statue of a dog and handler on a pedestal, we could be given space to build it on the museum grounds. I decided to continue our search.

It had been in the back of my mind that if we could not build it in Washington, then perhaps Lackland Air Force Base in San Antonio, Texas, might be a viable site. After all, Lackland is where the Department of Defense had been training dogs and handlers of all the U.S. armed services since 1958. It was also the home of the world's largest veterinary hospital for military working dogs.

Russell Santella set up a meeting with officials at Lackland. I gave a presentation about the monument and how we had arrived at considering Lackland as its home. The audience was very enthusiastic about the opportunity to acquire the monument. The civil engineers had mapped out several sites that could handle the 5,000 square feet we needed. After a tour of potential sites, we picked a perfect spot on the corner of a huge parade field.

On June 26, 2013, Timothy K. Bridges, Deputy Assistant Secretary of the Air Force (Installations) at the Pentagon, signed the final letter of approval. The conditions were that JBMF, Inc. gift the national monument, estimated value $2,000,000, to Joint Base San Antonio Lackland,

Texas. JBMF, Inc. would also assume full responsibility for the maintenance of the national monument in perpetuity in accordance with Section 2877 of Public Law 110-181. Both sides accepted the terms.

National monument site at Lackland Air Force Base,
San Antonio, Texas. Black dot marks the location.

Building the monument at Lackland Air Force Base did not satisfy some folks. No matter how many times I tried to explain why it could not be built on the National Mall in Washington, they continued to demand that it be situated there. Unless people had gone through what I had experienced, they'd never fully understand the process of government and its many-layered bureaucracy. I was very satisfied with the monument being located at Lackland. We had tried our best to get it on the National Mall, but it was not to be.

I received a call from Doug Miller, DoD canine program manager, HQ Air Force Security Forces Center, Lackland AFB. Mr. Miller said that after having read *Dog Tags of Courage* he understood why I was leading the charge for a national monument. We conversed about my service as a dog handler in Vietnam and about what the school was doing to train dog teams for the war on terror.

Mr. Miller informed me of a Joint Service Military Working Dog Committee meeting at the Security Forces Center Headquarters Building on Lackland AFB. He invited me to give a thirty-minute presentation about the monument project. The U.S. Department of Defense Military Working Dog Program Managers representing each of the armed services would be in attendance, as would other officials. I accepted the invitation and gave my presentation to a very receptive audience of decision makers.

Master Sergeant Chris LaLonde, a highly decorated combat veteran dog handler of the Iraq and Afghanistan Wars, attended the meeting. Afterward, he escorted me on a visit to the dog handler basic training school. He had also read my book while in Iraq and we had communicated via email during his tour there. Master Sergeant LaLonde was the top sergeant in charge of the student population of trainees. He introduced me to several classrooms of students. They looked so young and so eager to be dog handlers. I spent several hours telling them stories of the heroic dogs of several wars, and then inscribed a copy of my book for each student.

U.S. Army Master Sergeant Chris LaLonde,
dog handler, with John Burnam.

After the classroom tour, I toured the huge number of dog kennels. There must have been 500 dogs housed there. I also visited the nearby Holland Military Working Dog Hospital. It was a very impressive veterinary care facility with state-of-the-art comprehensive healthcare equipment and expert veterinary staff. The hospital cares for approximately 900 dogs and puppies. I am so happy to have included the veterinary corps as part of the national monument because they have been such an integral part of the military working-dog program since WWII.

Lackland had turned out to be the right place to build the national monument. I envisioned that after the monument was in place that it would become the beacon location for all dog handlers, veteran and active duty, and their families to gather on Memorial Day, Veterans Day, and other special remembrance days and events.

U.S. Air Force Sergeant Len Anderson and his military working dog, Azza, and John Burnam, San Antonio, Texas, March 6, 2013. An American warrior wounded in Afghanistan, Len lost his right hand and incurred other severe wounds. Len was a graduate of the Lackland AFB military dog-training school.

Chapter 30

Monument Fundraising

U.S. Air Force Master Sergeant (RET.) Ken Licklider, veteran military working-dog handler, and John Burnam at a JBMF fundraiser in Washington, D.C., 2012.

WE HAD ALL THE CONTRACTORS in place waiting to construct the various components of the national monument at Lackland Air Force Base. Now we needed to raise the rest of the $2,000,000 to make it all happen.

Each member of the JBMF team pitched in to find people, organizations, and events where we could raise money. We developed a simple tri-fold brochure and tri-fold tabletop mobile displays about the monument. Our goal was to raise the funds needed to finish construction in time to dedicate the monument in October 2013.

Larry Chilcoat volunteered to start a letter campaign to acquire celebrity endorsements and donations. His effort brought in some donations and some key endorsements from the Oak Ridge Boys, General Colin L. Powell, General H. Norman Schwarzkopf, author Dean Koontz, and a number of Hollywood celebrities.

I developed a list of private businesses and corporations that provided products and services for the U.S. military working-dog programs and sent them introductory letters. I received only a few responses with small donations. I wrote articles that were published in newspapers and magazines promoting the monument and directing readers to visit the JBMF website and make donations. I was able to get an official endorsement from the American Veterinary Medical Association (AVMA), which resulted in some contributions from their membership.

The JBMF website (www.jbmf.us), which was created and managed by our secretary, Richard Deggans, started to receive a consistent flow of donations. Our website store sold hats and T-shirts and miniature bronze and resin models. We also received a steady flow of donations via our website's PayPal account. Richard contacted various veterans' associations and dog organizations, and used Facebook to generate more interest. We were on a roll, and public interest was growing at a fast pace. Everyone's efforts helped raise funds, but nowhere near the hundreds of thousands of dollars we needed. We realized that a big part of the problem was due to a poor economy that affected the discretionary funds available to businesses and family budgets across the country.

I will never forget the ten-year-old girl who walked up to the display table I was tending and, with a big smile, placed a handful of coins and a dollar bill into the donation jar. It made my day. That wasn't the only time children and other young people had made donations like that, and then shared a story with me about their pet dog.

WWII, Korean War, and Vietnam War veterans who were not dog handlers would stop by the display table and share their stories about having seen dogs on the battlefields. I thoroughly enjoyed doing fund-raising and educational events so I could meet people and share dog stories.

In July 2007, Congressman Jones interviewed me about *Dog Tags of Courage* and my quest for a national monument. The twenty-minute interview was recorded for a segment on his monthly TV program *Washington Watch with Congressman Walter B. Jones.* I was given a copy of the interview and had more copies made to distribute to my team and several close supporters. We used the interview to help promote the monument and raise funds.

On December 28, 2011, my employer, Bart and Associates, Inc., was among the corporate sponsors of the 2011 Military Bowl at RFK Stadium in Washington, D.C. The NCAA football game featured the University of Toledo Rockets vs. the Air Force Academy Falcons. My company wanted to do something special for the monument, so they asked me to interview for a 30-second promotion that would be televised during the game. I was thrilled. The promotion was to air several times on national TV during the ball game and on the jumbo screen inside the stadium.

I was invited as an honored guest to attend the game, so I asked Richard Deggans, secretary of JBMF, to join me. Before the game, we set up a display table outside the stadium, with hats and T-shirts and a miniature bronze model. We had many visitors and met a lot of military personnel and their families. We also had great seats — on the fifty-yard line — to enjoy the game. When the advertisement appeared on the jumbo screen, it got roaring applause from the fans. The game was an exciting one start to finish. The final score was Toledo Rockets 42 and Air Force Falcons 41 after the Falcons' failed attempt at a two-point conversion on the final play.

Several of the executive staff at Bart and Associates purchased limited editions of the numbered miniature bronze models of the monument. As a result of this event, sales and donations brought in $30,000.

A significant fundraising event occurred in May 2011 when I first met Joey Herrick, president of Natural Balance Pet Foods, Inc. I had received an email from an associate producer of *Who Let the Dogs Out,* an Animal Planet TV show funded by Natural Balance. The show followed Tillman, the famous skateboarding bulldog who was named after Patrick Daniel "Pat" Tillman. Pat was a former star in the National Football League who gave up professional football to join the army in the aftermath of the September 11, 2001 attacks. Pat, an Army Ranger, was killed in action in Afghanistan by friendly fire.

Tillman the bulldog had performed his skateboarding stunts nation-wide and had appeared on *The Today Show,* ESPN, *Fox and Friends,* and iPhone ads, and was featured in *Time* magazine's top 50 YouTube videos. The producer of *Who Let the Dogs Out* wanted to interview me about my book *A Soldier's Best Friend* and how I became involved with the national monument project. I agreed to be interviewed on the grounds of the WWII Memorial in Washington.

Afterward, Joey Herrick stepped out of the crowd of onlookers and introduced himself. He complimented my interview performance and then asked if I had a corporate sponsor for the monument. I told him that I was working on several leads. After a brief discussion, Mr. Herrick offered to be a JBMF corporate sponsor and team with Petco to help raise significant donations. I gratefully accepted his offer and we shook hands in agreement. It was my lucky day!

Since we were at the WWII Memorial and a short distance from the

Rayburn House Office Building, I asked Mr. Herrick if he would like to meet Representative Walter B. Jones, the legislative sponsor of the national monument project. He immediately said yes, so I called the congressman's office and we met with him that afternoon. After the meeting, Tillman was turned loose on his skateboard and went flying up and down the third-floor corridor. It wasn't long before congressional staffers poured out of their office doors and lined up against the walls to watch and cheer Tillman's antics. What an exciting day it turned out to be for everyone!

Joey Herrick, president, Natural Balance Pet Foods, Inc.;
U.S. Representative Walter B. Jones, NC; Carrie Ask,
vice president, PETCO; John Burnam.

To help expose the monument to a wider American and international public, Mr. Herrick proposed the idea for a national-monument float in the 2013 Rose Parade in Pasadena, California. He said that his company had entered a different theme float each of the past four years, and would fully fund the construction of the proposed float. I agreed, and worked with the staff at Natural Balance on the float's design, which would feature the four dogs and dog handler, and with the supporting cast of working-dog teams from each U.S. armed service.

When the float was completed, it was judged in a competition with all the other Rose Parade floats and won the President's Trophy. Articles about the parade and the monument appeared in the *Los Angeles Times* and other publications and blogs. The national publicity provided enormous exposure and increased visits to the John Burnam Monument Foundation website and Facebook page.

Joey Herrick, president, Natural Balance Pet Foods, and John Burnam promote the sketch of the Rose Parade float "Canines with Courage" at a Lackland Air Force Base military working-dog competition, May 2012.

2013 Rose Parade National Monument float "Canines with Courage."

The entire JBMF team of Larry Chilcoat, Kristie Dober, and artist Paula Slater attended the parade on January 1, 2013. I rode on the float with active duty dog handlers and a WWII dog handler. It was great fun riding down the street exchanging hand waves with the estimated one million people that lined the five-mile parade route. At the end of the parade route, the floats were parked in a large staging area so the public could visit and take photos.

Parked alongside the float was a large trailer housing the newly minted large bronze statues of the national monument's four dogs and dog handler. The exhibit was a huge hit and we all pitched in to take photos with the visiting public and tell them about the monument project.

Group of dog handlers who accompanied the float with their dogs, and other veteran dog handlers at the post-parade bronze statue display.

A national road tour was planned for the bronze statues from April through August 2013, but funding from the sponsors didn't materialize and JBMF had no funds to support the tour. However, the statues did make one stop at a Petco store in Phoenix, Arizona, on their way to Lackland Air Force Base. JBMF board member Jim Frost organized the Phoenix stop. Several hundred people visited Petco that day to see and take photos of the bronze dogs and handler.

Cori Solomon, reporting for *Dogster,* wrote an article titled "We Interview the People Behind the First U.S. National Monument to Military Dogs." Cori wrote in part:

> I went behind the scenes and interviewed the people involved with creating the float. I was amazed by the passion I saw in John Burnam, a decorated Vietnam War veteran, scout-dog handler, and founder of John Burnam Monument Foundation. "Riding on the float humbled me," said Burnam, his eyes beaming with pride, seeing people standing and clapping, the mass of people was an experience that only happens once in a lifetime. I am honored to be part of this national monument.
>
> Burnam chose sculptress Paula Slater to create the immense work depicting a military handler, a Doberman pinscher, Labrador retriever, German shepherd, and Belgian Malinois. Slater said she reviewed pictures of the breeds, met with breeders, and examined dogs so she could understand the nuances of each. The first was the Doberman, she said, and it was the most difficult. Next was the German shepherd, which was also a challenge because the American German shepherd today is quite different from the dogs used by the military in Vietnam. Having owned a Labrador made that sculpture easiest for Slater.
>
> As an animal artist myself, viewing the majestic bronzes of these breeds made it clear Slater had accomplished her goal. It is a testament to her work that I was drawn to touch, feel, and pet the lifelike bronze dogs as if they were real.

Natural Balance Pet Foods and Petco collaborated on the idea to create Natural Balance Limited Edition Jerky Bark Treats and sell them at Petco stores nationwide and online as a fundraiser for the monument. Part of our agreement was to display a graphic image of the monument and language that supported it on each package of treats. The promotion was a huge hit with the American public, and the stores kept running out of inventory.

Together, Natural Balance Pet Foods and Petco raised $850,000 for the national monument.

John Burnam and Ken Licklider,
founder and president, Von Liche Kennels.

I received a phone call from Kenneth Licklider, president and owner of

Von Liche Kennels, in reply to my letter requesting his support of the monument. Ken invited me to visit his working-dog training facility in Denver, Indiana. Ken had a contract with the Department of Defense to train military working dogs and handlers for the wars in Iraq and Afghanistan. I met with Ken and his staff of expert trainers and toured their extensive facilities — about 600 acres of property with buildings, a warehouse, schools, open fields, and old vehicles mocked up for tactical dog-team training.

I was extremely impressed with Ken's operations, management, and training. Ken introduced me to a group of young trainees working their dogs through some techniques, and I said a few words about how training had helped me survive in Vietnam.

Ken was a senior master sergeant in the U.S Air Force and a veteran sentry-dog handler. He's also a highly skilled master trainer, and we hit it off like old friends. Before I left, Ken invited me to a cookout with his family and staff. I spoke briefly during the party, and then Ken handed me a check for $8,000. Ken has made several more sizeable donations since.

As the project progressed, more people learned about it and I answered many more emails. I tried to stay focused and not get overwhelmed by how much work and detail the project involved. I remember an email from someone presented an interesting fund-raising idea: he suggested that selling brick pavers with personalized engravings of the names of the dogs and handlers could raise enough money to pave the monument's entire 3,000-square-foot plaza area.

It was a great idea, but it would have been impossible to gather the contact information to give this opportunity to every dog and dog handler, trainer, veterinarian, and vet tech who had ever served with dogs dating back to WWII and forward to the Korean War, Vietnam War, Gulf War, and the wars in Iraq and Afghanistan. Also, I didn't want to see visitors bent over to search thousands of brick pavers for an individual name instead of focusing their attention on the bronze statues, the history wall, the dog water fountain, and the meaning of the entire design.

In 2012, Kristie Dober became a member of the JBMF board of directors. I met Kristie at the Joint Service Military Working Dog Committee meeting on May 4, 2010 at the Security Forces Center Headquarters Building on Lackland Air Force Base. After my presentation there, Kristie provided me a list of commercial companies that had business with the military working-dog programs.

Kristie Dober, secretary, JBMF, Inc.

Kristie had grown up with German shepherds since childhood. She joined the U.S. Army to become a military working-dog handler, and graduated from the Dog Handlers Course at Lackland AFB in 1990. After Kristie's military service commitment, she applied her knowledge and experience as a commercial consultant for the U.S. Army Military Working Dog program, developing training techniques, capabilities, equipment requirements, and program analysis. Kristie's military, government, and commercial business contacts in the working-dog world was immediately put to work, and her enthusiastic style was instrumental in expanding awareness of and interest in the monument project, and generated significant contributions.

✳

In January 2012, I met with Jim Diven, sales & marketing representative, Garrett Container Systems, Inc., to discuss planning a fundraiser for the monument. Jim's company was organizing a Department of Defense Worldwide Joint Service Canine Trials and Training Seminar to take place at Lackland Air Force Base from April 30–May 5, 2012.

The weeklong gala included a competition among forty military working-dog teams, kennel masters, and trainers. Senior military leaders representing the Military Police, Combat Engineers, Infantry, and Special Forces communities were in attendance. Garrett Container Systems recruited twenty commercial vendors to help sponsor the event. The vendors set up exhibition booths to display and demonstrate military working-dog products, services, and training. It was a huge hit.

The vendor donations for the monument ranged from $2,000 to $10,000. At the end of the fundraiser, Garrett Container Systems presented JBMF a check for $65,000. In recognition of their exceptional efforts, JBMF presented Garrett Container Systems an eighteen-inch bronze model of the national monument's pedestal figures.

One of the most important phone calls I received was in March 2012 from Rich Avanzino, president of Maddie's Fund (www.maddiesfund. org), a family foundation funded by Dave and Cheryl Duffield, the founders of Workday® and PeopleSoft®, which are widely used information technology/human resources enterprise systems.

The Duffields established Maddie's Fund in memory of their beloved family dog Maddie. Maddie's Fund helps create a no-kill nation where all healthy and treatable shelter dogs and cats are guaranteed a loving home. Mr. Avanzino said that the Duffields learned of my book and the monument project after reading an article I'd written. Rich Avanzino interviewed me over the phone; he asked a series of questions about my background and the monument project. Later, he called again to tell me that Mr. and Mrs. Duffield wanted to meet with me.

I flew to California and gave a formal presentation to Mr. and Mrs. Duffield and their board of directors, after which we had a productive exchange of questions and discussion points. I flew back home with a positive impression that we could team with Maddie's Fund for financial support. Soon, JBMF and Maddie's Fund entered into a sponsorship agreement, during the course of which I developed a great working relationship with Mary Ippoliti Smith, vice president of operations. Maddie's Fund contributed nearly $1 million to fund construction of the monument.

Mr. Dave Duffield, founder of Maddie's Fund,
with John Burnam.

The growth of funds increased the work required to manage admin-istrative operations and hire contractors to begin production. To help with the added workload, I recruited Jim Frost in 2012. JBMF board members Larry Chilcoat and Kristie Dober immediately approved him. Jim had been supporting the monument project since we met in 2004.

During the Vietnam War, Jim was commander of the 981st Military Police Company (Sentry Dogs), and has been a staunch advocate of military working dogs ever since. In 2001, he joined the Grand Canyon German Shepherd Dog Club of Arizona. They started a "Salute to the Military Canines" with an entry in the annual Phoenix Veterans Day Parade in downtown Phoenix, Arizona. Year after year, the number of dogs marching in the Veterans Day Parade grew as more dog clubs joined the march with their dogs. I had the honor of having been invited to march in the parade several times with a German shepherd dog and to speak at various patriotic functions.

Jim Frost, Promotions / Sales, JBMF, Inc.

Jim contacted Gold Star families of fallen dog handlers to join the walk in the parade to honor the memory of their sons' service and sacrifice in the Iraq and Afghanistan wars. The Gold Star families were loudly cheered as they marched past the reviewing stands and the thousands of spectators that lined the streets.

Jim had assembled a collection of memorabilia about the history of war dogs since WWII. He took his collection and display on the road to many Arizona dog events for years. His passion and drive to educate the American public was incredible. Jim's relentless efforts raised thousands of dollars in public donations to support the monument project. He has never taken a dime in payment for contributing his time after work and on weekends and holidays. Jim is a passionate volunteer for the dogs and a great friend.

U.S. Air Force Sergeants Alltop and Bravo, military working-dog handlers, and John Burnam participating in the Phoenix Veterans Day Parade, November 11, 2011.

With significant funds provided by Maddie's Fund, we hired Keith Monument Company to provide the many tons of granite needed to construct the monument's 3,000-square-foot plaza consisting of a large wall, three different-sized pedestals, and all the granite pavers. John Keith and Rich Urbach, senior executives, helped select the type of granite, sizes, and placement, and explained the general construction process. Their many years' experience in the granite business helped me better understand the size and complexity of the procedure.

Drew Johnson, graphic artist/engineer, Keith Monument Company, provided scaled color renderings and computer-aided designs (CADD), which were blueprint type drawings with detailed engineering specifications, dimensions, and engraving for each granite component.

John Keith and Rich Urbach, Keith Monument Co., with John Burnam.

I traveled to Elizabethtown, Kentucky, to tour the manufacturing operations and meet the staff and craftsmen of Keith Monument Company. After a tour of their facility, there was no doubt in my mind I had picked the right people to provide the granite. I also made a trip to the granite quarry in Montpelier, Vermont, where Rich Urbach and Robert Boulanger, vice president, Rock of Ages manufacturing operations, gave me a tour of the granite quarry and plant operations. It was amazing to watch the stone craftsmen use their hand tools and giant machines to extract, move, cut, inscribe, and polish the giant granite components of the monument. To see how the process actually worked from start to finish was an invaluable experience.

After evaluating several bids for construction of the monument's foundation, we chose Ahern Construction Corporation to construct the reinforced foundation for the granite and bronze components. Owner Tim Ahern is a talented and experienced artist and designer of complex projects. He had designed and built spectacular outdoor pools,

*John Burnam standing on half of the four-piece solid granite
pedestal (20 feet × 16 feet × 20 inches when assembled). The
pedestal features four large bronze dogs and a nine-foot dog
handler. Rock of Ages granite manufacturing plant, Montpelier,
Vermont, August 15, 2013.*

spas, fountains, and waterfalls using concrete, marble, and granite.
Tim's artistic landscapes were beautifully designed and masterfully
integrated with the surrounding structures and vegetation.

Before the work began, I invited Tim Ahern and John Keith of Keith
Monument Company to assemble their teams and meet me at Lackland
Air Force Base to visit the site where the monument was to be constructed so everyone could get acquainted and discuss their particular
aspects of the project. We also had a pre-construction meeting with
members of the Lackland Civil Engineers Department and toured the
approved construction site on the corner of the parade field. After several more meetings in preparation for digging the foundation, Lackland
AFB Civil Engineers gave JBMF approval to begin work on July 1, 2013.

Tim's company constructed a deep reinforced foundation to support
the heavy weight of all the granite and bronze. Tim's team installed

the in-ground lighting, flagpoles, sprinkler system, and vegetation, and connected the water supply to the bronze dog water fountain and sprinklers.

Tim Ahern, Ahern Construction Corporation.

John Keith's team installed 3,000 square feet of granite components over the foundation. Artist Paula Slater and a team from the Mussi Artworks Foundry in Berkley, California, installed the five bronze dogs and two dog handlers on the granite pedestals.

The in-ground lights were tested, the flags were raised, the vegetation was planted around the perimeter of the granite plaza, and the dog water fountain was fully functional. The entire national monument had been built in four months. The granite was cleaned and the bronze statues were given a final polish. It was time to build the stage, unfold the chairs, and invite the public to the dedication ceremony on October 28, 2013.

Chapter 31

Dedication of National Monument and Public Access

National Monument covered, no flags flying, before the dedication ceremony, 28 October 2013 (source: AceK9).

IT TOOK SEVERAL MONTHS to plan the national monument's formal dedication ceremony, which took place on 28 October 2013. A priority for me was to ensure that the ceremony would have all the pomp and circumstance the monument foundation could afford and the military could support.

The last major component, the "Not Forgotten Fountain" was installed two weeks before the dedication; it was a big hit with the visitors and their dogs.

Lieutenant Colonel Jason Harris and TSgt Christopher Dion of the 341st Training Squadron (Military Working Dog Training School) were assigned as my primary points of contact for the dedication planning. Together, we worked out the list of speakers, security, logistics, public access, parking, military resources, band, protocol, and public affairs requirements.

During one of my conversations with Lt Col Harris, I mentioned that I was in the process of searching for a master of ceremonies for the dedication. Without hesitation, he volunteered, and his performance was nothing less than outstanding.

(Center) Master of ceremonies Lt Col Jason Harris, Commander, U.S. Air Force, 341st Training Squadron, Lackland AFB, San Antonio, Texas (source: AceK9).

TSgt Christopher Dion, Team Chief and MWD handler and trainer, 341st Training Squadron, Lackland AFB. TSgt Dion coordinated the logistics, administrative tasks, and personnel resources during the site's construction and the preparation of the dedication ceremony (source: AceK9).

I searched for an event-planning company and settled on the proposal submitted by Great Events, a full-service company located in San Antonio, Texas. They provided everything on the long list of items I'd compiled to stage a large-capacity outdoors event for an expected 1,000 attendees. Some of the major items included a large stage under a large tent with seating for 500, portable toilets, trash receptacles, bottled water, audio/visual, personnel resources, signage, escorts, and staging crews. Their price point on each item was very reasonable compared to those of the competitors I evaluated.

Christina Alvarado-Morales, Senior Account Executive for Great Events, worked directly with me on a daily basis to plan and map out the details. Christina and the videography and audio staff attended all the meetings with the military to coordinate every aspect of the dedication ceremony. Christina's cheerful upbeat personality, professional skill set, and tireless initiative as the chief orchestrator of the staff and resources were a huge reason why the ceremony was so successful. We couldn't have picked a more capable event-planning person and company to handle the job.

I designed the dedication invitation, and Larry Chilcoat, treasurer of JBMF, Inc., mailed over 700 to our list of donors, organizations, and businesses. Public invitation announcements were also placed on our website, www.jbmf.us, and Facebook page (source: author).

With the help of longtime supporter and personal friend Kris "Lady Dog" of San Jose, California, we created a formal press release and media alert. Kris distributed them to local and national media outlets nationwide, including military media channels.

Dog-loving people of all ages got the word and traveled from many parts the country to attend the ceremony and reunite with friends. There were several hundred veteran dog handlers of different wars, including active-duty dog handlers representing the U.S. Army, U.S. Marine Corps, U.S. Navy, U.S. Air Force, and U.S. Coast Guard.

All 500 chairs under the big tent were filled. Hundreds of people stood alongside the edges of the tent, behind the tent, and on the grassy areas around the monument.

Emotions ranged from tears to excitement when the national monument was unveiled and the flag of each military service was raised to the theme music of that service.

Local and national media, including several documentary filmmakers, were in attendance to record the historic event. Several of us veterans and active-duty dog handlers, and Paula Slater (bronze sculptor), were interviewed on-camera by the media before and after the ceremony.

Great Events set up professional audiovisual equipment and camera crews to film the entire ceremony in HD (high definition). The final edited version was archived for historical purposes.

We enlisted the voluntary photography services of John and Becki Johnston of AceK9 in Jupiter, Florida. They snapped hundreds of photos capturing every aspect of the ceremony. Many of the photos taken are included herein.

The dedication ceremony program was designed and assembled by Kris "Lady Dog" and distributed to the attendees. The program contained the list of speakers, photos, narrative description of the national monument, activities, and list of contractors and technical support.

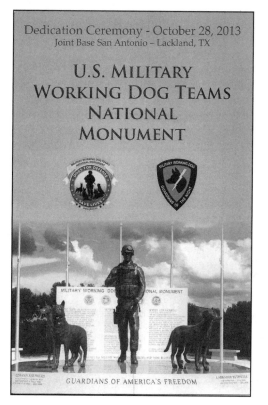

Dedication program cover (source: author).

Speaker Sequence

- Welcome Remarks: Colonel Mark D. Camerer, Commander, U.S. Air Force, 37th Training Wing, Lackland AFB, Texas (source: AceK9)

- Lieutenant General James M. Holmes, U.S. Air Force represented U.S. Representative Walter B. Jones, North Carolina, who could not attend. Representative Jones sponsored Congressional legislation for the national monument (source: AceK9)

- John C. Burnam, founder and president, John Burnam Monument Foundation, Inc.

- Brigadier General John L. Poppe, Chief, U.S. Army Veterinary Corps

- Paula B. Slater, bronze sculptor

- David Duffield, founder of Maddie's Fund

- Susan Kogut, executive director, Petco Foundation

- Rick Rockhill, senior vice president, Dick Van Patten's Natural Balance Pet Foods

- Tech Sergeant Leonard Anderson, U.S. Air Force military working-dog handler and Afghanistan wounded warrior

- Sergeant Mike Dowling, U.S. Marine veteran military working-dog handler and author of *Sgt Rex: The Unbreakable Bond Between a Marine and His Military Working Dog*

- Sergeant Ron Aiello, U.S. Marine Corps Vietnam veteran scout-dog handler and president, U.S. War Dogs Association

- Presentation of bronze model of national monument to the 341st Training Squadron by Larry Chilcoat, Jim Frost, and Kristie Dober, directors of the John Burnam Monument Foundation

- Acceptance of the Military Working Dog Teams National Monument: Brigadier General Robert D. LaBrutta, Commander, U.S. Air Force, 502nd Air Base Wing and Joint Base San Antonio.

Commemorative coin designed by John Burnam and Challenge CoinsRUs. Each person who attended the dedication was given a coin (source: author).

Commemorative lapel pin as designed by John Burnam and produced by Great Events. Each person who attended the dedication was given a lapel pin (source: author).

Commemorative dedication patch designed by Natural Balance Pet Foods and Petco (source: author).

Stage setup before ceremony; to provide a theme and backdrop for the ceremony and speakers, I decided to use the assembled collection of authentic war-dog-team images on the back of the monument's granite history wall (source: author).

The U.S. Air Force Band provided music for the ceremony (source: AceK9).

John Burnam, Fern Zappala, and
Brigadier General Robert D. LaBrutta
(source: AceK9).

Front row of dignitaries and speakers (source: AceK9).

*Speakers: (L) Mike Dowling, Kristie Dober, Joey Herrick,
Larry Chilcoat, Ron Aiello (source: AceK9).*

*Speakers: (L) Rick Rockhill, unidentified attendee,
Susan Kogut, Dave Duffield, Paula Slater (source: AceK9).*

John Burnam giving keynote address and relating stories of his experiences in Vietnam (source: Veronica Burnam, John's sister-in-law).

The following are a few of the many comments I received upon returning home after the dedication ceremony:

> *Mary and I were very impressed with the whole ceremony, and it was a real pleasure to meet Fern and have a little quality time with both of you. I must say that your talk during the ceremony was a highlight for me. You gave me a sense of what it must have been like, particularly out in front of a main unit all by yourself, totally relying on your dog. Several sections brought tears to my eyes.*
>
> Larry and Mary Brown

> *We — the public, your friends, and especially the military dogs from past to the present day—thank you, John. Because of all your hard work and dedication there is now a place to go and honor all war dogs at a national monument. You made it happen! Jim and I knew the moment we met you*

that you were the one for this job. Well done to you, soldier, and to your faithful dog Clipper. He touched your heart so deeply that you were chosen to be that special person to see this through.

— Terry Waldron and Jim Tottenham

JBMF, Inc. board of directors: (L) Larry Chilcoat, treasurer; Kristie Dober, secretary/promotions; Jim Frost, promotions/sales (source: AceK9).

Speaker: Sergeant Mike Dowling: U.S. Marine veteran military working-dog handler and author of Sgt Rex: The Unbreakable Bond Between a Marine and His Military Working Dog *(source: AceK9).*

*John Burnam cutting ribbon to open the national monument
for the unveiling ceremony. (L) Colonel Mark D. Camerer, Lieutenant
General James M. Holmes, Brigadier General John L. Poppe,
Brigadier General Robert D. LaBrutta (source: AceK9).*

*(L) U.S. Coast Guardsman, Airman, Sailor, Marine, Soldier.
Honor guard waiting to hoist the service flags up the poles at
the rear of the monument after the unveiling. Flags were hoisted
to the theme music of each military service (source: AceK9).*

Flags Raised and Memorial Wreath Placed – The U.S. Military Working Dog Teams National Monument (source: author).

Bronze dedication plaque seated on solid granite pedestal at entrance of monument's granite plaza (source: author).

Gold Star Family: Darrell and Kathy Rusk, son Brady, and veteran military working dog Eli. Darrell and Kathy's son, U.S. Marine Private First Class Colton Rusk, age twenty, was killed in action in the Helmand Province of Afghanistan on 5 December 2010 while operating with Eli, who survived. Under his senior photo in the Orange Grove High School yearbook, Colton had written: " Don't be afraid to go after your hopes and dreams, but don't be afraid to be willing to pay the price". (source: AceK9).

Crowd gathered around the national monument after the unveiling (source: Rich Urbach).

John Burnam and Dave Duffield, founder of Maddie's Fund and corporate sponsor of the national monument (source: author).

Jimmy Van Patten, John Burnam, Paula Slater (sculptor), and Rick Rockhill, Senior VP, Natural Balance Pet Foods, Inc. Jimmy's father, Dick Van Patten, was a longtime Hollywood TV star who founded Natural Balance Pet Foods, a corporate sponsor of the national monument (source: AceK9).

*Ray A. Burnam and John C. Burnam, brothers
(source: author).*

*Ariana Barger, John Burnam's granddaughter,
and Fern Zappala, John's wife (source: Mary Brown).*

Dr. Larry M. Kornegay, former president, American Veterinary Medical Association (AVMA) and official endorser of the national monument, Paula Slater, sculptor, and John Burnam (source: author collection).

Van Wilson, Vietnam combat-infantry veteran, and John Burnam. Under enemy fire, Van lifted John off the battlefield to safety after he was wounded in Vietnam in 1966. A year later, John teamed up with scout dogs Timber and Clipper in Vietnam (1967–1968) and was wounded a second time (source: author).

Waving: Ron Aiello, U.S. Marine Corps veteran scout-dog handler of the Vietnam War, president of the U.S. War Dogs Association, and dedication ceremony speaker. Standing behind in white shirt is Chris Slater, husband of sculptor Paula Slater (source: AceK9).

Tech Sgt Leonard Anderson, U.S. Air Force military working-dog handler and Afghanistan wounded warrior. A key speaker during the dedication, TSgt Anderson drew a standing ovation (source: AceK9).

Jesus Madrano, John Burnam, and Paul Mangus. Jesus and Paul are senior executives at Bart & Associates, Inc., an information-technology firm in McLean, Virginia, where John is employed as a senior technical writer/editor (source: author).

Joey Herrick, former president, Natural Balance Pet Foods, and Tim Ahern, Ahern Construction Company. Joey was a corporate sponsor of the monument. Tim's company built the foundation, installed the lighting, installed the "Not Forgotten Fountain," and planted the vegetation around the monument (source: AceK9).

Shane Laaz and family, and J. Burnam. Shane was the architect and engineer of the monument's reinforced foundation, the in-ground lighting system, and plumbing for the sprinkler system and the "Not Forgotten Fountain" (source: Jim Seitz).

(L) Julie Urbach, Paula Slater, John Burnam, Rich Urbach. Rich was the contractor who supplied and installed the tons of Vermont granite for the monument (source: Rich Urbach).

Harris Done, documentary filmmaker, setting up equipment for interview with John Burnam after the dedication ceremony on Tuesday, 29 October 2013 (source: author).

On a Tuesday morning I sat for a formal on-camera interview with Harris Done, a professional documentary filmmaker. Harris was assembling candidates for a feature-length film about Vietnam veteran dog handlers. He had already completed two major documentaries: *Always Faithful,* which follows the stories of U.S. Marine Corps dog teams deployed in Iraq and Afghanistan, and *War Dog of the Pacific,* which chronicles the stories of Marine Corps dog teams operating in the Pacific theater of World War II.

Public Access to National Monument

After the September 11, 2001 terrorist attacks on the World Trade Center and the Pentagon, access to military installations and bases throughout the military was restricted to the point where public access required an officially approved need and sponsor. Knowing this during the time I was working on the legislation with U.S. Representative

Walter B. Jones, I wanted language written into the final bill to reflect that the monument must be accessible to the public and their dogs. That language became part of the final bill, which was signed into law by President George W. Bush on 28 January 2008.

Briefing and working with the officials at Joint Base San Antonio–Lackland Air Force Base, public access to visit the national monument presented a problem for their existing security policies and procedures. In the end, however, the following official letter was signed and released three days after the dedication ceremony on October 28, 2013.

DEPARTMENT OF THE AIR FORCE
502D AIR BASE WING
JOINT BASE SAN ANTONIO

3 1 OCT 2013

MEMORANDUM FOR RECORD

FROM: 802 SFS/CC
        2445 George Avenue, Suite 4
        JBSA Lackland, TX 78236-5228

SUBJECT: Military Working Dog (MWD) Teams National Monument Public Access Policy

1. In accordance with Public Law 110-181, Section 2877, reasonable accommodations must be made to ensure that civilians and their dogs are able to visit the MWD Teams National Monument located on JBSA-Lackland.

2. Effective immediately, civilians requesting to visit the national monument will be directed to the Luke East Visitors Control Center (VCC) where they will be issued a four hour pass assuming no derogatory information arises during criminal history check. Additional time may be granted at the discretion of the VCC staff not to exceed eight hours. 802 SFS/CC will be the sponsor for all national monument visitors.

3. Point of contact for this matter is the undersigned.

SCOTT M. FOLEY, Lt Col, USAF
Commander, 802d Security Forces Squadron

Official public access authorization document to visit the Military Working Dog Teams National Monument (source: author).

Conclusion

I have long believed that worse than for a dog or dog handler to die on the battlefield is to be forgotten, which I could not allow to happen to all the dogs and handlers who, though wounded in combat, found the strength and courage to survive and carry on with their lives.

In honoring the dogs and dog handlers with a national monument, we also honor the countless thousands of lives they have saved since WWII. And there is no way we can put a number on all those American servicemen's children, grandchildren, and great-grandchildren who were born because America gave her sons and daughters life-saving dogs during wartime.

A share of the credit for our nation's freedom belongs to the war dog serving alongside his master on the battlefield. Together, they have always strived valiantly, as a team, to defend their ground, because they knew that, in the end, victory is saving American lives.

And when death befalls his master on the battlefield, there you will find his dog, eyes sad but vigilant, protecting his master to the very end.

I have now accomplished my mission by building a national monument to honor them all forever!

—*John C. Burnam*

Fully functional "Not Forgotten Fountain": Original concept design by John Burnam; sculpted in bronze by Paula Slater. Vietnam dog handler modeled from photos; German shepherd dog modeled in likeness of "Sadie," beloved companion of David and Cheryl Duffield (source: author).

Medal of Honor —
Robert W. Hartsock

THE CONGRESSIONAL MEDAL OF HONOR is the highest military decoration for bravery that the United States of America can bestow upon a U.S. military service member.

U.S. Army Staff Sergeant Robert W. Hartsock, 44th Infantry Platoon Scout Dogs, 3rd Brigade, 25th Infantry Division, is the only war-dog handler awarded the Medal of Honor during the Vietnam War. Sergeant Hartsock was born on January 24, 1945 in Cumberland, Maryland. He entered the U.S. Army at Fairmont, West Virginia.

Staff Sergeant Hartsock was awarded the Medal of Honor posthumously for extraordinary heroism in the Hau Nghia Province, Republic of Vietnam, on February 23, 1969 (see photo 15 of insert). The citation reads:

> For conspicuous gallantry and intrepidity in action at the risk of his life above and beyond the call of duty. Staff Sergeant Hartsock distinguished himself in action while serving as section leader with the 44th Infantry Platoon Scout Dogs. When the Dau Tieng Base Camp came under a heavy enemy rocket and mortar attack, Staff Sergeant Hartsock and his platoon commander spotted an enemy sapper squad, which had infiltrated the camp undetected. Realizing the enemy squad was heading for the brigade tactical operations center and nearby prisoner compound, they concealed themselves and, although heavily outnumbered, awaited the

approach of the hostile soldiers. When the enemy was almost upon them, Staff Sergeant Hartsock and his platoon commander opened fire on the squad. As a wounded enemy soldier fell, he managed to detonate a satchel charge he was carrying.

Staff Sergeant Hartsock, with complete disregard for his life, threw himself on the charge and was gravely wounded. In spite of his wounds, Staff Sergeant Hartsock crawled about 5 meters to a ditch and provided heavy suppressive fire, completely pinning down the enemy and allowing his commander to seek shelter. Staff Sergeant Hartsock continued his deadly stream of fire until he succumbed to his wounds. Staff Sergeant Hartsock's extraordinary heroism and profound concern for the lives of his fellow soldiers were in keeping with the highest traditions of the military service and reflect great credit on him, his unit, and the United States Army.

U.S. War-Dog Handlers Killed In Vietnam

In Memory of War Dog Handlers and War Dogs Killed in Action.
Original oil on canvas by Julie Parker, 2003 (author collection).

APPROXIMATELY 10,000 WAR-DOG HANDLERS and 4,000 war dogs served during the ground war in South Vietnam. Though their number was quite small compared to the several million American men and women who rotated in and out of that country from 1964–75, the war-dog-team mission and record for saving lives was very significant.

German shepherds became the dogs of choice for military scouting and sentry duty, while Labrador retrievers were selected for tracking. Both breeds were well suited because of their intelligence, learning ability, accommodating dispositions, ability to work with multiple handlers, and adaptability to variable climates, terrain, and work environments.

Each dog's ear was branded with a four-character alphanumeric service number for identification and accountability. Each dog had an official military medical, training, and service record established upon entry into military service. The records were maintained by the veterinarian or veterinarian technician assigned to support the war-dog unit.

War Dog Handlers Killed in Vietnam

Name	Age	Unit	Home	Died	Vietnam Memorial Panel
Ahern, Robert	27	37th SPS – Air Force	Laconia, NH	03/30/1969	28W-89
Alcorn Jr., Dale	19	60th Mine/ Booby Trap	Redondo Beach, CA	09/06/1969	18W-45
Amick, Richard	19	57th Scout Dogs	Nashville, TN	05/12/1969	25W-59
Anderson, William	21	66th Combat Tracker	Mt. Vernon, AL	11/06/1969	16W-36
Armstrong, Robert	20	Marine Scout Dogs	Fayetteville, TN	01/16/1969	34W-14
Atkins III, Joshua	19	Army Scout Dogs	Washington, DC	04/26/1967	18E-89
Baker, Donald	20	Marine Sentry Dog	Huntington Park, CA	09/06/1967	26E-5
Baker, Gary	21	Army Scout Dogs	Monroe City, MO	05/11/1970	11W-16
Baldoni, Lindsay	21	39th Scout Dogs	Detroit, MI	08/22/1967	25E-29
Banaszynski, Richard	22	59th Scout Dogs	Pulaski, WI	10/25/1968	40W-31
Barkley, Earl	21	Army Scout Dogs	Indian Head, PA	11/09/1971	02W-64
Beauregard, Richard	19	Army Scout Dogs	Woonsocket, RI	04/24/1971	03W-11
Beaver, James	20	50th Scout Dogs	Bradenton, FL	03/16/1968	44E-65
Beck, Terrence	18	Marine Scout Dog	Ft. Atkinson, WI	12/20/1967	32E-29

Name	Age	Unit	Home	Died	Vietnam Memorial Panel
Beesley, Gary	21	43rd Scout Dogs	St. Louis, MO	06/22/1967	22E-036
Behrens, Peter	26	Marine Scout Dogs	Newburg, MO	12/04/1970	06W-105
Belcher, Robert	22	Marine Scout Dogs	Winthrop, MA	04/11/1968	49E-19
Bell, Mark	19	Marine Scout Dogs	Redondo Beach, CA	06/09/1969	22W-117
Bennett, John	20	Army Scout Dogs	Columbus, OH	10/14/1969	17W-76
Berge, James	24	50th Scout Dogs	Portland, OR	01/23/1968	35E-13
Best, Billy	18	Marine Scout Dogs	Baltimore, MD	03/03/1969	30W-19
Beuke, Dennis	21	Combat Tracker Team-8	Chicago, IL	10/11/1967	27E-87
Bevich Jr., George	22	377th SPS– Air Force	Summit Hill, PA	12/04/1966	13E-9
Blaauw, James	21	Army Scout Dogs	Grayling, MI	03/22/1968	45E-54
Blair, Charles	20	64th Combat Tracker	Orlando, FL	05/14/1970	11W-38
Bost, Michael	20	42nd Scout Dogs	Grand Rapids, MI	05/14/1967	19E-115
Bowman, Stephen	18	Army Scout Dogs	Alta Loma, CA	06/02/1968	61W-10
Boyd, James	22	3rd SPS– Air Force	Winston Salem, NC	02/28/1968	41E-25
Boyer, James	20	Combat Tracker Team-2	St. Louis, MO	09/22/1967	26E-111
Bozier Jr., Willie	21	Army Scout Dogs	New York, NY	07/09/1970	08W-1
Brede, Robert	24	Combat Tracker Team-2	Alexandria, MN	11/16/1967	29E-104

Name	Age	Unit	Home	Died	Vietnam Memorial Panel
Brophy, Martin	24	41st Scout Dogs	Buffalo, NY	05/05/1968	55E-4
Brown, Charles	21	40th Scout Dogs	South Amboy, NJ	03/09/1967	16E-43
Browne, Walter	21	41st Scout Dogs	Haiku, HI	08/02/1969	20W-85
Buckingham, Keith	22	43rd Scout Dogs	Minneapolis, MN	02/25/1969	31W-44
Bullwinkel, Alden	20	61st Combat Tracker Team	Dunellen, NJ	09/11/1969	18W-66
Burdette Jr., Hilburn	19	Army Scout Dogs	Simpsonville, SC	07/12/1970	08W-11
Burk, Jimmy	21	43rd Scout Dogs	Littlefield, TX	11/30/1969	15W-9
Burlock Jr., Kenneth	23	Army Scout Dogs	Jacksonville, NC	09/17/1969	18W-100
Burnette Jr., Archie	20	Army Scout Dogs	Aberdeen	01/31/1968	35E-89
Cabarubio, James	20	Marine Scout Dogs	Odessa, TX	06/18/1969	22W-73
Cain, Douglas	23	43rd Scout Dogs	Sioux City, IA	07/14/1968	52W-27
Camp, Anthony	21	Marine Scout Dogs	Dallas, GA	06/04/1969	23W-62
Campbell, William	21	49th Scout Dogs	Silver Hill, MD	03/03/1967	16E-8
Carinci, Joseph	20	Marine Mine/ Booby Trap	Derby, CT	12/30/1970	05W-7
Carrillo, Melvin	19	48th Scout Dogs	Roswell, NM	03/03/1968	42E-48
Carter, Merle	20	Navy Sentry Dogs	Sapulpa, OK	10/22/1967	28E-49
Castle, Russell	34	40th Scout Dogs	Woodbridge, VA	07/02/1967	22E-097
Chisholm, Ronald	21	Marine Sentry Dog	Jacksonville, FL	05/11/1967	19E-89

Name	Age	Unit	Home	Died	Vietnam Memorial Panel
Clark, Walter	20	Army Scout Dogs	Roseville, MI	10/29/1967	28E-95
Clokes, Robert	21	40th Scout Dogs	New York, NY	12/04/1968	37W-38
Colford, Darrell	25	38th Scout Dogs	West Chicago, IL	11/08/1970	06W-45
Collier, Steven	19	Army Scout Dogs	Branford, CT	10/27/1968	40W-42
Conklin, Michael	22	Army Scout Dogs	Midland, MI	06/24/1970	09W-88
Conner, Jack	25	557th Combat Tracker	El Monte, CA	04/04/1970	12W-92
Conners Jr., Ralph	22	41st Scout Dogs	Washington D.C.	05/22/1969	24W-74
Connors, Jack	23	557th Combat Tracker	Filion, MI	08/21/1969	19W-85
Cox Jr., Edward	20	76th Combat Tracker	Shreveport, LA	02/15/1969	32W-36
Crawford, Bobby	22	43rd Scout Dogs	Buncombe, IL	01/10/1968	34E-16
Crawford, Gordon	24	Army Scout Dogs	Ft. Wayne, IN	02/01/1971	05W-71
Creaghead, Clarence	21	49th Scout Dogs	Bessemer, AL	05/22/1969	24W-74
Cumbie, William	19	Marine Scout Dogs	Jacksonville, FL	02/09/1969	33W-92
Currier Jr., Gordon	22	Veterinarian-Army	Independence, MO	01/31/1968	36E-4
Czarnota, Christopher	20	Army Scout Dogs	Perth Amboy, NJ	03/22/1971	04W-65
Davis, Abronl	20	Marine Scout Dogs	Youngstown, OH	01/11/1969	35W-69
Davis, Alan	21	48th Scout Dogs	Tulare, CA	03/21/1971	04W-63
Davis, Eligah	19	Marine Mine/ Booby Trap	Cecil, GA	04/05/1970	12W-96

Name	Age	Unit	Home	Died	Vietnam Memorial Panel
Deitrick, George	19	41st Scout Dogs	Antioch, CA	06/23/1969	22W-118
Dell, Kenneth	21	49th Scout Dogs	E. Candergrift, PA	11/05/1968	39W-21
Detrick, Gary	20	47th Scout Dogs	Wapakoneta, OH	04/13/1969	27W-72
Dillinder, Randy	19	34th Scout Dogs	Dearborn, MI	12/10/1967	31E-72
Doria, Richard	21	48th Scout Dogs	White Plains, NY	08/19/1969	19W-67
Doyle, John	19	59th Scout Dogs	Prospect, CT	08/25/1966	10E-37
Drobena, Michael	23	Marine Scout Dogs	Temple, TX	02/23/1969	32W-96
Drum, Thomas	21	62nd Combat Tracker	Johnson City, NY	03/04/1970	13W-81
Drysdale, Charles	19	Marine Scout Dogs	Birmingham, AL	01/26/1969	34W-83
Ducote Jr., Lonnie	22	34th Scout Dogs	Corpus Christi, TX	08/13/1967	24E-107
Duff, Phillip	20	Army Scout Dogs	Cornelia, GA	07/07/1972	01W-53
Duke, Douglas	23	Veterinarian-Army	Rush Springs, OK	12/20/1968	36W-49
Dunning, William	24	Veterinarian	Bridgeport, CT	06/22/1970	09W-78
Elliott, Robert	24	Marine Mine/ Booby Trap	Woodbury, NJ	08/09/1970	08W-97
Erickson, Russell	24	59th Scout Dogs	Franklin Park, IL	07/24/1968	51W-49
Esterly, Lawrence	20	Marine Scout Dogs	Lisbon, OH	07/18/1969	20W-14
Eubanks, George	21	25th Scout Dogs	Barboursville, WV	12/07/1967	31E-57
Evans, Ronald	24	44th Scout Dogs	Morrow, OH	04/29/1971	03W-17

Name	Age	Unit	Home	Died	Vietnam Memorial Panel
Farley, Marshall	20	44th Scout Dogs	Folsom, CA	09/19/1967	26E-92
Ford, Bernard		35th SPS– Air Force	Oak Lawn, IL	07/05/1967	23E-10
Ford, Richard	22	35th Scout Dogs	Surf City, NJ	01/18/1970	14W-42
Fox, Gary	18	25th Scout Dogs	Pittsburgh, PA	04/30/1967	18E-121
Fraley, Eugene	28	Navy Seal Team Dogs	Lansing, MI	01/21/1968	35E-5
Fraser, William	20	Marine Scout Dog	Manchester, NH	12/28/1967	32E-86
Freeman, David	20	34th Scout Dogs	Putnam, CT	08/11/1969	19W-1
Freeman, Jeffrey	23	39th Scout Dogs	Lakewood, OH	04/08/1970	12W-107
Freppon, John	20	35th Scout Dogs	Cincinnati, OH	02/02/1969	33W-38
Fritz, Gerald	20	56th SPS– Air Force	Junction, TX	05/13/1975	01W-125
Fuller, Gary	21	366th SPS– Air Force	The Plains, OH	02/27/1967	15E-105
Fuller, Stanley	21	76th Combat Tracker	Fullerton, CA	12/12/1968	36W-11
Gaspard Jr., Claude	21	33rd Scout Dogs	Short Hills, NJ	05/20/1968	60E-4
Giberson, Jerry	21	Army Scout Dogs	Donnellson, IA	06/20/1970	09W-72
Glenn, Livingston	28	57th Scout Dogs	Boston, GA	12/09/1967	31E-68
Goudelock, William	19	57th Scout Dogs	Meridian, CA	03/18/1968	45E-22
Green, Billy	22	Army Scout Dogs	Los Angeles, CA	06/24/1966	08E-85
Grieve, Michael	21	Army Scout Dogs	Hazel Park, MI	01/31/1968	36E-11

Name	Age	Unit	Home	Died	Vietnam Memorial Panel
Griffin II, William	23	63rd Combat Tracker	Pontiac, MI	12/15/1970	06W-122
Groves, William	20	Army Scout Dogs	Seattle, WA	11/30/1967	31E-12
Grundy, Dallas	23	Army Scout Dogs	San Jose, CA	11/05/1966	12E-28
Gyulveszi, Theodore	24	42nd Scout Dogs	Lincoln Park, MI	02/10/1969	32W-6
Hales, Raymon	27	58th Scout Dogs	Springville, UT	07/19/1969	20W-19
Harding, John	19	557th Combat Tracker	Benton, AR	10/08/1967	27E-72
Harris, Jessie	22	Veterinarian-Army	Peoria, IL	01/31/1968	36E-13
Hartsock, Robert	24	44th Scout Dogs	Cumberland, MD	02/23/1969	31W-3
Hartwick Jr., Floyd	20	Marine Scout Dog	St Charles, MO	07/15/1967	23E-75
Hatcher, David	21	63rd Combat Tracker	New York, NY	11/12/1970	06W-54
Henshaw, Patrick	21	Army Scout Dogs	Spokane, WA	12/19/1967	31E-23
Hernandez, Victor	24	57th Scout Dogs	Fullerton, CA	10/18/1968	41W-73
Hicks, Larry	22	Army Scout Dogs	St Ann, MO	09/24/1970	07W-87
Hilerio-Padilla, Luis	20	Army Scout Dogs	Yonkers, NY	11/13/1969	16W-69
Hilt, Richard	20	57th Scout Dogs	Minneapolis, MN	02/13/1969	32W-26
Holland, Wayne	21	Army Scout Dogs	Salemburg, NC	10/26/1968	40W-37
Holley, Glynn	20	Army Scout Dogs	Midland, TX	12/26/1969	15W-93
Holt, Herschel	23	Marine 1st Provisional	Nashville, TN	08/03/1966	09E-103

Name	Age	Unit	Home	Died	Vietnam Memorial Panel
Hoppough, Dennis	22	Marine Scout Dogs	Rochester, NY	07/16/1969	20W-9
Howard, James	20	44th Scout Dogs	Detroit, MI	11/09/1967	29E-59
Howard, Mark	21	Combat Tracker Team-2	St. Louis, MO	11/16/1967	30E-2
Huberty, William	21	44th Scout Dogs	St. Paul, MN	10/17/1966	11E-82
Hughes III, Edward	19	44th Scout Dogs	Garden Grove, CA	11/27/1967	30E-97
Hurksman, Wilhelm	20	43rd Scout Dogs	Rhinelander, WI	07/22/1968	51W-33
Ilaoa, Faleagafula	26	56th SPS – Air Force	San Francisco, CA	05/13/1975	01W-127
Ireland, Elmer	21	42nd Scout Dogs	Star, ID	07/01/1969	21W-42
Jenkins, Clayton	21	Marine Sentry Dogs	Pembine, WI	06/03/1969	23W-53
Jenkins, Steven	21	981st MP Dogs	Santa Ana, CA	01/15/1969	34W-8
Jenks, James	20	45th Scout Dogs	Concord, MI	03/02/1968	42E-33
Jesko, Stephen	20	Army Scout Dogs	Hereford, TX	10/16/1970	06W-3
Joecken, Richard	22	44th Scout Dogs	Columbus, OH	08/28/1969	18W-2
Johnson, Arnold	20	Combat Tracker Team-2	Rochelle, IL	11/16/1967	30E-3
Johnson, Carl	19	34th Scout Dogs	Wakefield, MI	06/22/1968	55W-19
Johnson, Freddie	26	1st Combat Tracker Team	Selma, AL	12/07/1966	12E-18
Johnson, Herbert	19	Army Scout Dogs	Poughkeepsie, NY	07/05/1968	53W-20

Name	Age	Unit	Home	Died	Vietnam Memorial Panel
Johnson, James	22	39th Scout Dogs	Jersey City, NJ	07/01/1969	21W-42
Johnson, Larry	19	Army Scout Dogs	Anaheim, CA	11/14/1968	39W-68
Karau, Ronald	21	Army Scout Dogs	Lewisville, NM	03/20/1971	04W-61
Kiefhaber, Andrew	20	65th Combat Tracker	New York, NY	02/23/1969	31W-7
Kimbrough, Golsby	20	35th Scout Dogs	Philadelphia, PA	07/06/1969	21W-70
King, Alexander	21	557th Combat Tracker	Woodbine, GA	01/20/1969	34W-42
Kobelin, John	24	40th Scout Dogs	Cheyenne, WY	03/06/1969	30W-56
Koon, George	20	Combat Tracker Team-2	Baltimore, MD	11/16/1967	30E-4
Kuefner, John	20	35th Scout Dogs	Duluth, MN	08/14/1969	19W-40
Kuehn, Lloyd	20	40th Scout Dogs	Stillwater, MN	03/09/1967	16E-46
Kunz, Anthony	21	Army Scout Dogs	Kerrville, TX	05/04/1967	19E-38
Lagodzinski, Roger	22	57th Scout Dogs	Buffalo, NY	05/19/1970	10W-65
Land, David	19	Marine Scout Dog	Panama City, FL	06/07/1967	21E-69
Lane, Richard	23	Army Scout Dogs	Fontana, CA	06/16/1968	56W-5
Lawton, Edward	19	75th Combat Tracker	Thermopolis, WV	09/27/1968	42W-30
Lebrun, Robert	21	Army Scout Dogs	Woonsocket, RI	03/22/1971	04W-68
Lee, Edward	20	44th Scout Dogs	Belmont, MA	05/13/1968	59E-25
Levins, Frederick	23	76th Combat Tracker	Naples, FL	06/16/1970	09W-57

Name	Age	Unit	Home	Died	Vietnam Memorial Panel
Lindholm, Dan	20	Army Scout Dogs	Lindsborg, KS	09/08/1968	44W-4
Lindsay, Stephen	23	Marine Scout Dogs	Shreveport, LA	01/24/1971	05W-63
Lipton, Joseph	18	Marine Scout Dog	Floral Park, NY	05/01/1967	19E-6
Lockhart, Harlan	23	35th Scout Dogs	Fredricktown, OH	11/09/1966	12E-48
Loftis, Joel	22	35th SPS-Air Force	La Marque, TX	06/07/1969	23W-104
London, Dennis	26	56th SPS-Air Force	Sparks, NV	05/13/1975	01W-127
Lovellette, Gary	23	45th Scout Dogs	Fergus Falls, MN	12/29/1969	15W-107
Lumsden, William	19	Combat Tracker Team-3	Compton, MD	05/21/1967	20E-77
Magruder, David	21	Army Scout Dogs	Utica, NY	05/16/1970	11W-52
Mahurin, Elmer	19	Combat Tracker Team-8	Goodman, MO	10/11/1967	27E-90
Mansfield, John	21	Army Scout Dogs	New York, NY	03/09/1967	16E-47
Marasco, Joseph	22	62nd Combat Tracker	Somers, NY	07/22/1969	20W-34
Marchant, Paul	22	Army Scout Dogs	Moline, IL	10/18/1969	17W-88
Markey Jr., James	23	63rd Combat Tracker	Warminster, PA	01/26/1971	05W-65
Marrufo Jr., Rodney	20	66th Combat Tracker	Stewarts Point, CA	05/23/1968	66E-11
Marshall, Clifford	21	43rd Scout Dogs	Richmond, KY	02/19/1971	05W-121
Marshall, Mark	18	Marine Scout Dogs	South Euclid, OH	03/29/1969	28W-83

Name	Age	Unit	Home	Died	Vietnam Memorial Panel
Martin, Kenneth	20	40th Scout Dogs	Kalamazoo, MI	03/05/1969	30W-47
Martinez, Juan	25	41st Scout Dogs	Pueblo, CO	05/05/1968	55E-22
Mason Jr., Benjamin	18	Marine Sentry Dog	Piscataway, NJ	09/04/1967	25E-104
Matel, Ronald	20	1st Combat Tracker Team	Duluth, MN	06/09/1969	22W-9
Mattson, Paul	23	59th Scout Dogs	Lake Bluff, IL	04/20/1968	51E-9
Maurer, Walter	20	Army Scout Dogs	Whittier, CA	11/01/1970	06W-33
May, Robert	20	34th Scout Dogs	Buffalo, NY	02/12/1968	39E-8
Mazzone, Joseph	23	Army Scout Dogs	Hicksville, NY	09/22/1968	43W-54
McCarty, Glenn	21	Army Scout Dogs	Texas City, TX	02/20/1971	05W-126
McFall, Gary	24	34th Scout Dogs	Northridge, CA	09/13/1968	44W-51
McGrath, Edward	20	43rd Scout Dogs	Crestview, FL	10/06/1967	27E-60
McIntosh, Donald	19	Army Scout Dogs	Hutchinson, KS	11/08/1970	06W-46
McLaughlin, James	23	Army Scout Dogs	Bangor, ME	04/16/1971	04W-129
Merschel, Lawrence	20	Army Scout Dogs	Wayne, PA	05/01/1968	53E-35
Meyer, Leo	20	61st Combat Tracker Team	Fond du Lac, WI	10/05/1968	41W-14
Michael, James	21	Army Scout Dogs	Gainesville, GA	02/13/1971	05W-101
Miller, Timmy	21	Marine Scout Dog	Stockton, KS	11/24/1968	38W-51
Mills, Rodney	22	Army Scout Dogs	Alma, MI	05/05/1970	11W-104

Name	Age	Unit	Home	Died	Vietnam Memorial Panel
Montano, William	19	Marine Scout Dogs	Deer Park, NY	11/19/1970	06W-71
Morrison, James	20	39th Scout Dogs	Grand Rapids, MI	02/02/1969	33W-42
Mugavin, Martin	20	48th Scout Dogs	Cincinnati, OH	02/23/1967	15E-80
Munch, Michael	20	57th Scout Dogs	Council Bluffs, IA	05/13/1969	25W-107
Munoz, Jose	19	1st Combat Tracker Team	Detroit, MI	12/07/1966	13E-19
Murray, Harry	20	1st Combat Tracker Team	Baltimore, MD	12/07/1966	13E-19
Myers, Richard	20	39th Scout Dogs	Glenmoore, PA	11/13/1967	29E-91
Newell, Tim	24	47th Scout Dogs	Des Moines, IA	09/09/1970	07W-49
Nicolini, Peter	21	44th Scout Dogs	Chicago, IL	05/16/1967	20E-9
Norris, Robert	18	42nd Scout Dogs	Towanda, PA	12/19/1969	15W-72
Nudenberg, David	24	63rd Combat Tracker	Caldwell, NJ	11/12/1970	06W-55
Nurzynski, Joseph	24	59th Scout Dogs	Buffalo, NY	05/12/1969	25W-79
Oaks, Robert	20	Army Scout Dogs	Lamesa, TX	11/11/1969	16W-59
Ohm, David	20	Army Scout Dogs	Alden, MN	07/20/1968	51W-20-
Olmstead, John	21	48th Scout Dogs	Warren, IL	07/15/1967	22E-077
Orsua, Charles	19	35th SPS – Air Force	Sunnyvale, CA	07/15/1969	20W-2
Palacio, Gilbert	21	34th Scout Dogs	San Antonio, TX	05/06/1969	25W-14
Park, Irving	23	12th SPS – Air Force	Ft Wayne, IN	03/06/1970	13W-88

Name	Age	Unit	Home	Died	Vietnam Memorial Panel
Parker Jr., Carter	23	Army Scout Dogs	Monroeville, AL	10/24/1970	06W-19
Parrish, Billy	32	Veterinarian	Tacoma, WA	05/23/1968	67E-1
Payne, Howard	24	59th Scout Dogs	Doraville, GA	04/27/1971	03W-15
Payne, Robert	24	Marine Scout Dog	Hampshire, IL	03/18/1968	45W-24
Payne, Terry	22	Army Scout Dogs	La Crosse, WI	08/05/1970	08W-85
Pearce, Marvin	19	47th Scout Dogs	Capitola, CA	08/25/1968	46W-19
Petersen, Harry	21	Army Scout Dogs	Salt Lake City, UT	11/09/1970	06W-48
Piasecki, John	22	Army Scout Dogs	Chicago, IL	11/29/1969	15W-7
Pierce, Oscar	23	40th Scout Dogs	Pauls Valley, OK	03/09/1967	16E-47
Plambeck Jr., Paul	22	39th Scout Dogs	Austin, TX	11/13/1969	16W-70
Plattner, Ernest	23	44th Scout Dogs	Marathon, NY	11/08/1968	39W-37
Poland Jr., Leon	20	Marine Scout Dog	West Paris, ME	03/26/1967	17E-54
Porter, Richard	21	Marine Mine/ Booby Trap	Hanover, NH	01/24/1971	05W-64
Pretter, Thomas	20	38th Scout Dogs	New York, NY	06/08/1967	21E-76
Pulaski Jr., Peter	23	42nd Scout Dogs	Howard Beach, NY	01/04/1970	15W-126
Quinn, Thomas	21	45th Scout Dogs	Minneapolis, MN	04/04/1969	27W-12
Randolph, Michael	20	1st Combat Tracker Team	Cumberland, MD	03/29/1970	12W-58
Rathbun, Gary	27	42nd Scout Dogs	Cosmos, MN	05/25/1967	
Ratliff, Billy	20	76th Combat Tracker	Pomeroyton, KY	09/24/1970	07W-87

Name	Age	Unit	Home	Died	Vietnam Memorial Panel
Ray, William	21	58th Scout Dogs	De Mossville, KY	07/04/1970	09W-119
Rhodes, Robert	19	Marine Scout Dog	Scituate, MA	05/27/1970	10W-110
Rivera, James	20	62nd Combat Tracker	New York, NY	03/09/1968	43E-69
Roberts, Virgil	21	557th Combat Tracker	Aztec, NM	01/22/1969	34W-61
Robinson, Charles	21	49th Scout Dogs	Easthampton, MA	01/07/1969	35W-51
Rosas, Jose	27	Marine Scout Dog	Weslaco, TX	05/08/1967	19E-65
Roth, John	21	50th Scout Dogs	River Rouge, MI	03/09/1967	16E-48
Rowe, Michael	20	Army Scout	Statesboro, GA	02/19/1969	32W-63
Sandberg, Charles	30	44th Scout Dogs	Philadelphia	05/13/1968	60E-2
Schachner, David	20	40th Scout Dogs	Charlotte, NC	05/14/1969	24W-11
Schmid, Robert	23	44th Scout Dogs	Hartsdale, NY	08/16/1966	10E-13
Schossow, Dennis	21	Marine Mine/ Booby Trap	Sheldon, ND	01/22/1971	05W-61
Schwab, Richard	21	57th Scout Dogs	Medford, OR	09/06/1970	07W-42
Schyska, Leroy	18	46th Scout Dogs	Moline, IL	12/06/1967	31E-54
Scott, Dave	21	Army Scout Dogs	Junction City, KS	01/24/1968	35E-27
Segundo, Pete	22	Marine Scout Dogs	Oceano, CA	09/05/1969	18W-42
Selix, James	24	47th Scout Dogs	Colorado Springs, CO	10/30/1971	02W-56
Severson, Paul	23	Army Scout Dogs	Glenwood, IL	08/25/1968	46W-22
Sheldon, William	19	Navy Sentry Dogs	Chicago, IL	05/05/1968	55E-31

Name	Age	Unit	Home	Died	Vietnam Memorial Panel
Shelton, Bobby	23	38th Scout Dogs	Flag Pond, TN	09/29/1967	27E31
Shepard, Raymond	24	Marine Scout Dogs	Chicago, IL	08/03/1966	09E-104
Sheppard, Ronald	22	49th Scout Dogs	Webster Groves, MO	09/20/1968	43W-50
Simpson, Edward	19	45th Scout Dogs	Collinsville, IL	05/11/1968	58E-26
Sims, William	21	60th Mine/ Booby Trap	Compton, AR	07/16/1969	20W-8
Smith, Gary	21	39th Scout Dogs	Santa Ana, CA	02/27/1967	15E-109
Smith, Michael	19	59th Scout Dogs	Omaha, NE	04/28/1968	52E-44
Smith, Ronald	20	Veterinarian-Army	Dearborn, MI	03/03/1967	16E-14
Smith, Stephen	22	Army Scout Dogs	Convoy, OH	06/21/1970	09W-76
Smith, Winfred	22	Army Scout Dogs	Greenville, VA	06/08/1970	09W-30
Smoot, Robert	19	557th Combat Tracker	Sacramento, CA	01/05/1968	33E-54
Soto, Concepcion	20	25th Scout Dogs	New York, NY	05/06/1969	25W-15
Southwick, John	19	Marine Scout Dogs	Spokane, WA	10/19/1969	17W-91
Spangler, Max	19	45th Scout Dogs	Dallas, TX	01/12/1968	34E-39
Spencer Jr., Daniel	23	Army Scout Dogs	Bend, OR	11/12/1968	39W-57
Steptoe, Raymond	20	35th Scout Dogs	Navasota, TX	08/15/1966	10E-11
Sturdy, Alan	22	41st Scout Dogs	Redwood City, CA	07/02/1967	22E-116
Sullivan, Donald	22	40TH Scout Dogs	Princeton, NC	01/29/1967	14E-96

Name	Age	Unit	Home	Died	Vietnam Memorial Panel
Sullivan, Jeremiah	21	38th Scout Dogs	Ardmore, PA	10/23/1967	28E-55
Sunday, James	22	43rd Scout Dogs	Garfield Heights, OH	09/29/1967	27E-32
Sweat Jr., Herbert	20	34th Scout Dogs	Palatka, FL	02/21/1969	32W-74
Sweatt, Theodore	22	25th Scout Dogs	Terre Haute, IN	11/27/1968	38W-79
Tallman, George	21	Army Scout Dogs	Huntington Beach, CA	04/09/1967	18E-7
Taranto, Robert	21	57th Scout Dogs	New York, NY	11/29/1968	37W-8
Taylor, Mark	20	44th Scout Dogs	Chesterton, IN	06/02/1971	03W-62
Teresinski, Joseph	20	557th Combat Tracker	Oneida. WI	02/06/1971	05W-82
Thibodeaux, Michael	19	Army Scout Dogs	Crowley, LA	07/19/1970	08W-32
Tosh III, James	23	25th Scout Dogs	Mobile, AL	08/21/1969	19W-89
Triplett, James	22	Marine Scout Dogs	Orlando, FL	04/17/1969	27W-104
Truesdell, John	21	Army Scout Dogs	Enid, OK	03/20/1971	04W-62
Van Gorder, William	20	57th Scout Dogs	Markham, IL	06/21/1968	55W-16
Vancosky, Michael	19	Marine Scout Dog	Scranton, PA	05/04/1970	11W-98
Vogelpohl, Rex	21	57th Scout Dogs	Butler, IN	01/11/1971	05W-41
Waddell, Larry	20	Army Scout Dogs	Richmond, OH	03/09/1967	16E-49
Ward, Danny	21	43rd Scout Dogs	Downey, CA	06/01/1968	61W-8
Ward, David	20	981st MP Dogs	Las Vegas, NV	07/04/1968	53W-14

Name	Age	Unit	Home	Died	Vietnam Memorial Panel
Webb, Howard	24	42nd Scout Dogs	Rehoboth, DE	06/08/1967	21E-77
Whetham, Vernon	25	43rd Scout Dogs	Glasgow, MT	11/30/1967	31E-19
White, Garson	21	Marine Scout Dogs	Sontag, MS	02/13/1969	32W-30
White, John	21	57th Scout Dogs	Saraland, AL	01/22/1968	35E-12
Whitehead, Alfred	25	44th Scout Dogs	Harlan, KY	06/16/1968	56W-11
Whitten, Robert	21	Army Scout Dogs	Ft Myers, FL	05/08/1968	57E-12
Wickenberg, Erik	20	43rd Scout Dogs	Bertha, MN	07/06/1967	22E-024
Winningham, Richard	20	Army Scout Dogs	Battle Creek, MI	01/07/1969	35W-49
Wood, Robert	21	Marine Scout Dog	Ft. Benning, GA	04/09/1968	49E-7
Yeager, Michael	19	Marine Mine & Booby	Baltimore, MD	04/08/1970	12W-10
Yochum, Lawrence	19	59th Scout Dogs	Burney, CA	02/13/1970	13W-5
Young, Jon	22	43rd Scout Dogs	San Luis Obispo, CA	04/04/1968	48E-14

U.S. War Dogs Killed or Died in Vietnam

48th Infantry Platoon Scout Dogs (IPSD), U.S. Army, South Vietnam. The handlers maintained the cemeteries as hallowed ground (photo courtesy of Richard Claggett, Vietnam veteran scout-dog handler. This was his unit's cemetery).

War Dog	Ear Tattoo	Died	Unit	U.S. Service
Alex	0K64	09/16/69	47th Scout Dogs	Army
Alf	K088	11/23/70	48th Scout Dogs	Army
Amigo	043A	03/10/70	48th Scout Dogs	Army
Andy	5A48	01/09/70	50th Scout Dogs	Army
Arko	K094	12/12/68	45th Scout Dogs	Army
Arras	K072	01/12/68	45th Scout Dogs	Army
Arras	K015	11/27/70	57th Scout Dogs	Army
Artus	K012	12/11/70	42nd Scout Dogs	Army
Astor	K092	11/10/70	39th Scout Dogs	Army
Axel	K059	03/31/70	58th Scout Dogs	Army
Axel	84A6	01/29/71	39th Scout Dogs	Army
Bark	5A35	06/16/67	42nd Scout Dogs	Army
Baron	0X81	02/23/67	25th Scout Dogs	Army
Baron	53X9	04/07/69	39th Scout Dogs	Army
Bizz	16M6	03/21/69	47th Scout Dogs	Army
Black Jack	498M	09/23/71	48th Scout Dogs	Army
Blackie	3A33	12/07/67	25th Scout Dogs	Army
Blackie	03X7	03/21/69	49th Scout Dogs	Army
Blackie	38A3	09/09/70	47th Scout Dogs	Army
Blitz	X239	10/04/67	43rd Scout Dogs	Army
Bo-Bear	025M	11/12/68	58th Scout Dogs	Army
Bobo	7M25	07/24/69	40th Scout Dogs	Army
Bobo	66A5	12/26/70	43rd Scout Dogs	Army
Bootsy	9X64	09/19/67	48th Scout Dogs	Army
Bozo	9X40	09/12/67	377th SPS - Sentry Dog	Air Force
Brandy	323M	06/25/71	42nd Scout Dogs	Army
Britta	0X47	11/27/68	25th Scout Dogs	Army
Bruno	26X8	07/16/67	48th Scout Dogs	Army
Bruno	8M05	01/30/69	35th Scout Dogs	Army
Brutus	46M2	03/17/69	43rd Scout Dogs	Army

War Dog	Ear Tattoo	Died	Unit	U.S. Service
Buck	61X2	11/24/68	47th Scout Dogs	Army
Buck	7X74	06/02/70	Marine Scout Dogs	Marine Corps
Buck	UNK	09/01/71	58th Scout Dogs	Army
Buckshot	23X9	05/13/68	44th Scout Dogs	Army
Buddy	80X5	12/15/68	43rd Scout Dogs	Army
Buddy	6M61	09/02/70	59th Scout Dogs	Army
Buddy	898M	11/12/70	48th Scout Dogs	Army
Butch	6M36	11/08/70	38th Scout Dogs	Army
Caesar	3A55	05/19/68	38th Scout Dogs	Army
Caesar	5X56	03/04/68	39th Scout Dogs	Army
Caesar	07A2	04/10/70	50th Scout Dogs	Army
Cap	4K87	06/27/71	34th Scout Dogs	Army
Chase	98X6	08/20/68	57th Scout Dogs	Army
Chief	3M42	12/09/69	57th Scout Dogs	Army
Chooch	06M3	04/24/70	48th Scout Dogs	Army
Claus	K024	06/18/69	40th Scout Dogs	Army
Clipper	12X3	Unknown	44th Scout Dogs	Army
Colonel	1A96	03/01/71	981st MP-Sentry Dogs	Army
Commander	X482	04/26/69	41st Scout Dogs	Army
Cookie	41X5	09/28/68	50th Scout Dogs	Army
Country Joe	7K31	01/23/71	Mine & Booby Trap Dogs	Marines
Cracker	60X1	08/19/68	49th Scout Dogs	Army
Crazy Joe	X134	02/13/70	Marine Scout Dogs	Marine Corps
Crypto	8M63	02/23/69	45th Scout Dogs	Army
Cubby	612E	12/04/66	3rd SPS- Sentry Dog	Air Force
Danny	21M2	04/29/70	42nd Scout Dogs	Army
Deno	7M28	05/22/69	41st Scout Dogs	Army
Devil	Unknown	Unknown	Marine Scout Dogs	Marines
Diablo	X313	01/31/68	3rd SPS-Sentry Dogs	Air Force
Dix	M064	02/15/70	57th Scout Dogs	Army

War Dog	Ear Tattoo	Died	Unit	U.S. Service
Dug	112M	06/01/71	47th Scout Dogs	Army
Duke	9X60	01/15/67	41st Scout Dogs	Army
Duke	3A15	06/13/68	25th Scout Dogs	Army
Duke	5A23	04/07/68	35th Scout Dogs	Army
Duke	383M	12/06/69	57th Scout Dogs	Army
Duke	409M	02/23/69	49th Scout Dogs	Army
Duke	230M	03/24/70	57th Scout Dogs	Army
Duke	461A	06/03/70	48th Scout Dogs	Army
Duke	84A2	01/21/72	3rd SPS- Sentry Dogs	Air Force
Dusty	724M	07/28/70	37th Scout Dogs	Army
Dusty	62M6	04/27/71	58th Scout Dogs	Army
Dusty	23M8	10/17/71	48th Scout Dogs	Army
Dutchess	0565X	08/01/70	981st MP-Sentry Dogs	Army
Egor	751M	06/23/69	41st Scout Dogs	Army
Erich	3M92	01/18/70	35th Scout Dogs	Army
Erik	36X3	11/09/67	44th Scout Dogs	Army
Fant	K027	10/28/70	47th Scout Dogs	Army
Flare	X272	07/26/69	42nd Scout Dogs	Army
Frico	0H57	01/13/67	41st Scout Dogs	Army
Fritz	2M97	11/07/68	57th Scout Dogs	Army
Fritz	X740	10/18/68	57th Scout Dogs	Army
Fritz	4M69	10/15/69	47th Scout Dogs	Army
Fritz	999F	02/28/69	12th SPS-Sentry Dogs	Air Force
Fritz	M275	10/06/69	Marine Scout Dogs	Marine Corps
Fritzie	763F	01/26/69	35th SPS-Sentry Dogs	Air Force
Gar	789M	03/09/70	37th Scout Dogs	Army
Gretchen	3M32	11/18/68	44th Scout Dogs	Army
Gretchen	265A	090/3/70	39th Scout Dogs	Army
Gretchen	40X7	05/29/70	42nd Scout Dogs	Army
Gunder	1X07	08/13/67	34th Scout Dogs	Army

War Dog	Ear Tattoo	Died	Unit	U.S. Service
Hanno	0H03	02/16/67	33rd Scout Dogs	Army
Hasso	0K55	06/18/69	41st Scout Dogs	Army
Hector	X459	05/14/69	40th Scout Dogs	Army
Heidi	18A6	10/31/70	58th Scout Dogs	Army
Heidi	Unknown	09/01/70	Mine & Booby Trap Dogs	Marine Corps
Heidi	T031	11/12/70	63rd Combat Trackers	Army
Heidi	Unknown	02/19/71	43rd Scout Dogs	Army
Heidi	X017	04/23/71	57th Scout Dogs	Army
Hunde	M145	02/28/68	3rd SPS- Sentry Dogs	Air Force
Ikar	X682	07/02/69	40th Scout Dogs	Army
Jack	130M	10/18/68	57th Scout Dogs	Army
Jack	7X18	12/17/69	34th Scout Dogs	Army
Joe	6B54	06/15/70	45th Scout Dogs	Army
Kaizer	6M91	01/18/69	Combat Tracker Team-2	Army
Kat	00M3	04/30/70	48th Scout Dogs	Army
Kazan	7X51	06/15/68	57th Scout Dogs	Army
Keenchie	14X7	12/10/67	34th Scout Dogs	Army
Kelley	14X7	12/10/67	34th Scout Dogs	Army
Kelly	Unknown	05/18/70	34th Scout Dogs	Army
King	0K87	07/01/68	43rd Scout Dogs	Army
King	334X	02/10/68	981st MP-Sentry Dogs	Army
King	49X0	07/04/68	57th Scout Dogs	Army
King	58X3	12/23/68	41st Scout Dogs	Army
King	66X5	01/10/68	43rd Scout Dogs	Army
King	8X87	09/13/68	34th Scout Dogs	Army
King	245M	03/20/69	33rd Scout Dogs	Army
King	81M5	08/14/69	37th Scout Dogs	Army
King	8M51	05/18/69	49th Scout Dogs	Army
King	9A18	11/13/69	39th Scout Dogs	Army
King	07M6	05/19/70	42nd Scout Dogs	Army

War Dog	Ear Tattoo	Died	Unit	U.S. Service
King	2A15	02/16/70	48th Scout Dogs	Army
King	7A65	02/13/70	59th Scout Dogs	Army
King	A642	01/13/70	8th SPS-Sentry Dogs	Air Force
King	X200	04/08/70	39th Scout Dogs	Army
King	72M4	06/28/71	47th Scout Dogs	Army
Krieger	65M8	06/02/71	42nd Scout Dogs	Army
Kurt	6A92	06/22/68	34th Scout Dogs	Army
Lance	82A6	01/26/71	42nd Scout Dogs	Army
Lightning	0M40	05/11/70	981st MP- Sentry Dogs	Army
Little Joe	223M	02/22/70	47th Scout Dogs	Army
Lobo	58M4	02/15/69	43rd Scout Dogs	Army
Lodo	729M	06/25/70	37th Scout Dogs	Army
Lucky	2X37	10/17/66	44th Scout Dogs	Army
Lucky	7K37	09/01/70	Mine & Booby Trap Dogs	Marine Corps
Ludwick	1X74	08/22/66	377th SPS- Sentry Dog	Air Force
Lux	0K29	08/19/68	43rd Scout Dogs	Army
Machen	2X99	03/31/68	39th Scout Dogs	Army
Max	8X18	06/04/70	42nd Scout Dogs	Army
Mesa	103M	08/24/69	49th Scout Dogs	Army
Mike	4X64	07/02/67	41st Scout Dogs	Army
Mike	760M	11/10/69	57th Scout Dogs	Army
Ming	X528	05/11/68	45th Scout Dogs	Army
Mister	3M13	06/01/70	58th Scout Dogs	Army
Money	32X3	01/24/69	50th Scout Dogs	Army
Notzey	X405	04/25/70	33rd Scout Dogs	Army
Paper	684M	06/26/69	42nd Scout Dogs	Army
Penny	9M96	10/05/70	34th Scout Dogs	Army
Pirate	8X71	12/02/68	34th Scout Dogs	Army
Prince	182X	12/09/65	3rd SPS- Sentry Dog	Air Force
Prince	30X7	03/02/67	48th Scout Dogs	Army

War Dog	Ear Tattoo	Died	Unit	U.S. Service
Prince	43X3	09/02/67	44th Scout Dogs	Army
Prince	703M	03/15/69	37th Scout Dogs	Army
Prince	271M	06/12/70	37th Scout Dogs	Army
Prince	288A	10/26/70	981st MP-Sentry Dogs	Army
Prince	74X1	01/30/71	47th Scout Dogs	Army
Prince	9A38	07/27/69	Marine Scout Dogs	Marine Corps
Princess	1M20	04/13/69	47th Scout Dogs	Army
Princess	45X9	02/02/69	39th Scout Dogs	Army
Princess	49A1	08/03/69	39th Scout Dogs	Army
Princess	764M	04/19/70	39th Scout Dogs	Army
Ranger	787M	03/16/69	37th Scout Dogs	Army
Reb	21X8	02/23/67	48th Scout Dogs	Army
Rebel	Unknown	12/04/66	377th SPS- Sentry Dog	Air Force
Rebel	X202	07/19/69	47th Scout Dogs	Army
Rebel	94A3	03/08/70	50th Scout Dogs	Army
Reggie	3A57	03/10/68	981st MP-Sentry Dogs	Army
Rennie	7K34	09/01/70	Mine & Booby Trap Dogs	Marine Corps
Renny	A548	01/11/68	35th SPS- Sentry Dogs	Air Force
Rex	8X60	05/25/67	33rd Scout Dogs	Army
Rex	0K11	02/07/68	43rd Scout Dogs	Army
Rex	4A85	05/04/68	40th Scout Dogs	Army
Rex	X306	02/07/68	43rd Scout Dogs	Army
Rex	5A77	02/22/69	35th SPS-Sentry Dogs	Air Force
Rex	83X4	03/06/70	48th Scout Dogs	Army
Rex	93M9	05/29/70	34th Scout Dogs	Army
Rinny	185E	07/04/68	212th MP- Sentry Dogs	Army
Rolf	K086	06/17/70	42nd Scout Dogs	Army
Rommell	52X6	06/10/70	50th Scout Dogs	Army
Rover	M075	09/07/68	57th Scout Dogs	Army
Rover	475A	09/19/70	33rd Scout Dogs	Army

War Dog	Ear Tattoo	Died	Unit	U.S. Service
Royal	19X8	09/10/70	48th Scout Dogs	Army
Rusty	6A97	08/30/69	42nd Scout Dogs	Army
Sam	544M	05/06/70	57th Scout Dogs	Army
Sam	5A84	09/24/70	62nd Combat Tracker Team	Army
Sam	66A7	12/16/70	635th SPS - Sentry Dogs	Air Force
Sarge	292M	10/29/69	34th Scout Dogs	Army
Sarge	934M	01/12/71	57th Scout Dogs	Army
Sargent	6X81	11/27/67	44th Scout Dogs	Army
Satch	M-164	01/31/68	212th MP-Sentry Dogs	Army
Savage	M263	09/28/68	49th Scout Dogs	Army
Sgt. Bilko	8X00	10/25/68	Unknown	Army
Shack	9X28	01/28/69	Marine Scout Dogs	Marine Corps
Shadow	9X00	11/09/67	44th Scout Dogs	Army
Shadow	X622	05/27/70	Scout Dogs	Army
Shane	711M	02/18/69	Scout Dogs	Army
Sheba	7X54	08/27/71	48th Scout Dogs	Army
Shep	48X8	01/24/69	50th Scout Dogs	Army
Shep	69A3	01/29/70	47th Scout Dogs	Army
Sheps	8X63	01/13/67	41st Scout Dogs	Army
Silber	1M57	11/27/68	35th Scout Dogs	Army
Silver	X101	07/24/68	59th Scout Dogs	Army
Sissy	441A	01/26/71	43rd Scout Dogs	Army
Skipper	288M	07/25/70	50th Scout Dogs	Army
Smokey	1A82	09/18/66	25th Scout Dogs	Army
Smokey	X121	06/01/68	43rd Scout Dogs	Army
Smokey	36M0	05/13/69	57th Scout Dogs	Army
Smokey	X817	01/27/69	57th Scout Dogs	Army
Smokey	7M50	04/26/70	47th Scout Dogs	Army
Spade	3A43	12/17/68	Marine Sentry Dogs	Marine Corps
Spike	M004	03/01/71	981st MP-Sentry Dogs	Army

War Dog	Ear Tattoo	Died	Unit	U.S. Service
Storm	01M3	04/23/69	39th Scout Dogs	Army
Stormy	476M	Unknown	Marine Scout Dogs	Marines
Suesser	0K81	01/21/68	42nd Scout Dogs	Army
Taro	287M	08/30/71	59th Scout Dogs	Army
Tasso	0K40	05/26/70	25th Scout Dogs	Army
Tempo	50A7	12/02/70	48th Scout Dogs	Army
Teneg	T012	03/12/70	62nd Combat Tracker Team	Army
Thor	335A	06/03/70	42nd Scout Dogs	Army
Thor	326M	04/09/71	63rd Combat Tracker Team	Army
Thunder	4A45	05/15/68	42nd Scout Dogs	Army
Tiger	3A17	08/09/66	25th Scout Dogs	Army
Tiger	3M78	08/14/70	57th Scout Dogs	Army
Tim	19X2	09/11/68	44th Scout Dogs	Army
Timber	Unknown	Unknown	44th Scout Dogs	Army
Toby	Unknown	12/04/66	377th SPS- Sentry Dog	Air Force
Toby	T036	01/25/70	63rd Combat Tracker Team	Army
Troubles	1X16	12/30/67	25th Scout Dogs	Army
Tye	341M	09/29/70	42nd Scout Dogs	Army
Willie	6M11	07/27/68	47th Scout Dogs	Army
Wolf	150X	05/22/68	Marine Scout Dogs	Marine Corps
Wolf	0K43	01/07/69	49th Scout Dogs	Army
Wolf	7X03	02/26/71	33rd Scout Dogs	Army
Ziggy	2M78	04/10/69	41st Scout Dogs	Army

About the Author

John C. Burnam, Master Sergeant, U.S. Army (Ret.) is a veteran combat infantryman and German shepherd scout-dog handler of the Vietnam War (1966–1968). His service awards include the Combat Infantryman Badge, Legion of Merit Medal, Bronze Star Medal, Purple Heart, Meritorious Service Medal, Vietnamese Cross of Gallantry with Palm Leaf, and many other awards and citations.

Burnam's firsthand accounts of combat in Vietnam have been featured in TV documentaries that include *War Dogs, America's Forgotten Heroes* (Discovery Channel); *Dogs of War* (CNN); *Hero Dogs* (History Channel); *Clipper – War Dog* (*Dogs with Jobs* – National Geographic); *Who Let the Dogs Out* (Animal Planet & Hallmark); and *11.11.11, Documentary of Veterans* on Veterans Day 2011.

John Burnam is the founder of the U.S. Military Working Dog Teams National Monument. Congressional legislation was sponsored by U.S. Representative Walter B. Jones, NC and signed into public law by President George W. Bush on January 28, 2008. Representative Jones subsequently amended the law to authorize the John Burnam Monument Foundation, Inc. (JBMF) to build and maintain the national monument. President Barak Obama signed the amendment into public law on October 28, 2009.

As cofounder and president of JBMF, John Burnam led the national monument project from inception, design concept and development, public funding, and final construction at Lackland Air Force Base, San Antonio, Texas. Lackland is where the Department of Defense (DoD) has been training military working dogs and dog handlers of the Army, Marine Corps, Navy, Air Force, and Coast Guard since 1958. The project's fundraising and construction (3,000-square-foot granite and bronze plaza) took three and a half years and cost approximately $2,000,000. The national monument was dedicated on Monday, October 28, 2013 before a large audience and the national media.

Since his retirement from military service in 1984, John Burnam has worked full-time as a civilian in the Information Technology field as a project manager, senior technical writer/editor, systems analyst, published author, and consultant.

Mr. Burnam enjoys golfing and lives in N. Bethesda, Maryland, and Naples, Florida.